STUDY GUIDES
General Editors: John Peck and Martin Coyle

Palgrave Study Guides

Authoring a PhD
Career Skills
Critical Thinking Skills
e-Learning Skills
Effective Communication for
 Arts and Humanities Students
Effective Communication for
 Science and Technology
The Foundations of Research
The Good Supervisor
How to Manage your Arts, Humanities and
 Social Science Degree
How to Manage your Distance and
 Open Learning Course
How to Manage your Postgraduate Course
How to Manage your Science and
 Technology Degree
How to Study Foreign Languages
How to Write Better Essays
IT Skills for Successful Study
Making Sense of Statistics
The Mature Student's Guide to Writing
The Postgraduate Research Handbook

Presentation Skills for Students
The Principles of Writing in Psychology
Professional Writing
Research Using IT
Skills for Success
The Student Life Handbook
The Palgrave Student Planner
The Student's Guide to Writing (2nd edn)
The Study Skills Handbook (2nd edn)
Study Skills for Speakers of English as
 a Second Language
Studying the Built Environment
Studying Economics
Studying History (2nd edn)
Studying Mathematics and its Applications
Studying Modern Drama (2nd edn)
Studying Physics
Studying Programming
Studying Psychology
Teaching Study Skills and Supporting Learning
Work Placements – A Survival Guide for Students
Write it Right
Writing for Engineers (3rd edn)

Palgrave Study Guides: Literature

General Editors: John Peck and Martin Coyle

How to Begin Studying English Literature
 (3rd edn)
How to Study a Jane Austen Novel (2nd edn)
How to Study a Charles Dickens Novel
How to Study Chaucer (2nd edn)
How to Study an E. M. Forster Novel
How to Study James Joyce
How to Study Linguistics (2nd edn)

How to Study Modern Poetry
How to Study a Novel (2nd edn)
How to Study a Poet
How to Study a Renaissance Play
How to Study Romantic Poetry (2nd edn)
How to Study a Shakespeare Play (2nd edn)
How to Study Television
Practical Criticism

HOW TO STUDY A NOVEL

Second Edition

John Peck

palgrave

First edition 1983
Reprinted nine times
Second edition 1995

Published by
PALGRAVE
Houndmills, Basingstoke, Hampshire RG21 6XS and
175 Fifth Avenue, New York, N. Y. 10010
Companies and representatives throughout the world

PALGRAVE is the new global academic imprint of
St. Martin's Press LLC Scholarly and Reference Division and
Palgrave Publishers Ltd (formerly Macmillan Press Ltd).

ISBN 0–333–63994–4

This book is printed on paper suitable for recycling and
made from fully managed and sustained forest sources.

A catalogue record for this book is available
from the British Library.

10   9   8
06   05

Printed and bound in Great Britain by
Antony Rowe Ltd, Chippenham and Eastbourne

For Alison

Contents

PART TWO

General editors' preface

EVERYBODY who studies literature, either for an examination or simply for pleasure, experiences the same problem: how to understand and respond to the text. As every student of literature knows, it is perfectly possible to read a book over and over again and yet still feel baffled and at a loss as to what to say about it. One answer to this problem, of course, is to accept someone else's view of the text, but how much more rewarding it would be if you could work out your own critical response to any book you choose or are required to study.

The aim of this series is to help you develop your critical skills by offering practical advice about how to read, understand and analyse literature. Each volume provides you with a clear method of study so that you can see how to set about tackling texts on your own. While the authors of each volume approach the problem in a different way, every book in the series attempts to provide you with some broad ideas about the kind of texts you are likely to be studying and some broad ideas about how to think about literature; each volume then shows you how to apply these ideas in a way which should help you construct your own analysis and interpretation. Unlike most critical books, therefore, the books in this series do not simply convey someone else's thinking about a text, but encourage you and show you how to think about a text for yourself.

Each book is written with an awareness that you are likely to be preparing for an examination, and therefore practical advice is given not only on how to understand and analyse literature, but also on how to organise a written response. Our hope is that although these books are intended to serve a practical purpose, they may also enrich your enjoyment of literature by making you a more confident reader, alert to the interest and pleasure to be derived from literary texts.

John Peck
Martin Coyle

Preface

ONE of the most common experiences of students of English Literature
is to read a novel and thoroughly enjoy it, but to be at an almost total
loss to say what the book is really about or what things in it are most
worthy of note. The natural tendency then is to rely on guidance from
teachers or critics, but this is a poor substitute for constructing a personal response. Developing an individual reading can, however, seem
extraordinarily difficult to the average student, even to the student who
is 'good at English'. For it is a difficulty which is not due to any lack of
intelligence on the part of the reader, but to inexperience of the nature
of criticism. Literary criticism is an activity, like any other, with its own
rules and well-established modes of conduct. But these rules are seldom,
if ever, explained to the newcomer. He or she is likely to be thrown in
at the deep end, and, in a confused sort of way, from the observation
of others, expected to establish what the rules are.

What this book attempts to do is to set out some of the rules for
studying a novel – or, at any rate, one version of the rules. It is indeed
the variety of approaches and methods that exists that makes teachers
reluctant to recommend any specific approach. But some general guidance about how to approach a novel must be better than none, and it
is in this spirit that the method suggested here is offered.

I do not claim that this book will make you an expert novel critic:
if anything, it can be compared to driving lessons. These teach you the
basics of handling a car, and how to proceed with reasonable assur-
ance, but even when you have passed your test there is still a lot to
learn. This book only attempts to illustrate some basic techniques of
handling a novel, although towards the end, when I look at recent
approaches to criticism of the novel, I do make some suggestions about
how you can advance further.

The criticism this book is open to is that it attempts to substitute a
mechanical form of study for the enjoyable experience of reading. And

it is perfectly true that the best way to find out about novels is to read as many as possible. But the pressure of studying several subjects at school, as well as outside distractions, means that very few school or university students have read as much as they feel they should have. In addition, studying novels for exams is a somewhat different activity from reading novels for pleasure, and does demand a certain sort of disciplined attention which the general reader is not obliged to bring to literature. A more positive defence of the approach recommended here is that it should not prove constraining. In some ways it is no more than a frame, in which it should be possible to articulate clearly a genuine response to any novel.

A word about the format of the first five chapters: in each chapter I discuss individual novels because I think that too much laying down of abstract principles is unlikely to prove helpful. Rules only begin to make sense when seen in operation. But this means, if you are going to find these chapters at all useful, that you may have to read analyses of novels that you have not read, and have no immediate intention of reading. In each example, however, the method employed is meant to be relevant to many novels, not just to the novel at the centre of the discussion; in the first chapter, for instance, you should find that the approach adopted with *Waverley* and *Sons and Lovers* could easily be adapted to the novel you are currently studying.

Chapters six and seven focus on the issue of how to write an essay; the skills of how to organise, pace and develop an argument are central to the whole activity of literary criticism. These two chapters attempt to provide some essential groundrules (they might even help you avoid that all too common student problem of going round and round in circles, never quite managing to say clearly what it is that you want to say). They are followed by three entirely new chapters, which appear for the first time in this 'Second Edition'. In recent years there has been a flood of new thinking in literary criticism, and a whole range of new approaches: students at university, in particular, soon become aware of terms such as deconstruction, feminist criticism and New Historicism. Chapters eight, nine and ten illustrate these new approaches in action, and suggest ways in which you can absorb this new thinking into your own work. Inevitably, these chapters push this book into what are, at times, difficult areas and difficult issues, but a point I try to keep clear is that even the most innovatory approaches must be built upon close examination of the text. By the end of this book, therefore, you might feel that you have arrived in unfamiliar ter-

ritory, but do try to see that the essential method is that outlined in
chapter one, of building your case from the evidence of specific passages; in other words, building an argument from the words on the
page.

University of Wales, Cardiff   John Peck

Part One

1

Tackling the text

Novels discussed:
Waverley, by Sir Walter Scott, published 1814
Sons and Lovers, by D. H. Lawrence, published 1913

I

I AM a student, at school, college or university, and have been told that the next book we are going to look at is *Waverley*, by Sir Walter Scott. I have heard of Scott, although the only thing I know about him is that he was Scottish, but I have never heard of *Waverley*. But, being a conscientious student, I decide to read the novel before the classes begin, and moreover, I hope to work out my own view of what it is about. Reading the book, I discover that it features a young man called Waverley who falls in with a group of Scottish rebels. At times it is very exciting, and moves along very quickly, but at other times it seems awfully wordy and slow. I enjoyed it, and think it might be about . . .

However, it is at this stage that I become very uncertain what to say, as I cannot decide what aspects of the book are most important. I lack any sort of confidence that the judgements I make can be accurate or worthwhile. And I feel particularly depressed as this does seem a relatively straightforward novel. I have tried my best, but I now decide to wait for lectures, when my teacher will guide me though the novel.

Obviously this is unsatisfactory. I should be able to produce my own response without immediately having to rely on help from another person. But I lack any sort of method that will enable me to develop my own view: I have lots of half-defined ideas about the novel, but I can't marshal them into any sort of pattern. Part of the problem is that the novel is so long that I am overwhelmed by sheer bulk. I just do not know where to begin. But this is where I can start to establish a method.

3

As length is a problem, it may help if I decide to concentrate on a few short passages in the novel, and try to work out from these to an impression of the work as a whole. No doubt there are limitations to such an approach, and it is going to have no value at all unless I have read the book beforehand, but it does seem a way of making a systematic start on coming to terms with the text. Further ideas about a critical method can develop as I go along.

Having decided to try this approach, my first task is to select useful passages. The logical thing to do would seem to be to start at the beginning, perhaps with a look at the first page of the novel, and then let my response to the opening determine my choice of where to look next. My hope, of course, is that the opening will introduce themes and ideas which will prove central to the work. So, I turn to the first page of *Waverley*. There, however, I encounter an immediate problem: the first chapter is entitled 'Introductory', and the opening does not seem very illuminating. But this is a problem that may often occur, particularly when the novel does not start with characters: in their absence it can prove difficult to find anything to hang on to. The answer is to turn on a few pages, until I find a passage that does present one or more of the leading figures. I can now formulate my first rule:

Step 1: After reading the work as a whole, take a close look at the opening page of the novel, or, if this proves unilluminating, at a passage fairly near the beginning featuring one or more of the principal characters.

Following this procedure, I discover that, after his introductory chapter, Scott moves on quickly to Edward Waverley, the hero of the novel, and I could choose any of a great number of passages describing this young man. The extract I select is just under a page in length: that is, long enough to say something substantial, but short enough to allow me to explore it in some detail:

His powers of apprehension were so uncommonly quick, as almost to resemble intuition, and the chief care of his preceptor was to prevent him, as a sportsman would phrase it, from overrunning his game, that is, from acquiring his knowledge in a slight, flimsy, and inadequate manner. And here the instructor had to combat another propensity too often united with brilliancy of fancy and vivacity of talent, – that indolence, namely, of disposition, which can only be stirred by some strong motive of gratification, and which renounces study as soon as curiosity is gratified, the pleasure of conquering the first difficulties exhausted, and the novelty of pursuit at an end. Edward would throw himself with spirit upon any classical author of which his preceptor proposed the perusal, make himself master of the style so far as to understand the story, and if that pleased or interested him, he finished the volume. But it was in vain to attempt fixing his attention on critical distinctions of philology, upon the difference of idiom, the beauty of felicitous expression, or the artificial combinations of syntax. 'I can read and understand a Latin author', said young Edward, with the self-confidence and rash reasoning of fifteen, 'and Scaliger or Bentley could not do much more.' Alas! while he was thus permitted to read only for the gratification of his amusement, he foresaw not that he was losing for ever the opportunity of acquiring habits of firm and assiduous application, of gaining the art of controlling, directing, and concentrating the powers of his mind for earnest investigation, – an art far more essential than even that intimate acquaintance with classical learning, which is the primary object of study.

[*Waverley* (Penguin, 1972), p. 46]

What do I say about this passage? Well, I am trying to be systematic, so it might be as well if I were to work out a standard procedure for looking at each extract. My analysis can fall into five stages:

(a) *A short statement of what the passage is about*
(b) *A search for an opposition or tension within the passage*
(c) *Analysis of the details of the passage, possibly relating them to the opposition already noted*
(d) *How the passage relates to the novel as a whole and/or novels in general*
(e) *A search for anything distinctive about the passage, particularly in the area of style, that has been overlooked in the previous stages.*

(a) The passage is about Edward Waverley, an enthusiastic young man, much attracted to literature, but who shows little application.

(b) There must always be some sort of conflict going on in a work of literature or there would be no story. Identifying a central opposition is one of the quickest ways of getting to grips with any novel, and, fortunately, this opposition is not only revealed in the work as a whole but to some extent is in evidence on every page. The opposition can take various forms. Most commonly, novels set the prevailing values of society against heroes or heroines who feel uncomfortable with these values: the novel records the quarrel between a particular individual and the society in which he or she lives. It is also possible, though, for novels to contrast different ways of living or the life-styles of different communities, or to set a traditional way of life against present-day life. Sometimes the opposition is less concrete – something familiar and knowable is set against something more vague. It is possible for any specific novel to combine a number of these oppositions, some of which will only become apparent as the work progresses, but one central opposition should be apparent at the outset.

This is certainly the case in *Waverley*. In this passage the opposition is between Waverley's lightness of approach, his casualness, and his lack of discipline, and an alternative set of values emphasising application, responsibility, and earnestness. These, presumably, are the values of society, whereas Waverley is a wayward, although very likeable, youth.

(*c*) There is no need to dwell on the details of this passage as the opposition just noted is so obviously repeated, with different illustrations, in sentence after sentence.

(*d*) So far I have established that Scott presents a pleasant but rather undisciplined young man, and sets against him notions of more sober and steady conduct. I now want to relate this to my sense of the work as a whole. From my knowledge of how the story develops, I feel confident in stating that this is, at least in part, a novel about how a young man like this fares in the world. That is quite a sufficient sense of the novel to be going on with, but if I had got more than just an awareness of the story out of the novel on my first reading I might well be able to extend this initial impression. The approach is to feed such ideas as I have formulated into my systematic analysis of the novel.

But for the moment I will move on to how this episode relates to novels in general. As already suggested, novels are often about the relationship between individuals and the society in which they live. Often these principal characters are young and naïve, idealistic and romantic, too impatient to have much time for conventional behaviour. Such novels frequently deal with the maturing of these young people and the scrapes they get into before they finally settle down. *Waverley* seems to be a novel of this kind: a novel about how a certain sort of romantic young man grows up.

Now it might be objected that what I have spotted so far would be obvious from the most casual reading of the book. What I have established, however, does have a certain solidity, as it is based on a real examination of the evidence. But also, and more importantly, these are only the early stages of my analysis. At some point I might begin to spot far less obvious characteristics of the novel.

(*e*) It is my impression that this is the case when I try to analyse what is distinctive about this passage. Scott is presenting a not untypical hero, and developing a fairly familiar theme, but his way of writing about such a character is unusual, or at least distinctive enough to demand attention. To me, it seems that Scott almost holds things back, with an excess of his own observations, which are presented in an elaborate style: look, for example, at a phrase such as 'of which his preceptor proposed the perusal'. The narrator also seems very confident, speaking with the voice of long and broad experience. Why does Scott choose to narrate the novel in this way? To work out why, it helps to return to the opposition already noted. Waverley is a reckless young man, whereas Scott, as narrator, presents himself as the voice of sagacity and application, with a concern for phrasing which is in direct contrast to Waverley's lack of concern for such matters. The narrator of the novel, then, can be said to represent a firm standard by which the behaviour of the hero can be judged.

Piecing everything together, I can now state that the novel will be about the romantic idealism of young Waverley, and the escapades he will become involved in as a result of being this sort of young man. The narrator views Waverley with something like amused detachment.

Step 2: Select and analyse a second passage

Looking at a first passage indicates a theme which should prove central to the novel. Selecting a second passage, I want to see this theme developed, which in this novel means choosing a scene where Waverley is becoming involved with the rebels. The passage I have chosen appears about a hundred pages on from the first extract – and, indeed, one of the most manageable ways of moving through any novel is to choose passages at about a hundred- or two-hundred-page intervals for analysis.

In this passage Scott describes some of the rebels and their refuge:

The interior of the cave, which here rose very high, was illuminated by torches made of pine-tree, which emitted a bright and bickering light, attended by a strong though not unpleasant odour. Their light was assisted by the red glare of a large charcoal fire, round which were seated five or six armed Highlanders, while others were indistinctly seen couched on their plaids, in the more remote recesses of the cavern. In one large aperture, which the robber facetiously called his *spence* (or pantry), there hung by the heels the carcasses of a sheep, or ewe, and two cows lately slaughtered. The principal inhabitant of this singular mansion, attended by Evan Dhu, as master of the ceremonies, came forward to meet his guest, totally different in appearance and manner from what his imagination had anticipated. The profession which he followed – the wilderness in which he dwelt – the wild warrior-forms that surrounded him, were all calculated to inspire terror. From such accompaniments, Waverley prepared himself to meet a stern, gigantic, ferocious figure, such as Salvator would have chosen to be the central object of a group of banditti.

Donald Bean Lean was the very reverse of all these. He was thin in person and low in stature, with light sand-coloured hair, and small pale features, from which he derived his agnomen of *Bean*, or white; and although his form was light, well-proportioned, and active, he appeared, on the whole, rather a diminutive and insignificant figure. He had served in some inferior capacity in the French army, and in order to receive his English visitor in great form, and probably meaning, in his way, to pay him a compliment, he had laid aside the Highland dress for the time, to put on an old blue and red uniform, and a feathered hat, in which he was far from showing to advantage, and indeed looked so incongruous, compared with all around him, that Waverley would have been tempted to laugh, had laughter been either civil or safe.

[pp. 140–1]

In looking at this section, I go through the same stages as in discussing the first extract.

The passage is about Edward's encounter with the rebels: just the sort of life he has dreamed about in his reading, but now we see this world in rather more realistic detail. The opposition I note in this passage is the difference between what Edward expected and the less impressive reality of the robber-chief. It is rather different from the initial opposition noted in the first passage, but has some resemblance to it in that the emphasis falls on the gap between how the hero would like life to be and how life really is.

Looking at the details, I must try to decide why Scott has selected the details he has chosen to include. There seems to be a great emphasis on how different all this is from Edward's comfortable background: the rebels live in a cave, rather than a house, and the size of the cave is difficult to determine. In addition, there is an uncertain light in which it is impossible to determine exact numbers. Initially Scott appears to be emphasising the mysterious romantic impression. But the dead meat hanging in the cave reminds us that the rebels are real people who have to eat, and the use of such a word as 'slaughtered' suggests how close to butchery the lives of such rebels are. Scott is beginning to take some of the glamour out of romance, and this process is continued when we are introduced to Donald Bean Lean, for he is not at all the sort of person Edward had expected.

Relating this to the novel as a whole, the chances are that many other scenes around this point are serving the same function of puncturing Waverley's daydreams. His education is now under way. As in the first passage, one of the most distinctive features is Scott's style. He is again eager to impress upon the reader that his range of experience and knowledge of the world is sufficient to put all this in context: as he talks of 'Salvator' and 'banditti' we gain a sense of a sophisticated and worldly narrator. He is never angered or exasperated by what he sees, but simply condescends to be amused. One of the nicest touches is the way he takes the language of the polite world – 'The principal inhabitant of this singular mansion . . .' – and uses it in a totally inappropriate setting.

Pulling all these strands together, what I can now state with some confidence is that this is a novel about a likeable, but immature, youth, who goes off in search of romance and adventure. He certainly finds adventure, as it is not every day that a Highland gang is encountered, but the truth about this way of life is less glamorous than Waverley expected. In the final sentence of this extract we see that Waverley, for all his eagerness to seek adventure, is still very much attracted to the ways of the polite world, for he shares the narrator's amusement at the absurd appearance of Bean Lean.

I seem to be making some progress with *Waverley*, but I can see a problem. I have drawn a certain set of conclusions from the evidence of the text, but another reader might draw different conclusions from the same passages, or, choosing different passages, might produce a wildly dissimilar reading. This doesn't really matter, however: a novel can support many interpretations. The first need is to arrive at a personal reading: at a subsequent stage this can be checked against the readings of classmates, teachers, and published critics.

Step 3: Select and analyse a third passage

From my reading of the novel as a whole I know that events now take a far more serious turn, as the Jacobite Rebellion of 1745 breaks out. Edward becomes more and more involved in the rebel cause, indeed becoming so highly regarded in Jacobite circles that it is not long before he meets the Pretender himself. The next passage I have chosen in fact features the Pretender, and also one of the rebel leaders, Fergus; I selected it because it seemed an interesting extract about two hundred pages on in the novel, but almost any other scene around this stage would prove just as rewarding to analyse:

Edward . . . had now been more than once shocked at the small degree of sympathy which Fergus exhibited for the feelings even of those whom he loved, if they did not correspond with his own mood at the time, and more especially if they thwarted him while earnest in a favourite pursuit. Fergus sometimes indeed observed that he had offended Waverley, but always intent upon some favourite plan or project of his own, he was never sufficiently aware of the extent or duration of his displeasure, so that the reiteration of these petty offences somewhat cooled the volunteer's extreme attachment to his officer.

The Chevalier received Waverley with his usual favour, and paid him many compliments on his distinguished bravery. He then took him apart, made many enquiries concerning Colonel Talbot, and when he had received all the information which Edward was able to give concerning him and his connections, he proceeded, – 'I cannot but think, Mr Waverley, that since this gentleman is so particularly connected with our worthy and excellent friend, Sir Everard Waverley, and since his lady is of the house of Blandeville, whose devotion to the true and loyal principles of the Church of England is so generally known, the Colonel's own private sentiments cannot be unfavourable to us, whatever mask he may have assumed to accommodate himself to the times.'

'If I am to judge from the language he this day held to me, I am under the necessity of differing widely from your Royal Highness.'

[pp. 354–5]

I look at this passage in the same way as I looked at the other extracts, but with one difference. So far I have been anxious to pull everything into a simple pattern. I must now be prepared to make this pattern more complex. I have latched on to what I take to be the central issue of the novel, but the more I look the more I should try to see some of the nuances of Scott's presentation of his theme.

This passage is about two of the rebels. The main opposition is between the rather rough manner of Fergus and the gentlemanly demeanour of the Pretender, but there is also an opposition between the Pretender's idea about where Talbot's loyalties must lie and the reality of his allegiance.

Looking first at Fergus: Scott here seems to continue his undermining of romantic notions, for Fergus, although in some respects a glamorous figure, is cruel and insensitive; he lacks that consideration for others which is one feature of a polite society. Part of the skill of the novel, it is becoming clearer, is Scott's ability to present a full and convincing impression of the manners and morals of the rebels. It is the English who, for the most part, have an exclusive possession of gentlemanly behaviour, whereas the Scots, although brave, are coarse and brutal.

But the picture gains in subtlety with the introduction of the Chevalier. Calling him the Chevalier establishes a sympathetic tone, for it is an acceptance of the term the rebels themselves use. This is followed by references to his manners, his bearing as a leader, and his recognition of sterling qualities. The paragraph could easily have been slanted against him, but the intention is to present him in a favourable light. The most touching feature is his misconception about the degree of popular support he enjoys: he cannot but believe that Talbot is secretly one of his supporters, and Edward has to offer a tactful refutation of the assumption. The impression is of a courageous and honourable man, but one who is sadly unaware of the realities of his situation.

To relate this to the novel as a whole, at first Scott seems to have nothing but contempt for the rebels, scorning them with his clever and cultivated use of a superior language. But, as the text progresses, he establishes in some detail the different natures of the protagonists, and begins to indicate their strengths as well as their shortcomings.

The three passages considered have shown me that the novel deals with the experiences of Waverley; I have noted the differences between the English and the Scots; and, in looking at this third passage, I have begun to realise that Scott has a sensitive understanding of the various impulses that inspire the Scots. This added dimension can now become the main focus of my reading, for an interpretation of any novel is only going to be really valuable if it captures something of the complexity of the picture offered, rather than just the simplest outline of the text.

Step 4: Select and analyse a fourth passage

I want a passage now that will endorse, and possibly extend, what I have spotted so far. (Sometimes, of course, even after looking at three passages, I will still be far from clear about the direction the novel is taking. I deal with this problem later.) I move forward about a hundred pages and start to look for a suitable scene: I find one at the point where the rebellion has collapsed, and some of the principal figures are being brought to trial. Edward, though, has been granted a royal pardon. The scene I have chosen is the trial of Fergus and his kinsmen:

> Fergus, as the presiding Judge was putting on the fatal cap of judgement, placed his own bonnet upon his head, regarded him with a steadfast and stern look, and replied in a firm voice, 'I cannot let this numerous audi-

ence suppose that to such an appeal I have no answer to make. But what I have to say, you would not bear to hear, for my defence would be your condemnation. Proceed, then, in the name of God, to do what is permitted to you. Yesterday, and the day before, you have condemned loyal and honourable blood to be poured forth like water. Spare not mine. Were that of all my ancestors in my veins, I would have peril'd it in this quarrel.' He resumed his seat, and refused again to rise.

Evan Maccombich looked at him with great earnestness, and, rising up, seemed anxious to speak; but the confusion of the court, and the perplexity arising from thinking in a language different from that in which he was to express himself, kept him silent. There was a murmur of compassion among the spectators, from the idea that the poor fellow intended to plead the influence of his superior as an excuse for his crime. The Judge commanded silence, and encouraged Evan to proceed.

'I was only ganging to say, my Lord,' said Evan, in what he meant to be an insinuating manner, 'that if your excellent honour, and the honourable Court, would let Vich Ian Vohr go free just this once, and let him gae back to France, and no to trouble King George's government again, that ony six o' the very best of his clan will be willing to be justified in his stead; and if you'll just let me gae down to Glennaquoich, I'll fetch them up to ye mesell, to head or hang, and you may begin wi' me the very first man.'

[p. 465]

The passage is about the response of Fergus and Evan to the sentence passed on Fergus (who is also known as Vich Ian Vohr). The opposition in the passage could be said to be the contrast between Fergus and Evan – Fergus his usual braggart self, Evan revealing some of the nobler qualities of the rebels – but there is also an opposition between those passing sentence and those being sentenced. Looking at the details, Fergus is presented as bravely accepting his sentence, but there is also a slightly ridiculous side to him as he makes his self-congratulatory defiant speech. But with Evan we see another side of the rebels. There is an impressive mixture of naïvety, bravery and loyalty in his speech to the court, the most astonishing feature of which is his offer to sacrifice his own life if they will spare his chief. He is so unsophisticated, though, that he genuinely believes the court will accept his word that, if they release him, he will return with other men, all of whom will be prepared to make the supreme sacrifice.

The attitude of the English is also included. As opposed to a rough and ready system of loyalty and oaths, the English, represented by the court, have institutionalised things. And the fairness of this is indicated in that both of the rebels are given a sympathetic hearing. With the Highlanders, we might well believe, justice would be swifter and crueller, with less opportunity for a person to speak in their defence or plead for mercy.

The overall development of the novel is that Scott has shown the defeat of one side and the victory of the other. A 'civilised' English way of life has triumphed. But if at the outset of the novel Scott seemed simply to pour scorn on the rebels, by the end he is full of admiration for their admirable qualities. Edward has now become a member of the English side again, so the novel has completed its early promise of looking at his education, but it has also broadened out to take a very impressive look at the difference between two cultures, and how one yields to the other. I suggested earlier that novels often deal with heroes or heroines who feel themselves to be at odds with the society in which they have been brought up, but this usually goes hand in hand with a look at the differences between different societies, or different classes, or people from different backgrounds. The novel is, it would seem, the ideal form for examining these social and personal tensions which always exist in some shape or form at all times in all societies. An analysis of a novel can always begin with a broad consideration of the distinctive way in which it examines such tensions.

Step 5: Have I achieved a sufficiently complex sense of the novel?

Having looked at four passages, I have completed my basic consideration of the novel. But I now have to ask myself whether I am satisfied with this analysis or do I want to say more? Obviously, an analysis is never going to be totally satisfactory, as all criticism is selective and reductive, but I am reasonably pleased with my examination of *Waverley*. I feel that my view of the novel became more substantial when I looked at the third passage, and moved from a simple sense of Scott's attitude to a fuller awareness of how he handled and regarded the personal and social issues contained in the work. But progress through a novel will not always be as steady as my progress through *Waverley*. In that case, the answer is to keep on looking at additional passages until a reasonable sense of what the novel is about is achieved. Or it might be that I have what I feel are important ideas about the novel which have not yet found a place in my analysis: the answer here is to choose relevant passages and discuss them in such a way as to forge a link between my initial impressions and the conclusions I have drawn from my systematic analysis of the text.

Step 6: Pursuing aspects of the text

So far I have been concerned to work out a fairly straightforward view of what the book is about. If I wish to proceed further the best approach is to concentrate on some particular aspect of the text; a task which becomes easier if I give some initial thought to the elements that go into the writing and reading of a novel.

Four elements can be isolated. There is the **text** itself; it is written by somebody, the **author**; it is read by someone, the **reader**; and it tells us something about life, a factor in the make-up of a novel which I will refer to as the **world**. These four elements, and the related critical approaches, can be represented in a simple diagram:

Before looking at a particular aspect of the text it is useful to think about these elements. I will start with the **author**. One way of reading a novel is to see it as a reflection of the author's life: for example, by seeking parallels between incidents in the author's experience and events in the novel. The novel is read as a sort of veiled auto-biography. I propose to say nothing about this as an approach, as it has only a tangential relationship to the academic criticism of novels. Far more central is an approach which tries to deduce from the work what ideas the author has on social questions and life in general. This does not mean searching for a didactic message, as a simple message is not reconcilable with the subtlety and reticence of good art, but an author is likely to have certain ideas which will inform his or her work. In moral terms, for example, the writer might be interested in the advantages and disadvantages of certain forms of behaviour, or concerned to distinguish between acceptable and less acceptable modes of conduct. This, then, is one possible focus of interest: how to organise an analysis of such questions is a problem I will turn to in a moment.

But to continue the discussion of the elements that make up a novel, the most problematic approach is that through the **reader**. Different readers read books for different reasons: they are required to at school, or they read novels to pass time on holidays, or to get off to sleep at night. Different readers also derive varying impressions and ideas from the same novel. Focusing on the reader thus leads one into a very subjective area, although all criticism is of course subjective. But if you concentrate too much on the nature of your personal response you are likely to end up saying far more about yourself than the book. For this reason I will not discuss the reader any further as a practical approach to the discussion of individual novels.

Far more practical are approaches which look at the **text** itself and the **world** it presents. Taking **world** first: a novel tells us about life, but this can be subdivided into what it tells us about characters and what it tells us about society, although, of course, it is mainly concerned with the way the two interrelate; it is, however, often productive to focus a discussion on either character or society. By the **text** I mean the form of the book, how it is written, such things as its structure and the author's use of language. It must be pointed out, though, that no critic would concentrate exclusively on one aspect of a novel: observations on language, for example, would only be valuable if they related to other elements in the text. In my discussion of the four passages from *Waverley*, comments on Scott's attitudes, the characters, the societies the novel presented, and its structure and language all merged together without any particular distinction. But if you wish to proceed further with your study of a novel it is fruitful to lean in one direction, if only because questions in examinations and essays set by teachers often encourage you to do so. If you look through old A-level papers, for example, you will see that two questions are usually set on each novel, one of them generally a question about the society the novel presents and the other a question about the characters. A view of the author's attitudes and ideas is usually implicit in such questions; but questions about form are uncommon at A-level unless the novel being studied is one (such as James Joyce's *A Portrait of the Artist as a Young Man*) where the technique is so unusual as to demand attention. At university, however, there will almost always be a question about the form of the novel.

These, then, are the aspects of a novel that I might decide to concentrate on. But, having decided to look more closely at, say, character, how do I proceed? The answer is obvious. Having looked at four passages to establish a general view of the novel, I now select another four passages featuring a character or characters that interest me, and analyse these four passages in exactly the same way as I considered the first group of extracts. This may seem time-consuming, but it is far quicker than laboriously noting masses of criticism. Moreover, as you read and analyse more novels, it will become more instinctive, more a natural part of the process of reflecting on the work. In *Waverley* I might decide that I wanted to discover more about Waverley himself. I would remember what I had established already, but could now look at four additional passages featuring Edward, and add my impressions to the view I had developed so far.

I could look at other aspects of the novel in exactly the same way – finding four passages which I felt filled out the social picture of the novel, or four passages where it seemed to me that Scott's attitudes were made clear. Such passages would be fairly easy to select, as my initial analysis would have already revealed to me the general direction of the novel. It is, though, slightly more difficult, especially for the inexperienced reader, to talk about the form of a novel – this being the reason why questions· about language and structure are seldom set at school. But at university you will be expected to cope with such issues, and really it should not prove all that much of a problem. Discussing the language of a novel simply amounts to explaining why the novelist chooses to write in the way he or she does. Something along these lines has already been done in my discussion of the first four extracts from *Waverley*: Scott's own cultivated manner was emphasised, and a reason was found for his decision to write in this sort of way. The argument already launched could be extended by looking at four further extracts. The best way to choose them would be to select passages where his style is eye-catching, and thus seems to demand analysis.

Talking about structure is more difficult, for there is less possibility here of working from short extracts. By structure I mean the overall shape of the book and the shape of individual scenes. The first is easier to cope with, and, in fact, quite a few assumptions about overall structure have informed the discussion so far. The principal one is that *Waverley* is an 'education' novel, which organises itself around the early development of a character, up to the point where he achieves a reasonable degree of maturity. The essence of this very common kind of novel is that it thrusts the leading character into a series of incidents in which he or she can be tried and tested.

It is easy to spot this as the main structural feature of *Waverley*, but only a lot of reading of a great many novels – or an innate gift for getting the 'feel' of a novel – will enable you to speak with any confidence about the shape of individual scenes in a work. One feature of *Waverley*, for example, is the large number of settings and characters introduced. Edward is continually in new places, encountering new people, and finding out new things. This is an effective way of rendering the confused and exciting nature of the times. But this sort of perception about how the novel is structured is not likely to be obvious when you are still struggling to unravel a meaning from the work. If coping with structure seems beyond you, don't worry about it; it is not essential for studying novels at school, while, if you go to university to read English, you will read a sufficient number of novels gradually to become confident in this area.

There are other threads through a novel that can be traced. You could pursue a certain image in the work, or concentrate on the references the author makes to other works of literature, or look at the ways in which the characters speak – the list could be extended almost without end. But these are rather specialised approaches (I touch on them more fully when discussing ways of writing an essay). They really only become appropriate when the groundwork on the text has been completed: groundwork which consists of gaining an overall sense of what the novel is about and attending to those aspects of the text which arouse your interest.

Step 7: Looking at critics

Many students make the mistake of looking at critics as soon as they have finished reading a novel (and, not uncommonly, before, or even instead of, reading the book). The time to look at critics is when you have done your own work on the text; you can then turn to critics in a spirit of 'prove me wrong' or 'show me what I have missed'. Criticism is extremely useful if used in this way and can be especially encouraging when it reassures you that your own reading of the novel is on the right lines. For example, when I had written my analysis of *Waverley*, I went to the library and found a reasonably up-to-date book on Scott – *Walter Scott* by Robin Mayhead. I was gratified to find that his view of the novel was fairly close to my own. But looking at his analysis of the novel was not simply reassuring, for he noticed things about the novel which could be added to my view. If, however, the views of the critics are at variance with your own, this does not mean that you are wrong. A literary text is a complex structure which can support many different readings: when you come across a totally different interpretation you have to decide whether you prefer it or your own, although a third possibility is to see whether the two readings can be reconciled.

Before concluding this discussion of a critical approach to *Waverley*, there is one important point I should add. I have written this analysis from a perspective of almost total blankness about the novel: as if I had managed to follow the story but had no idea at all what it might be said to mean. This is a fair representation of the almost total bewilderment I often felt as a student. But confusion is not always as absolute as this; often a student comes away from a novel with a great many ideas and impressions. If this is the case it is vital to integrate these impressions into your systematic analysis of the novel. Far too often students abandon their own best insights because they can't relate them to the view of the novel they are offered in class, yet these initial impressions are the ones most likely to make a student's work distinctive and impressive – provided that they are assimilated into a coherent overall view of the novel.

II

The critical approach outlined above goes through seven stages. It does seem an adequate method for coping with *Waverley*, but it will only be of real value if it can be applied to all novels. The best way to see whether it works is to test it in action, so I will now follow the same approach with D. H. Lawrence's *Sons and Lovers*.

> *Step 1: After reading the work as a whole, take a close look at the opening page of the novel, or, if this proves unilluminating, at a passage fairly near the beginning featuring one or more of the principal characters*

Sons and Lovers begins as follows:

> 'The Bottoms' succeeded to 'Hell Row'. Hell Row was a block of thatched, bulging cottages that stood by the brookside on Greenhill Lane. There lived the colliers who worked in the little gin-pits two fields away. The brook ran under the alder trees, scarcely soiled by these small mines, whose coal was drawn to the surface by donkeys that plodded wearily in a circle round a gin. And all over the countryside were these same pits, some of which had been worked in the time of Charles II, the few colliers and the donkeys burrowing down like ants into the earth, making queer mounds and little black places among the corn-fields and the meadows. And the cottages of these coalminers, in blocks and pairs here and there,

together with odd farms and homes of the stockingers, straying over the parish, formed the village of Bestwood.

Then, some sixty years ago, a sudden change took place. The gin-pits were elbowed aside by the large mines of the financiers. The coal and iron field of Nottinghamshire and Derbyshire was discovered. Carston, Waite and Co. appeared. Amid tremendous excitement, Lord Palmerston formally opened the company's first mine at Spinney Park, on the edge of Sherwood Forest.

About this time the notorious Hell Row, which through growing old had acquired an evil reputation, was burned down, and much dirt was cleansed away.

[*Sons and Lovers* (Penguin, 1981), p. 35]

This passage is about an area called 'The Bottoms': Lawrence presents it as it used to be, in the days when 'Hell Row' existed, but then goes on to describe how, with the coming of the industrial revolution, the old buildings were burnt down. The opposition is between how things used to be and how they changed with the advent of extensive coal-mining. Thus, the initial opposition in the novel is between two different kinds of society, on the one hand a settled and attractive way of life, on the other hand the brutal industrialised present.

Looking at the details, in the opening sentence, '"The Bottoms" succeeded to "Hell Row"', Lawrence suggests that something mean and vulgar has replaced something exciting. The name 'Hell Row' is tantalising: it suggests vitality and energy, but also something evil. The major part of the paragraph, however, is devoted to recreating a very positive sense of the past: the cottages bulged, and there was a gentle brook. Hell Row was close to Greenhill Lane: in this lost world religion was never very far away. What Lawrence is saying is best summed up in the long sentence beginning 'And all over the countryside were these same pits . . .', which emphasises, even celebrates, abundance and variety, and one thing co-existing with another. There were stirrings of industry, but the 'little black places' fitted in quite naturally 'among the corn-fields and meadows'. In this old world harmony seemed to reign.

Lawrence is setting up the past as a time of good order, but he does include negative elements. There are, for example, the tethered donkeys: it is a well-ordered world, but not an entirely free one. The dominating sense, though, is of something positive, particularly when the casual order of this lost world is set against the ugliness of the present. The industrial revolution thrusts in brutally in the second paragraph: in the first paragraph Lawrence uses present participles ('burrowing', 'making', 'straying'), giving a sense of activity and life, but in the second paragraph he uses aggressive verbs in the past tense ('elbowed', 'was discovered', 'appeared'). The sentences also become short and abrupt. In the past one long sentence could hold together a variety of concepts, but now, in a more violent and unpleasant world, one sentence can carry only one fact: 'Carston, Waite & Co. appeared.'

From this short passage, we can forecast that the novel will be concerned with how people survive in this new world where industry dominates. Lawrence, like Scott, is evidently concerned with social change, but whereas Scott seems reconciled to the changes taking place, Lawrence is unhappy about the way society is heading. Attempting to say what is distinctive about this passage, I am struck by how closely Lawrence focuses on what he describes, assuming an insider's knowledge (for example, using the word 'gin-pits' and not bothering to explain it to the reader). Scott seems to preserve a polite distance, but Lawrence is much more involved. Why this should be so, and what the effect of such an approach is, I cannot say yet, but it is something worth bearing in mind as I look at subsequent passages.

To piece together what I have established so far: I have not made all that much progress, principally because I chose to concentrate on this opening description of the locality, rather than on characters. But I have seen that Lawrence is writing about a coal-mining area, and that he laments the passing of an attractive way of life.

Step 2: Select and analyse a second passage

My choice of a second passage is easy: I must discover how Lawrence presents the characters who live in this area. I know from reading the novel as a whole that it concentrates on Paul Morel, specifically on his relationship with his mother and his first romantic encounters. What I need to do is to look at a passage featuring Paul. The extract I have chosen, about a hundred pages on in the novel, deals with a trip to Nottingham made by the mother and son. Many other passages featuring Paul would serve just as well for analysis, but this seems quite an interesting one as he has just got his first job – as a 'junior spiral clerk at eight shillings a week'. To celebrate, Paul and his mother go for a meal in a restaurant:

It was felt to be a reckless extravagance. Paul had only been in an eating-house once or twice in his life, and then only to have a cup of tea and a bun. Most of the people of Bestwood considered that tea and bread-and-

butter, and perhaps potted beef, was all they could afford to eat in Nottingham. Real cooked dinner was considered great extravagance. Paul felt
rather guilty.

They found a place that looked quite cheap. But when Mrs Morel
scanned the bill of fare, her heart was heavy, things were so dear. So she
ordered kidney pies and potatoes as the cheapest available dish.

'We oughtn't to have come here, mother,' said Paul.

'Never mind,' she said. 'We won't come again.'

She insisted on his having a small currant tart, because he liked sweets.

'I don't want it, mother,' he pleaded.

'Yes,' she insisted, 'you'll have it.'

And she looked round for the waitress. But the waitress was busy,
and Mrs Morel did not like to bother her then. So the mother and son
waited for the girl's pleasure, while she flirted among the men.

'Brazen hussy!' said Mrs Morel to Paul. 'Look now, she's taking that
man *his* pudding, and he came long after us.'

'It doesn't matter, mother,' said Paul.

Mrs Morel was angry. But she was too poor, and her orders were
too meagre, so that she had not the courage to insist on her rights just
then. They waited and waited.

'Should we go, mother?' he said.

Then Mrs Morel stood up. The girl was passing near.

'Will you bring one currant tart?' said Mrs Morel clearly.

The girl looked round insolently.

'Directly,' she said.

'We have waited quite long enough,' said Mrs Morel.

In a moment the girl came back with the tart. Mrs Morel asked
coldly for the bill. Paul wanted to sink through the floor. He marvelled at
his mother's hardness. He knew that only years of battling had taught her
to insist even so little on her rights. She shrank as much as he.

[pp. 138–9]

The passage is about Mrs Morel and Paul going for a meal in Nottingham, and the way in which they were snubbed in the café. The opposition is between everything we might associate with Nottingham and
the poverty of the Morels. From the details of the passage we receive a
lot of fascinating documentary information about what it must have
been like to come from a small village to the city. We also gain interesting psychological insights into the two characters, the mother determined to stick up for herself, the boy in his mother's shadow, sensitive
and embarrassed, but also impressed. Now, relating this to the first
passage, the conviction begins to develop that Lawrence's main interest
is in people as victims of industrial society. The initial opposition noted
was one between past and present, and here Lawrence seems interested
in class differences and social tensions.

But, as anyone who knows the novel well will realise, I am over-looking the intense psychological and personal tussles, which are argu-ably of far greater importance than the more directly social elements. But my partial misrepresentation of the work does not matter. When I discussed *Waverley*, the first passages I looked at led me to notice per-sonal features, in particular Waverley's nature, but as I went on I began to notice the broader social issues dealt with in the novel. It so happens, in looking at *Sons and Lovers*, that it is the social dimension that has caught my attention first, but as I go on I am bound to dis-cover more about the characters as individuals rather than just as representative figures. If after looking at four passages I still feel that my discussion of the novel leans too much in one direction I can easily correct this by looking at a couple of additional extracts.

For the moment I will continue with my systematic analysis of this second passage. Relating it to novels in general, this extract does seem to reflect the ability of the novel form to represent social differences and tensions in a particularly vivid way. Searching for what is dis-tinctive about Lawrence's way of writing, I am most struck by the sim-plicity and immediacy of his method. He uses an ordinary situation, with mundane facts, but conveys the feelings of the characters very tell-ingly. In a simple way – 'Mrs Morel asked coldly for the bill. Paul wanted to sink through the floor.' – Lawrence indicates the personal and emotional strain of the situation. Scott was always aloof, but Law-rence gets close to familiar feelings by referring directly to the char-acters' emotional responses.

What I can piece together so far must take account of this final impression. I have seen that the novel presents a convincing account of the experiences of ordinary people as victims of industrial society. As Paul is the main character I can venture to say that the novel con-centrates on what one young man in particular makes of his life in such a world. But I have also spotted a quality of emotional intensity in the writing which suggests to me that the novel as a whole will con-centrate just as much on the mind of the main character as it will on his actions. This is a vague impression so far, but I can add to it as I turn to a third passage.

Step 3: Select and analyse a third passage

I know that the novel deals with Paul's relationships with his mother and with two girlfriends, Miriam and Clara. I have looked, albeit briefly, at his relationship with his mother, so now it would seem sensible to look at his relationship with Miriam. A scene where they are playing on a swing seems promising.

It is Paul's turn first:

> He set off with a spring, and in a moment was flying through the air, almost out of the door of the shed, the upper half of which was open, showing outside the drizzling rain, the filthy yard, the cattle standing disconsolate against the black cart-shed, and at the back of all the grey-green wall of the wood. She stood below in her crimson tam-o'-shanter and watched. He looked down at her, and she saw his blue eyes sparkling.
> 'It's a treat of a swing,' he said.
> 'Yes.'
> He was swinging through the air, every bit of him swinging, like a bird that swoops for joy of movement. And he looked down at her. Her crimson cap hung over her dark curls, her beautiful warm face, so still in a kind of brooding, was lifted towards him. It was dark and rather cold in the shed. Suddenly a swallow came down from the high roof and darted out of the door.
>
> [p. 200]

Then it is Miriam's turn:

> She felt the accuracy with which he caught her, exactly at the right moment, and the exactly proportionate strength of his thrust, and she was afraid. Down to her bowels went the hot wave of fear. She was in his hands. Again, firm and inevitable came the thrust at the right moment. She gripped the rope, almost swooning.
>
> [p. 200]

These extracts are about the different responses of Paul and Miriam to the swing, and the opposition is between his energetic and enthusiastic response and Miriam's far more nervous reaction. The farmyard is presented in rather surprising terms: as the novel is set in and around industrial Nottingham, the farm might be offered as an idyllic alternative, but the farmyard is as gloomy and depressing as everything else. Paul on the swing, however, is associated with courage and a free unrestrained rhythm that transcends the setting: he swings out, above and beyond his miserable surroundings, and can momentarily cast them aside. My sense of the overall direction of the novel is now beginning to change: possibly Lawrence is interested not only in his characters as victims, but also in how they can escape from this grim world. This adds extra significance to the scene where Paul and his mother went for a meal; it can now be viewed as a passage in which Paul's mother was shown aspiring to rise above her class, but it is a frustrating battle, for she is simply too poor to make her mark in the city. Paul, however, is finding liberation, although it is of a different kind, more metaphoric, more emotional: swinging out of the barn door, he is associated with the bird making its dash for freedom.

Looking at Miriam's response to the swing, it can be see that the whole scene could stand as an extended analogy for sexual intercourse, with Paul thrusting and Miriam nervously following his orders. Part of Paul's path of discovery seems to be associated with liberation through sex. But Miriam is hesitant. How can this be interpreted? Possibly that Miriam is more of a victim, more trapped by conventional standards, without Paul's ability to find a way of transcending the life he is born into. Paul seems to be making a sort of statement of his individuality and freedom.

I can now see how the novel employs the familiar pattern of presenting a hero or heroine at odds with the world he or she inherits. But notice that Lawrence takes a line directly contrary to that of Scott: Scott argued for conformity, whereas Lawrence seems to be on the side of the person who rebels. These are, broadly speaking, the two directions novelists can take on social issues: they can be in favour of the status quo and argue for the advantages of social compromise, or they can attack society as presently constituted, and defend the individual who refuses to buckle under.

What is distinctive about Lawrence's way of presenting this scene? I notice the lyricism of his writing, and how the form is appropriate to the content. The sentences describing Paul's actions are bold and adventurous, whereas the sentences for Miriam are far more cramped and restrained; the sentences seem to enact their feelings. Compared to Scott's style, it is a far more adventurous way of writing: Scott writes in the polite style of society as a whole, whereas Lawrence needs a style which will show how he prefers an intense emotional and personal response to the world.

I am now, after looking at three passages, moving towards a more complex sense of the novel, beginning to understand something of the alternative Lawrence presents to the monotony and repression of a life dominated by industrialism.

Step 4: Select and analyse a fourth passage

Paul moves on from his relationship with Miriam to an affair with Clara. I have chosen a very short passage depicting a moment early in their relationship:

> Clara's hat lay on the grass not far off. She was kneeling, bending
> forward still to smell the flowers. Her neck gave him a sharp pang, such a
> beautiful thing, yet not proud of itself just now. Her breasts swung slightly
> in her blouse. The arching curve of her back was beautiful and strong;
> she wore no stays. Suddenly, without knowing, he was scattering a
> handful of cowslips over her hair and neck . . .
>
> [p. 295]

The passage is about Clara, and Paul's impetuous scattering of flowers
over her. It may seem rather difficult to find an opposition here, but
when this happens it helps to think of the themes raised so far in the
novel. The main opposition evident in the text could be said to centre
on the difference between being trapped and achieving some sort of
freer existence. In this passage Clara is clearly associated with freedom;
there is something casual and relaxed about her, which contrasts dramatically with Miriam's anxiety. The details present an intensely physical, even erotic, impression of Clara, again presumably with the
intention of contrasting her with the spiritual Miriam. Clara is very
free, something that is conveyed in the curious piece of information
that 'she wore no stays', whereas both Mrs Morel and Miriam seem
knotted-up and repressed. Looking more closely, my impression is that
Lawrence separates out the parts of the body, so that her neck, breasts
and back become almost independent things. Why present her in this
way? In a sense, it echoes the description at the opening of the novel of
the past when everything existed independently yet in harmony with
other things.

So, with reference to the novel as a whole, I can say that Paul
finds in Clara the freedom he desires; his reckless behaviour with the
flowers could be said to represent his awareness of how free a spirit
Clara is.

Step 5: Have I achieved a sufficiently complex sense of the novel?

Having looked at four passages, I now have to ask myself whether I
have achieved a reasonable sense of the novel. I have made considerable progress, but there are still questions that I have not answered.
Discussion of just one scene with each of the three women is only
scratching the surface. I have not really discovered why Lawrence
devoted so much space to the relationship with the mother, nor have I

determined why Paul finished his affair with Miriam, nor why the relationship with Clara also goes wrong. It will often be the case, though,
that a look at just four passages will be sufficient only to introduce the
book's themes, and that it will be necessary to look at further scenes to
get a fuller impression.

In this novel, I certainly need to look at one or more additional
scenes with the mother and the two girlfriends. Fairly short passages
will probably suffice, such as the following description of Paul and his
mother:

> Mrs Morel clung now to Paul. He was quiet and not brilliant. But still he
> stuck to his painting, and still he stuck to his mother. Everything he did
> was for her. She waited for his coming home in the evening, and then she
> unburdened herself of all she had pondered, of all that had occurred to
> her during the day. He sat and listened with his earnestness. The two
> shared lives.
>
> [p. 158]

The passage is about the mother and son. The opposition I see is
between their closeness and the sense of a wider world outside. What is
most striking in the passage is that Paul has taken the role normally
occupied by a husband. But there is also something stifling about the
scene (look at verbs such as 'clung' and the repeated 'stuck'), a cloying
intimacy that is troubling; words such as 'unburdened' and 'pondered'
have an oppressive heaviness.

This passage reflects the sense of oppressive emotional entanglement that characterises the novel as a whole. It suggests how close the
mother and son are, and helps to explain why he needs to break free
and yet finds it so difficult to do so. He is not only trapped by his
environment but also by his relationship with his mother. Presumably a
similar sense of entanglement, and possibly a sense of Paul's annoyance
at feeling trapped, would be evident in any passage featuring Paul and
Miriam that I might now select to discuss. As the relationship with
Clara also comes to an end, I would need to select a scene from the
later stages of the novel to see whether this problem is in evidence
again. When I had looked at all three relationships in this way I might
at last feel that I had caught something of the true nature of the text –
though even then my analysis would be incomplete, for I would have
made no reference to Paul's equally tangled relationship with his father.
But this is an element that is perhaps best pursued when I decide to
concentrate on one or more aspects of the text.

Step 6: Pursuing aspects of the text

Having formed a general impression, I could now proceed to investigate specific aspects of the novel. Character is the most inviting one. I have barely mentioned the father, but he is a very important person in the work. And there is a lot more that could be said about Paul's relationships with the three women, particularly that with his mother. If I did wish to investigate these matters further, my tactic would be to select and report on relevant scenes. This may seem a very time-consuming approach, but one of its great advantages is that what I discover could be transferred almost directly into an essay about the characters in the novel.

The same would be true of the material I might amass from a close look at how Lawrence presents industrial England – four appropriate scenes, full of valuable details, would be very easy to find. Or I might prefer to look at Lawrence's ideas, and the fact that he seems to be arguing the desirability, while fully recognising the difficulty, of breaking free. In every instance my approach would be to choose relevant scenes, and build upon the impressions I had formed in my initial analysis of the novel.

There is also, of course, the question of form. I have already mentioned Lawrence's direct and emotional style of writing, but my comments were far from exhaustive, and a look at four additional scenes would provide more evidence about his use of language. Structurally, the overall form of *Sons and Lovers* is that of an 'education' novel, but it is the local effects that are more interesting: most scenes in this work feature just two people, usually at odds with each other. There are many short scenes, circling around the same characters, showing their relationships at different moments, and different aspects of their relationships; this is an effective method of conveying the feeling of being trapped in circular and unproductive relationships.

Step 7: Looking at critics

When I feel that I have done all I can with the book on my own I turn to critics. Some writers are more complicated than others (Lawrence is probably a more complicated author than Scott), and criticism of these authors is likely to be more varied than criticism of easier authors. At first the volume and variety of Lawrence criticism may appear unnerving, but the important thing is not to be scared by critics. If I disagree with critics it is not necessarily the case that they are right and that I am wrong: I have, after all, worked systematically from the text, so it would be hard to prove me wrong. But when I come across new ideas, or comments on aspects of the text that I have overlooked, I can usefully incorporate them into my own response. The approach is to use critics rather than rely on them.

My seven-stage approach does seem to work just as well with *Sons and Lovers* as with *Waverley*, so I can reasonably hope that it will work with other novels. But there are vast differences between novels, so it is likely that I shall have to deal with problems not yet encountered. This is particularly the case in chapters three and four, where I deal with books written in a very distinctive, sometimes odd, style. But first, in the next chapter, I discuss two more novels, concentrating on the first stages of an analysis, so as to make clearer how I can arrive at a basic impression of what a book is about.

2

Constructing a basic analysis

Novels discussed:
Mansfield Park, by Jane Austen, published 1814
Jane Eyre, by Charlotte Brontë, published 1847

THE seven stages of constructing an analysis, as described in chapter one, are as follows:

Step 1: After reading the work as a whole, take a close look at the opening page of the novel, or, if this proves unilluminating, at a passage fairly near the beginning featuring one or more of the principal characters

Step 2: Select and analyse a second passage

Step 3: Select and analyse a third passage

Step 4: Select and analyse a fourth passage

Step 5: Have I achieved a sufficiently complex sense of the novel?

Step 6: Pursuing aspects of the text

Step 7: Looking at critics.

In this chapter I take another look at the first five steps, which are the crucial stages in establishing an overall view of a novel.

At each stage I keep roughly to the following sequence of analysis, also described in chapter one:

(a) *A short statement of what the passage is about*
(b) *A search for an opposition or tension within the passage*
(c) *Analysis of the details of the passage, possibly relating them to the opposition already noted*
(d) *How the passage relates to the novel as a whole and/or novels in general*

29

(e)   A search for anything distinctive about the passage, particularly in the area of style, that has been overlooked in the previous stages.

What I am trying to do is build up a picture of the novel as a whole, by relating small details to a developing overall sense of the work.

In the two analyses that follow, then, the method of analysis is exactly the same as in chapter one; the only difference is that I have cut out most of the discussion of the method itself, and concentrated on producing accounts that are closer in style to what might be expected in an academic essay.

I 'Mansfield Park'

Mansfield Park has as its heroine Fanny Price, a rather drab girl, who comes to live with her wealthier relatives at Mansfield Park. The novel examines her experiences, and her cousins' experiences, as children and young adults. Much of the focus is on visits from the Crawfords, a lively, if rather irresponsible, brother and sister from London, and the possibility of marriage between the two families. Henry Crawford for a while pursues Fanny, but eventually runs off with her cousin Maria, despite Maria's being engaged to a Mr Rushworth. Towards the end of the novel Fanny marries her cousin Edmund.

The novel begins:

> About thirty years ago, Miss Maria Ward of Huntingdon, with only seven thousand pounds, had the good luck to captivate Sir Thomas Bertram, of Mansfield Park, in the county of Northampton, and to be thereby raised to the rank of baronet's lady, with all the comforts and consequences of an handsome house and large income. All Huntingdon exclaimed on the greatness of the match, and her uncle, the lawyer, himself, allowed her to be at least three thousand pounds short of any equitable claim to it. She had two sisters to be benefited by her elevation; and such of their acquaintance as thought Miss Ward and Miss Frances quite as handsome as Miss Maria, did not scruple to predict their marrying with almost equal advantage. But there certainly are not so many men of large fortune in the world, as there are pretty women to deserve them. Miss Ward, at the end of half a dozen years, found herself obliged to be attached to the Rev. Mr Norris, a friend of her brother-in-law, with scarcely any private fortune, and Miss Frances fared yet worse. Miss Ward's match, indeed, when it came to the point, was not contemptible, Sir Thomas being happily able to give his friend an income in the living of Mansfield, and Mrs and Mrs Norris began their career of conjugal felicity with very little

less than a thousand a year. But Miss Frances married, in the common phrase, to disoblige her family, and by fixing on a Lieutenant of Marines, without education, fortune, or connections, did it very thoroughly.

[*Mansfield Park* (Penguin, 1966), p. 41]

The passage is about the Ward sisters and the men they married. Miss Frances, who made such an unfortunate marriage, is Fanny's mother. There is an opposition in the passage between the advantageous marriage made by one sister and the less desirable marriages made by the other two, although it could be said that the main opposition is between the socially acceptable marriages made by Maria and Miss Ward (the eldest sister) and the socially unacceptable marriage made by Frances. Thinking in terms of society and the individual, we can see that Maria and Miss Ward conform whereas Frances rebels against social convention. Austen thus seems to be setting up the familiar conflict that is at the centre of so many novels. How things will develop, though, is not yet clear: she may deal with a rebellious individual, or she may be more concerned to contrast the members of two different social classes. But it is already apparent that Austen, like all novelists, is interested in social orders and social conventions, and the advantages and shortcomings of various ways of ordering the world. Whether she is in favour of maintaining or challenging the established order should become apparent in time, but her own style is so polite and restrained that it is a reasonable assumption that she writes as one who accepts conventional values.

But what are these values? Essentially those of polite society. They may, however, strike us as rather limited values. The first striking detail of this passage is the very practical concern with money, as is suggested by the precise information about Maria's fortune; in fact, the financial and social aspects of marriage dominate completely, no mention being made of love as a factor in the relationship. Possibly Frances married for love, but no hint of that is given, the impression being rather that she made this marriage to spite her family. The materialistic emphasis is underlined in other details: characters are defined in terms of their place of residence and their social rank. And this society seems to have very elaborate rules, for how far Maria is short of any equitable claim to marry Sir Thomas can be fixed as precisely as three thousand pounds. There is, moreover, a sense of elegant correctness, which is not only evident in the facts presented but also in the style itself: Austen makes repeated use of balanced phrases such as 'comforts and consequences' and 'handsome house and large income'. Interestingly, the word 'handsome', used here to describe property, is used again to describe the sisters: by a sort of extension, women too seem to become property. This, then, is society as depicted on the first page of the novel, and Austen seems to write as an insider, sharing its values and vocabulary.

But the picture is so penetrating that it may well be that she is concerned to let us see the rather mercenary and unfeeling side of this well-ordered world. She certainly indicates one of the potential problems: that there is a shortage of men with money, so that women have to trade on their good looks and good luck to gain a suitable partner. Austen sets against conventional behaviour the marriage of Frances: her choice of a partner is totally unacceptable; the Lieutenant of Marines is entirely outside the social fold.

To sum up the impression so far, it seems that the novel will be about socially acceptable and socially unacceptable standards and behaviour, the narrator herself – with her precise and correct style – being a member, albeit a possibly critical one, of the polite world. But there is no indication yet of which characters will carry the burden of various roles. A reading of the novel as a whole, however, has indicated that Fanny is the central character, so it seems sensible to turn to her next. Along with her two female cousins, Maria and Julia, she features in the following passage:

> Maria, with only Mr Rushworth to attend to her, and doomed to the repeated details of his day's sport, good or bad, his boast of his dogs, his jealousy of his neighbours, his doubts of their qualification, and his zeal after poachers, – subjects which will not find their way to female feelings without some talent on one side, or some attachment on the other, had missed Mr Crawford grievously; and Julia, unengaged and unemployed, felt all the right of missing him much more. Each sister believed herself the favourite . . .
>
> Fanny was the only one of the party who found anything to dislike; but since the day at Sotherton, she could never see Mr Crawford with either sister without observation, and seldom without wonder or censure; and had her confidence in her own judgement been equal to her exercise of it in every other respect, had she been sure that she was seeing clearly, and judging candidly, she would probably have made some important communications to her usual confidant. As it was, however, she only hazarded a hint [to Edmund] and the hint was lost.
>
> [p. 142]

The first paragraph is about the Bertram sisters, and their boredom with their life at Mansfield Park. Both think of the attractive and agreeable Henry Crawford, a recent visitor at the house, and each imagines herself to be his favourite. The second paragraph features Fanny, who does not share their enthusiasm for Crawford, and who has reservations about the rather flirtatious relationship he has struck up with the two sisters. The opposition is clearly between the behaviour of the sisters and the attitude of Fanny.

The details of the passage make clear that the daily reality of life at Mansfield, at least as far as the two sisters are concerned, is not as orderly as suggested at the outset of the novel. Rather than being two young ladies contentedly playing their roles as daughters of the house, they are bored, and attracted by the idea of a flirtation, and with some justification for their feelings of discontent, as their lives are hardly fulfilling. Maria is saddled with the attentions of her dreary fiancé, Mr Rushworth, who is interested only in sport and squabbling with his neighbours; Jane Austen may be a spokeswoman for society but she can none the less see how empty Maria's life is. It is the same for the 'unengaged and unemployed' Julia. But the passage is not totally a defence of the two sisters, for there is a hint of mockery in Austen's choice of phrases: 'missed Mr Crawford grievously . . .' and 'Julia . . . felt all the right of missing him much more'.

The idea that there is something frivolous and irresponsible about their behaviour becomes all the more apparent when Fanny's moral reservations are introduced. Fanny is the daughter of Frances, who breached society's rules governing the choice of a suitable husband, but it is Fanny who seems to be the defender of traditional standards of behaviour. And Austen goes out of her way to support the essential correctness of Fanny's evaluation of the situation, drawing attention to the value of her instinctive judgements. What Fanny sees, and condemns, is Crawford's morally lax behaviour.

Relating these paragraphs to the novel as a whole: at the outset Austen seemed to be setting the ordered life of Mansfield Park against more wayward behaviour, but now things are reversed, for the reality of life at Mansfield is not as disciplined as we might have thought, and it is the outsider, Fanny, who seems to be the true embodiment of correct behaviour and proper judgement. The established society appears to have lost its sense of direction and purpose, and only a newcomer can show the others the error of their ways.

It is the Crawfords who have been instrumental in unsettling life at Mansfield, and as such they clearly require consideration. In the following extracts Mary and Henry Crawford are seen discussing Fanny –

Henry has developed an interest in her and wonders why she is so reluctant to respond. This is followed by comments from the narrator. First Mary talks about Fanny:

'I have always thought her pretty – not strikingly pretty - but 'pretty enough' as people say; a sort of beauty that grows on one. Her eyes should be darker, but she has a sweet smile; but as for this wonderful degree of improvement, I am sure it may all be resolved into a better style of dress and your having nobody else to look at . . .'

[p. 240]

Next Henry speaks:

'I do not quite know what to make of Miss Fanny. I do not understand her. I could not tell what she would be at yesterday. What is her character? – Is she solemn? – Is she queer? – Is she prudish? Why did she draw back and look so grave at me? I could hardly get her to speak. I never was so long in company with a girl in my life – trying to entertain her – and succeed so ill! Never met with a girl who looked so grave on me!'

[p. 240]

Then the narrator offers her comment:

And without attempting any further remonstrance, she left Fanny to her fate – a fate which, had not Fanny's heart been guarded in a way unsuspected by Miss Crawford, might have been a little harder than she deserved; for although there doubtless are such unconquerable young ladies of eighteen (or one should not read about them) as are never to be persuaded into love against their judgement by all that talent, manner, attention, and flattery can do, I have no inclination to believe Fanny one of them, or to think that with so much tenderness of disposition, and so much taste as belonged to her, she could have escaped heart-whole from the courtship (though the courtship only of a fortnight) of such a man as Crawford . . .

[p. 241]

These three extracts tell us something of the attitudes of Mary and Henry towards Fanny, and also offer an insight into the narrator's view of what is happening. The superficial and irresponsible attitude of the Crawfords contrasts dramatically with the more concerned attitude of the narrator. Mary's speech is characterised by frivolity, but it is also rather bitchy and condescending. She can judge only by externals, being concerned exclusively with the prettiness of a face or the improvement made by a dress. There is no awareness of Fanny as a person, no awareness that attraction to another person may be based on something deeper than appearance.

But Mary is simply silly. Her brother is a far more dangerous character, as can be seen in this speech of his, which is essentially villainous. His first three sentences all begin with the word 'I': his view of the world is totally egocentric, and therefore disturbing. Also disturbing is his repetition of the phrase 'a girl', which seems to consign all women to the category of plaything or object. His perversity is reflected in his belief that there must be something wrong with a girl if she does not like him.

In the speeches of these two characters, and in their actions throughout the novel, we gain a clear impression of why Austen clings to conventional standards of behaviour, for a disregard for the proprieties of life is likely to cause suffering. Henry and Mary are polite on the surface, but lacking any real sense of values they do not hesitate to think of misusing and exploiting others. Society is a delicately balanced mechanism, dedicated to serving the best interests of everybody, and the Crawfords represent a threat to such good order. They have already misled the Bertram girls, and now would be quite complacent about corrupting Fanny.

The case against the Crawfords is most explicitly presented in the narrator's comments, as seen in the third of these extracts. Following the remarks made by the Crawfords, the narrator seems compelled to make her own position clear. What is most interesting about these comments, though, is that they are extremely witty and humorous. But unlike the wit of the Crawfords, the 'talent' of the narrator is not disruptive but directed towards a socially positive end. She can mix vivacity – as in her comments on the usual heroines in novels – with an undisguised disdain for 'a man' such as Crawford: her tone in this long sentence is, for the most part, light and ironic, but, at the end, there is a more abrupt and aggressive snap of disapproval. Many readers of *Mansfield Park* feel that Fanny is a rather drab representative of correct values in the novel, but it becomes clear there that the side of right has another spokeswoman in the text – the narrator herself, who can combine all Fanny's correctness with a 'talent' to amuse that is far greater than that of Henry or Mary.

But what exactly is Fanny's function in the work – is she merely the representative of traditional standards, or does she have something distinctive that she can contribute? Her role becomes clearer in the latter stages of the novel, for example in the following scene in which Edmund, her cousin, tells Fanny, who secretly loves him, about the collapse of his relationship with Mary Crawford:

> and so, with the usual beginnings, hardly to be traced as to what came first, and the usual declaration that if she would listen to him for a few minutes, he should be very brief, and certainly never tax her kindness in the same way again – she need not fear a repetition – it would be a subject prohibited entirely – he entered upon the luxury of relating circumstances and sensations of the first interest to himself, to one of whose affectionate sympathy he was quite convinced.
>
> How Fanny listened, with what curiosity and concern, what pain and delight, how the agitation of his voice was watched, and how carefully her own eyes were fixed on any object but himself, may be imagined.
>
> [p. 440]

The passage presents Edmund's stumbling account of recent developments (his sister Maria has by this stage run off with Henry Crawford) and Fanny's fear that he might have reached an understanding with Mary. The opposition is between Edmund's manner and Fanny's. Edmund, in his speech, exhibits some of the failings of the traditional Mansfield way: the old order insisted on certain standards, but these were so cold and impersonal that love was often squeezed out. When characters at Mansfield do develop emotional feelings they act in a reckless way – as in Maria's going off with Crawford. The extremes seem to be a rather cold and characterless good behaviour and utterly reprehensible behaviour. And Edmund's difficulty in expressing himself sums up how difficult the established order finds it to talk of emotional matters. Fanny's response is very different, however; she embraces the polite forms of Mansfield, but brings with her, and preserves, a capacity for measured love and measured feeling. It seems that Austen is putting forward a sort of compromise – that the old forms can be given fresh life if feelings are allowed a place. Significantly, Sir Thomas Bertram is presented in the novel as something of a failure as a father, being almost exclusively concerned with matters of business, and showing no affection for his children. Fanny reintroduces feeling and by the end of the novel she has brought fresh energy into the Mansfield order, setting things on a better course.

This discussion of *Mansfield Park* has been constructed from a fairly careful following of the first four stages of the critical approach outlines in chapter one. Four passages have been selected and discussed in an attempt to build up a coherent view of the novel. The only difference between this analysis and those in the first chapter is that here I have concentrated on the novel, and tried to suppress any discussion of the method of analysis. The interpretation of the novel that has emerged may, of course, seem idiosyncratic, or even waywardly wrong, and if so I must ask myself whether I want to modify my reading. Having looked at four passages I would also have to ask myself whether I had formed an adequate impression of the novel. If I felt that my account was incomplete it would be very easy to look at additional scenes until I was satisfied.

To proceed further, it would be most profitable to concentrate on some particular aspect of the text: such as its treatment of character, society, the author's stance, or the novel's language or structure. In order to prepare for an examination I would need to be familiar with quite a few extracts, in order to be able to respond rapidly, and with appropriate material, to any question set. Of course, in an exam I would not be in a position to quote at length – but there are ways round this problem, which I deal with in the essay-writing chapters of this book. For the moment, I want to concentrate again on the task of constructing a basic analysis. The novel I have chosen is Charlotte Brontë's *Jane Eyre*. The method employed for analysing this work is the same as used in all the examples so far.

II 'Jane Eyre'

Jane Eyre is the story of an orphan, Jane, who is mistreated by her guardian and her guardian's family, and sent away to a charity school, where she endures great unhappiness, but then secures a job as a governess in the home of a rich man, Rochester, who eventually proposes marriage to her. The ceremony is interrupted, however, when it is revealed that Rochester already has a wife who, because of her madness, is kept prisoner in the attic of his house. Jane flees, but in the end returns to Rochester who has lost his sight in a fire that has destroyed his home. With his wife dead they are free to marry.

The novel begins:

> There was no possibility of taking a walk that day. We had been wander-
> ing, indeed, in the leafless shrubbery an hour in the morning: but since
> dinner (Mrs Reed, when there was no company, dined early) the cold

winter wind had brought with it clouds so sombre, and a rain so penetrating, that further outdoor exercise was now out of the question.

I was glad of it; I never liked long walks, especially on chilly after-
noons; dreadful to me was the coming home in the raw twilight, with
nipped fingers and toes, and a heart saddened by the chidings of Bessie,
the nurse, and humbled by the consciousness of my physical inferiority to
Eliza, John, and Georgiana Reed.

The said Eliza, John and Georgiana were now clustered round their
mamma in the drawing-room: she lay reclined on a sofa by the fireside,
and with her darlings about her (for the time neither quarrelling nor
crying) looked perfectly happy. Me, she had dispensed from joining the
group . . .

[*Jane Eyre* (Penguin, 1966), p. 39]

The passage is spoken, indeed the whole novel is narrated, by the
heroine, Jane. In the first paragraph she offers what appears to be a
fairly straightforward account of the day. In the second paragraph she
tells of her hatred of long walks. In the third paragraph she presents a
fairly vicious picture of the Reed family. Looking for an opposition, the
most obvious one is between Jane herself and the Reed family, but
there is also an opposition between social routine and convention and
anti-social behaviour: going for family walks, dining at a set hour,
sitting around the domestic hearth is set against disliking long walks,
being chided, quarrelling and crying. It seems to resemble the pattern
of other novels in setting conventional behaviour against rebellious
behaviour.

Looking at the details of this opening sequence, it can be said that
the whole emphasis of the first paragraph is social. The slightly
wayward word 'wandering' is undercut, both by the adverb 'indeed'
(which, rather than being emphatic, modifies or qualifies, by giving a
polite air to the sentence) and by the controlled extent of that wandering, made explicit in 'the shrubbery' (nature brought under control in a
garden) and by the set time-span (one hour). Social factors are further
underlined in the next sentence, where it is made clear that the day is
organised around social occasions, such as dinner. There is also the
idea of a group of people doing something together. But it is not only
the ideas that create the social impression, so too does the syntax. The
introduction of brackets signifies a social imagination, capable of thinking in subclauses, and introducing socially relevant asides. Thus, the
overwhelming impression in the first paragraph is of a social consciousness: the extreme weather that is referred to is, for the moment, pushed
into the background.

After this socially correct paragraph, the second paragraph is almost shocking. First, it is shockingly personal: 'I was glad of it . . . I never liked long walks . . . dreadful to me . . .'. Attention is thrust on to the concerns of one mind. But it is not only the personal pronouns that convey so strong a sense of the mind present: the rush of short clauses creates the impression of a mind racing along, feelings are pushed into a position of prominence, and these feelings are extreme. She could have written 'I disliked long walks', but prefers the more forceful 'I never liked'. Such effects help create the impression of an emotionally overwrought mind. But even if these features of style were overlooked, the same impression would emerge from the content. There is now a more emphatic concentration on harsh weather than in the first paragraph, the weather being so cruel that it makes a physical attack on her body. A sense of Jane's isolation comes across, that she can find no comfort in nature, nor can she turn to her companions, as they only chide her or make her feel inferior.

This sense of her isolation is underlined in the third paragraph, where she is excluded from the family circle as they warm themselves around the fire. The language of this paragraph differs, however, from what has gone before: Jane's tone now becomes satiric, as she mocks the delicate home environment. But at the end the intensely personal manner reappears: 'Me, she had dispensed from joining the group . . .'.

Piecing all this together, it is fair to say that there is already an impression of an extraordinary heroine, conveyed through the emotionally direct language. She seems isolated, excluded from love and affection. As in so many novels, this is a character at odds with society, but the distinctive feature here seems to be how completely Brontë gets inside her heroine's mind, and an extraordinary mind at that.

From the small amount of evidence looked at so far, it can be predicted that one of Brontë's strengths in the novel will be her insight into such a person. If the opening is a reliable guide, the style of the novel is likely to be intense, in order to convey this anti-social concern with self. Jane will probably be seen in conflict with the world she encounters. The novel may deal with how she eventually comes to terms with society (which would necessitate a change in the style of writing, as she comes to concentrate less on her self and more on the world around her), or possibly Jane may never change. If this is the case, she is bound to suffer, as it is always dangerous to flout society's rules.

As Jane is always at the centre of the novel, almost any scene would serve to illustrate how she fares in the world. I have chosen a short extract from her schooldays, where she is punished by being made to stand on a chair in front of the class. This extract concentrates on her reaction:

> Now I wept: Helen Burns was not there; nothing sustained me; left to myself I abandoned myself, and my tears watered the boards. I had meant to be so good, and to do so much at Lowood: to make so many friends, to earn respect, and win affection. Already I had made visible progress: that very morning I had reached the head of my class; Miss Miller had praised me warmly; Miss Temple had smiled approbation; she had promised to teach me drawing, and to let me learn French, if I continued to make similar improvement two months longer: and then I was well received by my fellow-pupils; treated as an equal by those of my own age, and not molested by any; now, here I lay again crushed and trodden on; and could I ever rise more?
>
> [p. 100]

The passage is about how distraught Jane is as a consequence of the punishment she has received. Her present unhappiness can be contrasted with how she had hoped to progress at the school: she had imagined herself making steady progress, winning the friendship of the others, but all this now seems impossible as she sinks crying to the floor. Clearly Jane desires affection, and wishes to be normal, but circumstances seem to conspire against her finding happiness. A vision of herself as a full member of society is set against her present awareness of isolation. The syntax helps support the idea, for the long central sentence devoted to the progress she hoped to make is steady and cumulative, but surrounded by her characteristic breathless short clauses.

But this is not the response of an ordinary girl suffering a temporary setback, for her experience is presented in extraordinarily dramatic and exaggerated terms. There is Jane's usual intense self-reference: the sentences seem structured to include the words 'I' and 'myself' as frequently as possible. And her suffering is presented almost as a physical assault on the self: 'molested' is a surprising but effective word to choose, suggesting a sort of sexual assault. It amounts to a highly overcharged view of herself as victim, the complement of which is an overardent desire to achieve the opposite: she does not just desire friendship and approval, but craves it.

Relating this to the novel as a whole, the impression formed in looking at the opening passage, that Charlotte Brontë has a tremendous gift for getting inside the mind of her heroine, is confirmed. Individual readers will disagree in their assessment of Jane: some will see her principally as a victim, who has every right to feel so desperately unhappy, while others will see something almost pathological in her response. Any attempt to forge links with other novels is difficult. The basic formula, of a young person at odds with the world, is familiar enough, but in most novels this is presented as principally a social problem, even though it may have psychological overtones. In Charlotte Brontë's novel the emphasis seems to fall entirely on the psychological nature of the heroine.

Consequently, our interest is always in what happens to Jane, and of central importance is her relationship with Rochester, the man she is to marry. The following passage occurs about a month before their planned wedding:

> Mr Rochester affirmed I was wearing him to skin and bone, and threatened awful vengeance for my present conduct at some period fast coming. I laughed in my sleeve at his menaces. 'I can keep you in reasonable check now,' I reflected; 'and I don't doubt to be able to do it hereafter: if one expedient loses its virtue, another must be devised.'
> Yet after all my task was not an easy one; often I would rather have pleased than teased him. My future husband was becoming to me my whole world; and more than the world; almost my hope of heaven. He stood between me and every thought of religion, as an eclipse intervenes between man and the broad sun. I could not, in those days, see God for His creature: of whom I had made an idol.
>
> [p. 302]

The first paragraph is about how she delights in thwarting Rochester, the second about how difficult this proves at times, for she worships him more than she worships God. The opposition is between the desire to vex him and her idealisation of him. Looking at the details of the passage, it is extremely odd that she should take such pleasure in manipulating him, and that she should even now plan strategies for doing so when married. It confirms, and makes even more explicit, the sense already received of Jane's perversity. When this instinct is set against the second paragraph's quite extraordinary, almost blasphemous, statement of her love, a fairly precise idea can be established of the way in which Jane is peculiar: she cannot conceive of a sensible middle course and seems incapable of forming a balanced relationship. When she loves someone her feelings run to a dangerous excess, but at the same time she is intent on vexing Rochester, and so preventing a natural trust and affection. There is no sense of balance or proportion in her personality. And it is Brontë's ability to imagine and present such a character that more than anything else accounts for the strength of the novel.

In this present book I am more concerned with illustrating a method of criticism than with providing full analyses of novels, and therefore I do not propose to take this discussion of *Jane Eyre* any further at this point (I look at *Jane Eyre* again in chapter eight). The remaining stages would be those outlined earlier in this chapter and in chapter one. I would look at a scene towards the end of the novel, to see if Jane changes in any way, and then ask myself if I was satisfied with my account of the book. If I felt I had not done it justice, I would look at some more scenes, always trying to fit my impressions on to what I had discovered so far, with the intention of establishing a coherent sense of the work as a whole. When I felt satisfied with my overall impression of the novel I could turn to particular aspects of the book: I might want to take a closer look at Rochester, or make a more extended study of the language Brontë employs. My tactics, as always, would be to choose short passages for close analysis. Finally, when I was happy with my own version of the novel, I would look at critics, to confirm or challenge my view, always realising that they might send me back to the novel to make fresh decisions about it.

A final point about the two novel readings in this chapter: it is possible that some of the textual analysis offered here may seem frightening; talk about syntactic features is, after all, rather intimidating. But you do not need to slant your discussions in this direction. The important thing is to describe what you notice in a passage. I have included slightly more technical details about style as I have gone on, to illustrate the range of ways in which a passage can be discussed. But it is quite sufficient, especially at school, simply to talk about the content of a passage. Another point worth reflecting on, if these discussions seemed at all frightening, is that they are the end result of a fair amount of rewriting: my first drafts were extremely long, untidy and confused. I was spotting things that I could not relate to any overall impression, and often making irrelevant or worthless judgements. The process of analysing a novel is likely to be untidy. It takes time and work for a coherent picture to focus.

But it is always possible to get to grips with a novel, however much you may lack confidence in your own abilities. The intention of these first two chapters has been to demystify the whole business of being an effective critic, by showing how much progress you can make if you adopt a systematic approach. The analyses in this chapter use exactly the same approach as described in chapter one, and each individual passage is examined to a set pattern. Sometimes, of course, there is more to say about one point than another, and sometimes there may be nothing one can find to say about some aspect of an extract, but if you look at the analyses in these first two chapters you will see how methodical the approach is. The only difference when analysing a novel yourself is that you might find it easier to work from longer extracts (say, a couple of pages at a time: this is how I would teach a novel in a seminar), but in a book like this it is more convenient to work with short passages.

3

Looking at aspects of a novel

Novel discussed:
The Portrait of a Lady, by Henry James, published 1881

IN this chapter I take a closer look at ways in which one can pursue an aspect of a text, such as characterisation or language. But, before looking at aspects of a novel, it is always necessary to make a basic analysis – employing the method outlined in the first two chapters – as any more detailed comments must develop out of a firm sense of what the novel is about, and in what ways it is distinctive. Consequently, the first part of this chapter is devoted to a brief general discussion of *The Portrait of a Lady*.

I 'The Portrait of a Lady': a basic analysis

The Portrait of a Lady is about an American girl, Isabel Archer, who comes to stay in Europe, and who rejects a couple of suitors before deciding to marry Gilbert Osmond, an American living in Italy. Their marriage is not a success, but at the end of the novel she decides that she must nevertheless stay with him.

The novel begins:

> Under certain circumstances there are few hours in life more agreeable than the hour dedicated to the ceremony known as afternoon tea. There are circumstances in which, whether you partake of the tea or not – some people of course never do – the situation is in itself delightful. Those that I have in mind in beginning to unfold this simple history offered an admirable setting to an innocent pastime. The implements of the little feast had been disposed upon the lawn of an old English country house in what I should call the perfect middle of a splendid summer afternoon. Part of the afternoon had waned, but much of it was left, and what was left was of the finest and rarest quality. Real dusk would not arrive for

many hours; but the flood of summer light had begun to ebb, the air had grown mellow, the shadows were long upon the smooth, dense turf. They lengthened slowly, however, and the scene expressed that sense of leisure still to come which is perhaps the chief source of one's enjoyment of such a scene at such an hour. From five o'clock to eight is on certain occasions a little eternity; but on such an occasion as this the interval could be only an eternity of pleasure. The persons concerned in it were taking their pleasure quietly, and they were not of the sex which is supposed to furnish the regular votaries of the ceremony I have mentioned.

[*The Portrait of a Lady* (Penguin, 1963), p. 5]

The passage presents a number of unnamed characters taking afternoon tea in the idyllic setting of the garden of an English country house. It is difficult to find an opposition, though, as everything seems so harmonious. But this is not a problem: when an opposition is difficult to pinpoint it helps to remember that novels often set conventional behaviour against rebellious behaviour or against a different set of social conventions. This is such a well-ordered setting that James may well be presenting it so that he can subsequently compare it with someone whose behaviour is wayward or with a division of society where life is less blissful. To take a closer look at this idyllic existence: the setting is a garden, which often in literature can stand as a representation of a perfect balance between what nature offers and what society brings under control. The choice of words in the passage – words such as 'finest', 'rarest', 'mellow' – serves to endorse the impression of exquisite harmony. But the sharp-eyed reader may notice certain negative elements: James begins with the phrase, 'Under certain circumstances . . .': perhaps circumstances are not always so happy. 'From five o'clock to eight is on certain occasions a little eternity . . .': again the fact that things are not always so pleasant is hinted at.

Trying to relate this to the novel as a whole, there is as yet little to work on. But thinking in terms of the contrast between accepted social behaviour and unconventional behaviour, *The Portrait of a Lady* does seem to set up a normative standard at the outset: the rituals and routines of life, such as afternoon tea, are presented as something of the first importance and a source of great pleasure. There are, however, slight hints that this order is not the whole truth, that such balance may be the exception rather than the rule.

What is most striking about the stylistic features of this passage is how elaborately James writes. Yet there is also a bathetic sense of anti-climax. The opening sentence begins grandly, as if it might be about something important, but the final words reveal that the narrator is simply talking about 'afternoon tea'. The pattern is repeated in the second sentence, which appears to be about to say something significant, making apparently important discriminations, only to end with the word 'delightful', which seems too trivial a conclusion. Another stylistic feature is James's elaborate use of euphemism, as in 'they were not of the sex which is supposed to furnish the regular votaries of the ceremony I have mentioned'. It seems fussy and excessive, but James has decided to write in this particular way, and the critic must decide why.

A possible explanation may be found in James's opposition between a particularly refined life and an, as yet unspecified, alternative life-style. His style in this opening passage seems as elaborate as the life he is describing; he appears to be a spokesman for this society. But he might also be intent on exposing the inadequacies of this life: there are more important things in life than afternoon tea, but these are members of a leisured class with nothing better to do. Perhaps the floweriness of the language is meant to parallel the elaborate attention they pay to trivial matters: an attractive life, but perhaps rather empty and purposeless.

The Portrait of a Lady, like many other novels, may then present a challenge to a settled order. And Isabel Archer, the heroine, must be the rebel. She first appears in the novel at a point when the men are still taking tea. A dog runs up to greet her:

> The person in question was a young lady, who seemed immediately to interpret the greeting of the small beast. He advanced with great rapidity and stood at her feet, looking up and barking hard; whereupon, without hesitation, she stooped and caught him in her hands, holding him face to face while he continued his quick chatter. His master now had had time to follow and to see that Bunchie's new friend was a tall girl in a black dress, who at first sight looked pretty. She was bareheaded, as if she were staying in the house – a fact which conveyed perplexity to the son of its master, conscious of that immunity from visitors which had for some time been rendered necessary by the latter's ill-health. Meantime the two other gentlemen had also taken note of the newcomer.
> 'Dear me, who's that strange woman?' Mr Touchett had asked.
> 'Perhaps it's Mrs Touchett's niece – the independent young lady,' Lord Warburton suggested. 'I think she must be, from the way she handles the dog.'
>
> [pp. 15–16]

The passage is about Isabel, and since it is the first impression of her offered in the novel, James may be expected to be particularly concerned to make every detail count. Looking for an opposition, we notice that Isabel's behaviour, in contrast to the orderly world of those in the garden, seems to have a freedom, an instinctive quality, that sets her apart.

James does not refer to Isabel by name, writing as if he does not know her, as if he is a close acquaintance of the men taking tea, and as puzzled as they are at the intrusion of this stranger. The sense of distance from Isabel is underlined by referring to her as 'a young lady' and 'a tall girl', whereas James appears to be sufficiently familiar with the Touchett family to know that Ralph's dog is called Bunchie. Why does he adopt this tactic? Possibly he wishes to identify himself as a member of, even a representative of, the established order, and to stand at a non-comprehending distance from this alien intruder. But in what ways is she an alien? Well, we know from other evidence in the book that she is an American, but so are the Touchetts. But there are differences. There is a quickness about Isabel that can be set against the slow steady pace of the characters encountered so far: James mentions how quickly she interprets the dog's greeting, how she stoops 'without hesitation'. Her openness is stressed, whereas the others are associated with enclosure and immunity. In some way she also seems to break the rules by being bareheaded.

How does this relate to the novel as a whole? A possible confrontation between opposing forces is being engineered, but as yet there is no indication of what form it will take. The next step in an analysis must be to seek a fuller picture of the sort of experience being examined in the novel. Just about any scene would provide clues, but, as *The Portrait of a Lady* is a very long work, I decided to turn forward about two hundred pages in search of a suitable scene for discussion. The passage I selected is one in which Henrietta Stackpole, a friend of Isabel's, is lecturing her. Henrietta has just accused Isabel of having too many 'graceful illusions':

> Isabel's eyes expanded as she gazed at this lurid scene. 'What are my illusions?' she asked. 'I try so hard not to have any.'
>
> 'Well,' said Henrietta, 'you think you can lead a romantic life, that you can live by pleasing yourself and pleasing others. You'll find you're mistaken. Whatever life you lead you must pay your soul in it – to make any sort of success of it; and from the moment you do that it ceases to be romance, I assure you: it becomes grim reality! And you can't always please yourself; you must sometimes please other people. That, I admit, you're very ready to do; but there's another thing that's still more impor-

tant – you must often *displease* others.You must always be ready for that – you're too fond of admiration, and you like to be well thought of. You think you can escape disagreeable duties by taking romantic views – that's your great illusion, my dear. But we can't. You must be prepared on many occasions in life to please no one at all – not even yourself.'

[p. 217]

The passage presents Henrietta's view of Isabel, and it is a penetrating view, presenting an opposition between how Isabel would like life to be and Henrietta's view of what it's really like. Isabel has romantic and adventurous ideas, but Henrietta points out the greater difficulty of accepting life as it is and that it is often necessary to displease other people. Isabel is too fond of being well thought of to accept that awkward fact.

This scene does seem to clarify a sense of the way in which this novel is distinctive. Many novels set an idealistic hero or heroine against the world, but James's presentation of this familiar conflict is marked by his interest in providing a particularly subtle, even ambiguous, picture of his heroine. Henrietta pinpoints the mixture of bravery and cowardice in Isabel, how she is just as much scared of the world as in rebellion against it. The bravery of her words is often likely to run ahead of the bravery of her actions. What, then, makes James's treatment of the familiar educational pattern of novels distinctive is his interest in the confusions and contradictions of his heroine's mind. If Scott seems to stand aloof, whereas Charlotte Brontë offers a sort of intense emotional insight, James can be characterised as providing a particularly subtle and discriminating analysis.

This should be apparent in his presentation of Isabel's most significant action in the book, her decision to marry Osmond. Any scene between the two could be used to examine the nature of their relationship, the nature of their attraction to each other. The particular scene I have chosen appears about a hundred pages on from the previous passage discussed. Isabel has now inherited a great deal of money, and is determined to use part of it to travel the world (again, that taste for adventure, which could also be interpreted as running away from the inevitability of having to commit herself and settle down). In this extract she is talking to Osmond about the life she has been leading:

She went on in the same tone, fretting the edge of her book with the paper-knife. 'You see my ignorance, my blunders, the way I wander about as if the world belonged to me, simply because – because it has been put into my power to do so. You don't think a woman ought to do that. You think it bold and ungraceful.'

'I think it beautiful,' said Osmond. 'You know my opinions – I've treated you to enough of them. Don't you remember my telling you that one ought to make one's life a work of art? You looked rather shocked at first; but then I told you it was exactly what you seemed to be trying to do with your own.'

She looked up from her book. 'What you despise most in the world is bad, is stupid art.'

'Possibly. But yours seems to me very clear and very good.'

'If I were to go to Japan next winter you would laugh at me,' she went on.

Osmond gave a smile – a keen one, but not a laugh, for the tone of their conversation was not jocose. Isabel had in fact her solemnity; he had seen it before. 'You have an imagination that startles one!'

[pp. 307–8]

It is difficult to say what the scene is about, as Osmond's manner and way of speaking are so odd. But a fairly clear opposition emerges between Isabel's nervousness – indicated, for example, by her fretting the edge of her book – and Osmond's perfect poise. She shows her usual taste for adventure and desire to travel, particularly to Japan, and perhaps she is attracted to Osmond because he also seems exotic. But she is agitated as she is on the verge of becoming more closely involved with him.

What of Osmond, though? He is an outsider, thoroughly unconventional in his life, style and ideas: this, in part, makes him attractive to Isabel. But, if he is a romantic figure, he also embodies some of the shortcomings of the romantic stance, for he wishes to retreat from the mess and unpleasantness of life. He is opposed to life and variety, concerned to make life as much like a work of art as possible.

To relate this to the novel as a whole, the crucial question is why Isabel marries Osmond. Positively, he is different, and she has always declared an interest in pursuing what is different. But, negatively, he too is scared of life, so she may be aligning herself with someone very much like herself, someone who would prefer to opt out. This is a possible reading, but one that may seem more confident than the facts of the scene allow. Here one has to come to terms with James's method, for, as the obliqueness of the scene suggests, his distinctive method is one of nuance and vague suggestion. Sometimes he will allow a character such as Henrietta to provide a sweeping interpretation of the heroine, but most of the time the reader is put in the position of having to respond to very small hints, with very little direct statement or explanation. Possibly part of James's intention may be that her reasons for marrying should remain obscure; he wishes to suggest rather than state. The reader only gets to know the heroine from piecing together, and making an individual interpretation of, a mass of clues.

Although I have not pursued the novel to its conclusion, it does now seem possible to draw some threads together. Here we have another novel concerned with youthful idealism, making a very searching exploration of the idea, indicating both positive and negative sides. But what seems most distinctive about the novel is how reticent James is in providing any easy understanding of his heroine, for the novel consists of hints rather than statements. Glancing ahead to the end of the novel: her marriage has gone sour, she returns to London where her cousin Ralph is dying, but then returns to Osmond in Italy. One can anticipate that James is unlikely to provide any clear or definitive explanation of her reasons. It will be up to the reader to interpret the details as he or she sees them.

II Pursuing an aspect of the text: the characters

I now have a general view of the novel. In order to strengthen it I could go through the work again, selecting another two or three scenes, with the object of endorsing, but at the same time extending, this impression. Or I could decide to concentrate on some aspect, or aspects, of the novel. The important point to remember, however, whatever course I take, is that what I say now must develop out of what I have already discovered in my initial analysis.

If I decide to look at an aspect of the text, there are five areas which can most fruitfully be considered: character, society, the author's attitudes or moral view, language, and structure. Given the sort of novel *The Portrait of a Lady* is, a closer look at one or more of the characters seems the obvious course to take. I may well feel that I have not yet done justice to Isabel and that it might be rewarding to look more closely at her. My method is simple: I choose three or four scenes that might provide further insight, and analyse them closely. I will not provide full analyses here, as it should prove just as informative to indicate some of the lines of analysis that could be followed.

An interesting scene appears early in the novel, in which Isabel is portrayed in her original home in Albany, in a room where she seems to seek refuge:

It was in the 'office' still that Isabel was sitting on that melancholy afternoon of early spring which I have just mentioned. At this time she might
have had the whole house to choose from and the room she had selected
was the most depressed of its scenes. She had never opened the bolted
door nor removed the green paper (renewed by other hands) from its
sidelights; she had never assured herself that the vulgar street lay beyond.

[p. 25]

For a full analysis I would choose a somewhat longer passage, but there
is plenty here to work on. The overall impression of Isabel is consistent
with what has already been discovered; we see her craving isolation,
locking herself away, perhaps choosing this particular setting because it
enables her to imagine herself in the role of suffering heroine. But,
whatever her thoughts, she's not interested in looking out at the real
world – she leaves the door bolted and does not remove the green
paper, preferring it to the real green of the outside world. Notice how
James uses settings as a clue to character – this is true throughout the
novel, from the garden at the outset, here in Albany, and particularly
vividly in the descriptions of Osmond's house in Italy. Consistently the
method is one of delicate suggestion, rather than one of hard statement. We can see why the novel is called *The Portrait of a Lady*: as in
responding to a picture, we interpret the visual evidence, the atmosphere, the details, trying to piece together an impression.

This delicacy of presentation is in evidence throughout the novel.
For example, scenes treating Isabel's relationships with her other
suitors, Lord Warburton and Caspar Goodwood, will probably show
James working with his delicate brush-strokes, suggesting, but never
spelling out, the confused mass of feelings that make up her personality.

The same quality is evident in scenes with her cousin Ralph. In
the scene below, Ralph and Isabel are discussing Osmond, shortly
before Isabel becomes seriously involved with him. Ralph says very
little about Osmond, but obviously has no liking for him. As this
extract opens, Ralph asks her why she does not ask Madame Merle for
her opinion of Osmond. Isabel replies:

'I ask you because I want your opinion as well as hers,' said Isabel.
  'A fig for my opinion! If you fall in love with Mr Osmond what will
you care for that?'
  'Not much, probably. But meanwhile it has a certain importance.
The more information one has about one's dangers the better.'
  'I don't agree to that – it may make them dangers. We know too
much about people in these days; we hear too much. Our ears, our minds,

our mouths are stuffed with personalities. Don't mind anything anyone tells you about anyone else. Judge everyone and everything for yourself.'

'That's what I try to do,' said Isabel; 'but when you do that people call you conceited.'

'You're not to mind them – that's precisely my argument; not to mind what they say about yourself any more than what they say about your friend or your enemy.'

Isabel considered. 'I think you're right; but there are some things I can't help myself minding: for instance when my friend's attacked or when I myself am praised.'

'Of course you're always at liberty to judge the critic. Judge people as critics, however,' Ralph added, 'and you'll condemn them all!'

'I shall see Mr Osmond for myself,' said Isabel. 'I've promised to pay him a visit.'

'To pay him a visit?'

'To go and see his view, his pictures, his daughter – I don't know exactly what. Madame Merle's to take me; she tells me a great many ladies call on him.'

[pp. 249–50]

The passage presents Ralph and Isabel discussing Osmond. There is an opposition between the confidence of Ralph's judgements and the more hesitant quality of Isabel's statements. Even within this short passage she seems to contradict herself: at one stage she says that she tries to judge everyone herself, but a moment earlier she has been anxiously soliciting Ralph's opinion. There is an emphasis on Isabel's wavering between independence and conformity – she likes to think for herself, but is worried that this may make her appear conceited. Always in evidence is that desire to be well thought of that Henrietta has commented on. The main contradiction in her personality – the assertive independence, which is never really free – is made most evident in her last two comments here: she declares boldly that she will pay Osmond a visit, but then it turns out that, instead of going independently, she is being led – Madame Merle is taking her. The apparent independence of her statement that she is going to visit him is also undercut by her comment that a lot of ladies call on him, as if there is really nothing very outrageous about her visit at all.

The emphasis, when related to the novel as a whole, is, as always, on the contradictions of Isabel's personality, the mixture of bravery and cowardice. Close examination of a passage shows how clearly James sets out the contradiction, consistently allowing one of her statements to qualify in some way the previous one, but the contradiction is far from mechanically presented. This effect is partly created by James's use of understatement – the conversation seems trifling; the impression is derived almost totally from the asides and what we make of them. The air of something intangible is also aided by the reticence of the author – there are very few 'stage directions'; the conversation continues unimpeded, with little more than an 'Isabel said'. The effect of such a technique is to create a complex psychological impression of the heroine – although the psychological emphasis is clearly different from what is found in a Charlotte Brontë novel. Charlotte Brontë presents the stormy extremes of mind, whereas James offers a more delicate, ambivalent picture.

This impression could be confirmed by looking at a couple more scenes from the novel; perhaps one at around the stage when Isabel realises that her marriage is going wrong, and one from the closing stages of the novel, when she decides to return to Osmond. They are likely to consist of delicate suggestions, often contradictory, rather than straightforward explanations of motive and action. At the end, for example, some may feel that she has changed sufficiently to accept the consequences of her actions, and thus face up to the reality of her disastrous marriage, but others may feel that she fails to make the break with Osmond because she is scared of embarking on a new and uncharted course.

So a consideration of a number of scenes featuring Isabel has allowed me to build up a fuller sense of her role in the novel. Obviously the same sort of approach could be adopted with any novel. The reading of character arrived at might, of course, be idiosyncratic, but it would be an interpretation based upon the evidence of the text, and therefore would have at least some degree of validity. This individual reading could then be checked against the readings of others. There is one more important point that I should add at this stage: it should be evident in this outline analysis of Isabel that I have not been concerned to discuss her as if she were a real person, but to view her as a character presented in a literary text, with a corresponding emphasis on the techniques employed to realise her. The reason for this is that Isabel is only one element in the novel; if I concentrated too much on discussing her as if she were a real person there would be a danger that I might lose sight of how the novel as a whole operates. Essentially, in discussing any character in any novel, one is not interested in that character as an individual, but is using that character to gain access to a richer sense of the work as a whole.

Obviously, Isabel is not the only character in the novel who could be used in this way. The novel could be approached through Ralph, or Warburton, or Goodwood, or Osmond, or any of the other characters. If I wished to do this, my approach, as always, would be to choose relevant scenes for analysis, fitting my impressions to the conclusions I had already reached in my initial analysis, and consistently striving to achieve a coherent overall impression.

III Pursuing an aspect of the text: language

The Portrait of a Lady is written with such obvious care that a look at its language should prove particularly rewarding. Looking at language means simply explaining why the novelist chooses to write in the way he does. Many incidental comments have already been made about James's style, but, if I wanted to take a more protracted look at his use of language, I would choose several additional passages and submit them to the sort of analysis already illustrated – but with a particular emphasis on his style. The assumption I can work from is that the form will support the content, being the way of writing which is most appropriate to the view of people and society contained within the novel.

The first passage I will discuss was chosen at random – on the basis that any passage chosen should illustrate characteristic features of the author's style. It is a scene where Warburton comes to visit Isabel, possibly with the intention of proposing:

> She put the letter into her pocket and offered her visitor a smile of welcome, exhibiting no trace of discomposure and half surprised at her coolness.
>
> 'They told me you were out here,' said Lord Warburton, 'and as there was no one in the drawing-room and it's really you that I wish to see, I came out with no more ado.'
>
> Isabel had got up: she felt a wish for the moment, that he should not sit down beside her. 'I was just going indoors.'
>
> 'Please don't do that; it's much jollier here; I've ridden over from Lockleigh; it's a lovely day.' His smile was peculiarly friendly and pleasing, and his whole person seemed to emit that radiance of good feeling and good fare which had formed the charm of the girl's first impression of him. It surrounded him like a zone of fine weather.
>
> 'We'll walk about a little then,' said Isabel, who could not divest herself of the sense of an intention on the part of her visitor and who wished both to elude the intention and to satisfy her curiosity about it. It had flashed upon her vision once before, and it had given her on that occasion, as we know, a certain alarm. This alarm was composed of

several elements, not all of which were disagreeable; she had indeed spent some days in analysing them and had succeeded in separating the pleasant part of the idea of Lord Warburton's 'making up' to her from the painful. It may appear to some readers that the young lady was both precipitate and unduly fastidious; but the latter of these facts, if the charge be true, may serve to exonerate her from the discredit of the former.

[p. 101]

The passage is about the arrival of Warburton, and Isabel's suspicion that he has come to propose. They are both trying to gain control of the situation. A detail bears this out: as he sits down she stands up, indicating a desire on her part to avoid a correspondence of position with Warburton, which might indicate a broader similarity and connection. As is so often the case in the novel, Isabel, however much she may wish to retreat, is forced to confront the world and the people who live in it. As always, the focus is on Isabel's mind.

This covers the bare bones of the passage: now I can discuss its distinctive style. First, a meticulous attention to detail is evident in the way James seems to delight in picking out, observing, and including, every gesture and movement. All these details are clues to character. Just as the gestures are presented in detail, extraordinarily full versions of the conversations are given. Warburton's opening speech indicates his correctness, his good form: he apologises for the slightest breach of convention. He is very much the confident social personality, unlike Isabel, who would prefer to retreat from the lovely day into the shadows.

What can we deduce from James's method in this scene? It corresponds with the impression already formed that he prefers to hint, rather than state, providing the reader with a mass of clues from which he or she can select at will. But more can be said about James's style: it is, for one thing, rather inflated, as in the phrase 'exhibiting no trace of discomposure'. Trying to explain why this should be so, we may think of the thematic concerns already noted: society is set against a rebel; James seems to write from the stance of society, but, by writing in a slightly fussy way, he can simultaneously mock society. Another point of thematic importance, though, is that Isabel is elusive: we cannot sum her up easily. And the archness of James's language, along with his hesitancy and asides to the reader, signals the difficulty language has in coping with such a personality.

This point may seem rather vague, so it is worth looking at a further passage to see whether James's method can be described any more precisely. In the following extract, which appears near the end of the novel, Isabel has heard that Ralph is dying. She bursts into Osmond's room to tell him that she must visit London to see her cousin:

> Isabel stood a moment looking at the latter missive; then, thrusting it into her pocket, she went straight to the door of her husband's study. Here she again paused an instant, after which she opened the door and went in. Osmond was seated at the table near the window with a folio volume before him, propped against a pile of books. This volume was open at a page of small coloured plates, and Isabel presently saw that he had been copying from it the drawing of an antique coin. A box of water-colours and fine brushes lay before him, and he had already transferred to a sheet of immaculate paper the delicate, finely-tinted disk. His back was turned towards the door, but he recognised his wife without looking round.
>
> 'Excuse me for disturbing you,' she said.
>
> 'When I come to your room I always knock,' he answered, going on with his work.
>
> 'I forgot; I had something else to think of. My cousin's dying.'
>
> 'Ah, I don't believe that,' said Osmond, looking at his drawing through a magnifying glass. 'He was dying when we married; he'll outlive us all.'
>
> Isabel gave herself no time, no thought, to appreciate the careful cynicism of this declaration; she simply went on quickly, full of her own intention. 'My aunt has telegraphed for me; I must go to Gardencourt.'
>
> 'Why must you go to Gardencourt?' Osmond asked in the tone of impartial curiosity.
>
> 'To see Ralph before he dies.'
>
> [pp. 534–5]

The passage presents Isabel coming to Osmond's study to tell him that Ralph is dying. James's opposition is between the concerned manner of Isabel and the ugly indifference of Osmond. Ralph is dying, and again Isabel has to accept that life is not a romantic dream but full of pain and suffering, and that demands are always being made on the feelings. On the feelings, that is, of everybody except Osmond, who refuses to show any interest or to offer his wife any expression of sympathy. His refusal to accept that Ralph is dying is interesting: he is happy to relate to a dead art object, the antique coin, but a real death is too painful to contemplate, so he simply denies it. And this idea of how he locks himself into a safe and unreal world is also present in the motif of the door. Osmond locks himself away in seclusion, but feelings, the sort of feelings being experienced by Isabel, demand that private doors sometimes be thrown open. Obviously this is a scene which could well be employed in a discussion of characters in the novel: it is sad and moving, suggesting delicately the wretchedness of her situation, what it must feel like to be trapped in marriage with such a man.

But at the moment I am more concerned with James's technique. One aspect of this is James's usual ability to use small details which work by implication. It is not an art of statement, but of showing, and, by showing so many of the details of the confrontation, an immensely complex sense of the experience is conveyed. Characters' statements, gestures, the setting, are all recorded in great detail, and the cumulative effect is one of delicate insights. But another aspect of the book is the intangibility of Isabel's character, and James's style also supports this impression. Every time Osmond performs any action, or says anything, James provides a fairly full commentary, but Isabel's speeches are usually accompanied by no more than a basic 'she said', if that. With Isabel, then, there is far less guidance from the narrator: we are presented with her words and actions, but there is not the same authorial presumption to explain her. This ties in with James's inflated style in the previous extract: when he describes his heroine he either uses a language which signally fails to cope with her, or, as here, withdraws from any attempt fully to analyse and explain her.

The implications of this lead in a direction which complicates our whole approach to the analysis of fiction, a direction that has become increasingly central in recent novel criticism, and which you will almost certainly have to take into account if you study English at university. To state the matter as concisely as possible: the implicit idea in the first two chapters of this book, and for the greater part of this chapter, is that the novel is the ideal form for presenting a picture of human experience, in particular the problems that beset the individual in society. So far the novel has been treated almost as a clear window on the world. Style has, for the most part, been treated as a tool for the novelist, that enables him or her to report in the fullest and most striking way.

But consideration of James's style has suggested that the narrator's perception of experience may be complex, and possibly beset with problems. It seems that experience cannot totally be 'read', that there is a very real, and potentially troublesome, gap between writing and life. Some novelists may, of course, wish to present the illusion that their novels offer a straightforward transcript of life, but it can be seen that the authority of the narrator is a suspect thing. James seems to be sceptical of his own authority when he refuses to read and explain fully his principal character for us. By questioning the role of the narrator in this way, James's novel indicates the possibility of a sort of criticism which concentrates on looking at the narrative procedures in fiction.

Not just in novels like *The Portrait of a Lady*, where the style obviously draws attention to itself, but in all novels, there is the possibility of looking more single-mindedly at how the fictional world is created rather than concentrating on a discussion of that imagined world. One consequence of examining the language or style of any novel is that questions about the status of the narrative procedures, most importantly the gap between the written word and life, can begin to loom large, as factors of tremendous importance. Thus, a decision to look at the language of a novel can significantly alter the overall emphasis of a discussion. Rather than being just another method of gaining access to a sense of the work as a whole, it tends to modify (some might say distort) one's sense of the work as a whole. For the human content of the work, the picture it presents of people in society, becomes something of less importance than questions of how the narrative works. To put it another way, a concentration on language is likely to lead to a greater emphasis on the 'art' of the novel and less emphasis on the 'life' of the novel.

To some extent, a similar modification occurs if one decides to concentrate on the author's ideas: an interest in the imagined world of the novel is likely to be downgraded, and in its place will be substituted an increased emphasis on the 'philosophy' informing the work. But this approach is less far-reaching in its overall implications than an approach which concentrates on language, for the latter begins to make a great deal of the gap between art and life, and possibly to stress the limitations of fiction rather than its reach. To take Jane Austen's novels as an example: rather than being interested in the vivid impression her novels offer of characters caught in difficult situations, or being interested in the moral values informing her novels, critics who concentrate on her language are likely to report on the way in which she uses a certain style, vocabulary and tone of voice to advertise her values. Critics following such an approach are less interested in the fictional illusion than in how language creates that illusion. To some, this may seem a cold and abstract approach, because it is one that refuses to become fully involved in the novel, preferring to stand detached, looking at the operations of the text. But, however academically sterile this approach may seem, it is one that has become increasingly popular in recent years, particularly in critical approaches that can be broadly labelled as 'structuralist'.

Critics who concentrate on language frequently draw attention to how often novelists discuss the problems of fiction within the novel itself, either explicitly, as in the novels of Sterne and Joyce, or implicitly, as in *The Portrait of a Lady*. They are likely to stress how exercised many novelists are by the problems inherent in narration – noting this feature in novelists such as, say, George Eliot, who, approached from a different angle, might seem a fairly transparent realist. All in all, critics who concentrate on language are likely to downgrade an interest in the reported and ethical world of the novel, and to highlight far more the question of how art relates to life.

If all this seems rather too much to take in, don't worry about it: such an approach is not very important in studying novels at A-level, where the emphasis is almost invariably placed on character, society and the author's views. At university such issues may become more central, but there is no point in trying to force unduly the pace of your own interest in fiction. You need to become familiar with many novels before any very great curiosity about the mechanics of fiction develops. What is most likely to happen is that, at some stage of your university course, and in response to the sort of ideas being put forward in lectures and critical books, you will find yourself developing an interest in these rather abstract questions of the aesthetics of novel-writing. It is, in fact, just such issues that are taken up in chapters eight and nine of this book, where I deal with structuralist approaches to fiction, but also go on to show how subsequent developments in criticism have moved beyond a focus on form alone and have revitalised our whole sense of the content, and significance, of novels.

For the moment, however, one reassuring point. As suggested, concentrating on the language of a novel can lead to a very different view of the work from the traditional content-based view: essentially, an interest in how a piece of writing relates to reality, rather than an interest in the imagined world of the novel. Straightforward concentration on the content of a novel normally reveals a fairly simple tension at the heart of the work: usually a tension between the individual and society. A consideration of the language of a novel begins and ends with an equally straightforward central idea: that art is neat, precise and finite, whereas life is messy, rambling and infinite. A discussion of the language of a novel will usually begin by focusing on the question of the extent to which the novelist is aware of this fact: the question of whether the writer reveals or attempts to conceal his or her artifice.

This is an issue and an approach which, in the case of many

novels, you can decide for yourself whether you wish to confront or not. But there are other novels where questions of the author's artifice do seem an unavoidable issue, and it is to such novels that I turn in the next chapter.

4

Coping with different kinds of novel

Novels discussed:
A Portrait of the Artist as a Young Man, by James Joyce, published 1916
Martin Chuzzlewit, by Charles Dickens, published 1843–4

THE easiest novel to read and study is the one that presents a seemingly realistic picture of ordinary life but there are many novels where the oddity, opacity or exaggeration of the writings is what most strikes the reader. Two such novels – one by Joyce, one by Dickens – are considered in this chapter, but the conclusions drawn should apply to many more novels which depart from the conventions of realism. The principal idea in this chapter is that, when the technique of the novel obtrudes (and this refers not only to an unusual style, but to such things as exaggerated characterisation or a very intrusive narrator), the reader is obliged to pay more attention to the manner and style of narration than is necessarily the case when studying a realistic novel.

Broadly speaking, in novels that depart from standard realism the approach is either more external (Dickens's comic narration is a good example of this) or more internal (as in the case of Joyce's *Portrait*). The reader, in coming to terms with such novels, is required to justify the choice of an internal or external method of narration. Some of the ideas informing the analyses in this chapter are summarised over the next few pages.

I

The realistic novelist – Austen is a good example – is concerned to produce a picture which will strike us as being very much like life as we normally understand it. The author produces a subtle and complex picture, indicating in a psychologically convincing way the various impulses that determine characters' actions, this being coupled with a believable picture of the society in which the characters live. The novelist is concerned to present his or her views about this society, but we are generally more struck by the credibility of the picture than by the preferences or prejudices of the author. Indeed, it could be argued that the author tests his or her hypotheses about people and society in the laboratory of the imagined real world of the novel.

But not all novelists are concerned to produce such a credible picture. One large group of novels which departs from this convention is popular fiction – detective stories, thrillers, romances, westerns, adventure novels. Writers of these books are more concerned with producing an ingenious, exciting or passionate story within the broad conventions of their genre, than with reproducing an entirely credible world. Thus, such novels can be said to be more external than the realistic novel, in that the form of the story itself is usually one of the most notable features of the work.

But it isn't only light fiction that is more external. So are some of the finest novels, in particular comic novels. In these works, issues and characters are presented in such a way as to make a comic impression, and often the narrator makes his or her self felt as a humorous presence. We can't respond to and evaluate such novels by the same criteria we apply to realistic novels, since accuracy and mimetic truthfulness are not a part of the author's intention. The novels appeal in other ways, and a large part of the appeal is the inventive and imaginative quality of the writing itself. This applies more to Dickens than to anybody else, but it is also relevant to novelists such as Fielding, Smollett, Peacock and Thackeray. So, when we read their works, it makes sense to pay more attention to the manner of the narration than we necessarily have to do with a realistic novelist.

An external approach is one option for the novelist. Another is to become more internal. This approach becomes particularly widespread in the early years of the twentieth century. Instead of concentrating on the world and characters as they might appear to an outsider, certain novelists (Joyce and Woolf are the most obvious examples) began to be interested in producing writing that attempts to get inside the mind and reproduce the flow of internal impressions. Such novels can be difficult to read because this internal flow is far less ordered and sequential than the world as reported by a realistic novelist.

This chapter looks at an external novel and an internal novel, and tries to suggest some ways of focusing a critical discussion of them. The easiest way of coping with such novels is to approach them as if they are conventional realistic novels, presenting the usual personal and social conflicts. But this will only provide an initial entry into the works: because their method differs from that found in a realistic novel, their distinctive character and appeal can be defined in terms of the ways in which they break or ignore the realistic conventions, and we shall soon reach the fairly simple conclusion that the author of an internal novel needs to find new ways of writing to represent the stream of consciousness of characters. The external or comic author, instead of aiming at a sympathetic insight into the reality of being caught in a certain situation, prefers to present a detached, perhaps mocking, view of human affectation, and possibly takes people less seriously than the realistic novelist. The realistic novelist occupies a sort of sensible middle ground between the internal and external approaches; external novelists tend to suggest that people aren't very complex, internal novelists that they are very complex indeed. Realistic novels suggest that they are complex, but can be understood if we take account of a comprehensive range of personal and social factors.

This should become clearer in the analyses of the novels by Joyce and Dickens, but, before turning to the books themselves, a further issue should be considered. As I suggested at the end of the last chapter, the internal or external novelist can become aware of the artifice involved in the creation of fiction, and can, within the novels, become very concerned about it. This is most obvious in the internal novel where the writer may find it very difficult, indeed suspect, to attempt to reproduce the complexities and confusions of the human mind, and so become conscious of the gulf between the written word and the reality of the mind. To some extent, as the previous chapter showed, this can happen in novels which, at first sight, seem close to conventional realism: Henry James became reluctant to 'read' his own heroine, realising that an author is not an all-seeing god. A number of realistic novelists become concerned with this question of the problem of knowing, James being only the most extreme case (particularly in his later novels). Others, such as Austen, do not draw attention to their own faulty or incomplete vision, but, as the previous chapter suggested, it is possible to look at a novelist such as Austen in a way that stresses the rhetorical surface of her work: instead of looking single-mindedly at the world she presents, or taking her moral view too seriously, the reader can concentrate on how she creates a certain authoritative, all-knowing, tone in her novels.

But, by and large, realistic novels can be studied fruitfully without the reader needing to consider the surface operations of the text. With an author such as Joyce, however, it is almost essential to consider the ways in which his novel discusses itself. Attempting to map the unmappable, such internal writers almost inevitably raise questions about the relationship between life and art. This need not become the central focus of the discussion of such a novel, but it is a dimension that the reader must recognise.

Only a few external novels lead towards a discussion of the difference between art and life, whereas most internal novels do. Most comic novelists are quite content to go on producing comic novels, but some of them become aware of the problem associated with their approach. Expressed simply, this is that a comic novel is likely to appear more shallow in moral terms than a realistic novel. The novelist has a comic view of the world, and employs all his or her imaginative skills to put that view across in an amusing way; the author is not concerned to note every variation and contradictory point that may exist in the real world. Thus, a comic novel is more detached, laughing, from on high, at human folly. This does not mean that a comic novel is necessarily less profound than a realistic novel; indeed, comic novels can be very disturbing, as they put in perspective the problems that beset humanity, and laugh at how seriously we take things which, viewed from a distance, do not appear very important at all. But the comic novelist can become aware that the comic is just one way of looking at the world, and perhaps a slightly suspect one, as it does not take full account of all the facts – a comic perspective, for example, can become a cruel one, as it may ignore how very real the suffering is for people caught in certain situations.

One response might be for the comic novelist to move towards realism, towards a more accurate and honest representation of life: and, in practice, comic novels do contain a great deal of realism. But another response is to move in the opposite direction, towards highlighting the difference between art and life, and some of the finest comic novels are self-referential in this sort of way. Two of the best examples are Fielding's *Tom Jones* and Sterne's *Tristram Shandy*: in both works the author discusses his own novel at length. The point of this self-referential approach is to highlight the difference between a work of fiction and the non-fictional nature of life in the real world. Comparing the two things, both Fielding and Sterne draw attention to how art stands as an artificial pattern imposed on experience. Both writers indicate the complexity of life by making obvious the nature, and limitations, of their own comic art.

I have discussed this issue at some length because it is an important one, and one which will come along at university as an initial step in recent developments in novel theory and criticism. Nevertheless, it is only one of several ways of approaching novels which depart from the conventions of realism, and the primary concern of this chapter is with other approaches, as the following analyses should make clear.

II 'A Portrait of the Artist as a Young Man'

The central character in Joyce's *Portrait* is Stephen Dedalus; the novel deals with his experiences at school and college, his troubled relationship with his family and the Catholic Church, and his youthful sexual encounters. At the end of the novel he decides to leave Ireland, hoping to make a clean break with his past. Clearly, this is yet another novel about the early development of a young man. But there might be problems in trying to discuss the novel in quite the same way as, say, *Waverley* or *Sons and Lovers*, because Joyce's manner of writing seems to stand like a barrier between us and the world presented. This is obvious from the very first page of the novel:

> Once upon a time and a very good time it was there was a moocow coming down along the road and this moocow that was coming down along the road met a nicens little boy named baby tuckoo. . . .
>
> His father told him that story: his father looked at him through a glass: he had a hairy face.
>
> He was baby tuckoo. The moocow came down the road where Betty Byrne lived: she sold lemon platt.
>
> *O, the wild rose blossoms*
> *On the little green place.*
>
> He sang that song. That was his song.
>
> *O, the green wothe botheth.*
>
> When you wet the bed, first it is warm then it gets cold. His motherv put on the oilsheet. That had the queer smell.
>
> His mother had a nicer smell than his father. She played on the piano the sailor's hornpipe for him to dance. He danced:
>
> *Tralala lala*
> *Tralala tralaladdy*
> *Tralala lala*
> *Tralala lala.*

Uncle Charles and Dante clapped. They were older than his father and mother but Uncle Charles was older than Dante.

Dante had two brushes in her press. The brush with the maroon velvet back was for Michael Davitt and the brush with the green velvet back was for Parnell. Dante gave him a cachou every time he brought her a piece of tissue paper.

[*A Portrait of the Artist as a Young Man* (Panther, 1977), p. 7]

Normally it would not be too difficult to say what a passage is about, and then to analyse it in detail, but one might feel rather frightened by the prospect of trying to do that here, as the technique is so peculiar. But, however strange or difficult a passage may appear, it is always worth trying to tackle it in the way described in previous chapters; certain oppositions and tensions are returned to so often in fiction that, however odd the novel may appear, the chances are that familiar themes will be present. The best approach to a stylistically difficult passage is, then, to ignore initially the oddities of presentation, in an attempt to get at the summarisable content.

Thus, approaching this passage in the usual way, we can see that it is about a child's early experience. The passage may seem too baffling for an opposition to be established with any certainty, but it helps to think of those oppositions which seem repeatedly to be at the heart of novels. Novels often contrast different societies; they often set rebellious individuals against society and its prevailing values; they often deal with people who are dissenting or departing from some social norm. At the opening of this passage, Joyce almost immediately offers the phrase about the 'nicens little boy' who met a 'moocow' coming down the road: there, in an encapsulated form, we have the idea of the individual coming into conflict with the wider world. This conflict, as yet barely in evidence, could develop as the novel continues, but for the moment an analysis can concentrate on seeing whether other details of the opening passage can be related to this individual-and-society pattern.

In the second paragraph the father is introduced, and subsequently his mother and uncle and aunt. It is as if the child is beginning to understand who he is, and how he relates to other people, gradually coming to know and understand the social structures within which he exists. These ideas can be drawn out of the passage, but at the same time I am using my knowledge of what novelists are interested in to help me spot such things; I know that they are interested in social structures and forms of social organisation, and how individuals relate to them, so can confidently expect to see such interests being presented in the early pages of any novel. This interest in how the world is ordered is not only evident in those items of content that I have noted, but also in the punctuation. The first paragraph is unpunctuated, but in the second paragraph Joyce does begin to punctuate, and the punctuation becomes more complex as the passage continues: at first, then, there is just a string of words, but, as we grow up, we begin to shape and organise things, dividing them up in standard ways, both when speaking and when thinking about the world we live in.

So, Joyce sets 'baby tuckoo' against the world at large, and gradually familiarises the child with the various ways in which we organise the world. The imposing of frames and structures is central throughout the passage: the song, for example, contrasts what is natural and unrestrained ('the wild rose blossoms') and humanity's artificially created order ('the little green place') – a social order is imposed upon luxuriance and wildness. By the end, the child is developing an awareness of, though no understanding of, politics and religion: two more of the ordering frames found in, or imposed on, the world.

It seems then that Joyce is as concerned with social conventions and patterns as any other novelist: *Portrait*, as a whole, will examine the family and the political and religious structures into which Stephen is born. I could, therefore, discuss *Portrait* as a reasonably straightforward novel about a young man coming to terms with society, but other novelists who address themselves to such matters do not write in this peculiar way, and if I am to do justice to the work, it does seem necessary to come to terms with, and justify, Joyce's technique.

This is where I can introduce the idea of 'internalisation'. One possible explanation of Joyce's method is that he wants a style that enacts the child's mind. The passage appears less difficult once this can be seen, and, thinking about the novel as a whole, I can see that at each stage Joyce finds a style appropriate to Stephen at that stage of his development. The conventional labels for this are 'interior monologue' or 'stream of consciousness'.

Now this does go some way towards explaining why Joyce chooses to write in this way, but possibly it doesn't explain enough. The opening sequence appears far more complicated and stylised than just the flow of a mind. What it seems to amount to is a very self-conscious examination of how language shapes, frames and presents the everyday world. It is as if Joyce has taken a step back to consider the relationship between language and life.

This is a view of the text I can develop as I look at subsequent passages, but it must be stressed at this point that this is not the only way of looking at the novel. I could get a great deal out of *Portrait* even if I totally ignored most of its oddities of form. Indeed, to get a firm grip on the novel I need, first of all, to come to terms with it at the level of content in a more traditional sense. So, for the moment, I will continue to discuss *Portrait* as a conventional realistic novel.

Although I have decided that Joyce is going to set Stephen against the world, I have not yet seen how Stephen rebels. I need a passage that will enable me to see Stephen more clearly; the one I have chosen is on the second page of the novel:

> The wide playgrounds were swarming with boys. All were shouting and the prefects urged them on with strong cries. The evening air was pale and chilly and after every charge and thud of the footballers the greasy leather orb flew like a heavy bird through the grey light. He kept on the fringe of his line, out of sight of his prefect, out of the reach of the rude feet, feigning to run now and then. He felt his body small and weak amid the throng of the players and his eyes were weak and watery. Rody Kickham was not like that: he would be captain of the third line all the fellows said.
>
> [p. 8]

This passage describes the way in which Stephen hangs back from the hurly-burly of the football game. It opposes Stephen, who remains on the fringes, and the rest of the boys, who participate vigorously and enthusiastically. Relating this to novels in general, we see here a hero who shies away from participation, and who prefers to remain on his own. I could develop this point by selecting scenes where Stephen comes in active conflict with those around him, and part of my interest would be in seeing in what ways, if any, he changes during the course of the novel.

But previous chapters have already shown how to construct a discussion of a novel along these lines, so there is no point in repeating a similar analysis here. It makes more sense to concentrate on the distinctive technique of the novel, either focusing on its internal dimension or extending the discussion of how Joyce is very self-conscious about the language of fiction. Almost any scene from the novel would serve to extend the discussion of either of these points; the one I have selected is a famous scene, at the end of chapter four, where Stephen, having just decided to reject the priesthood, encounters a girl wading in the water:

A girl stood before him in midstream, alone and still, gazing out to sea. She seemed like one whom magic had changed into the likeness of a strange and beautiful seabird. Her long slender bare legs were delicate as a crane's and pure save where an emerald trail of seaweed had fashioned itself as a sign upon the flesh. Her thighs, fuller and softhued as ivory, were bared almost to the hips, while the white fringes of her drawers were like feathering of soft white down. Her slateblue skirts were kilted boldly about her waist and dovetailed behind her. Her bosom was as a bird's soft and slight, slight and soft as the breast of some darkplumaged dove. But her long fair hair was girlish: and girlish, and touched with the wonder of mortal beauty, her face.

[pp. 155–6]

The passage is about a girl Stephen sees. The implied contrast is between the uneasiness he has been experiencing and the ecstasy of this moment. Detailed examination notices that the girl is associated with a bird, always a symbol of freedom, and that she seems enticing. It is like a vision, a vision of someone Stephen can communicate with, and so escape from his mundane life. Such moments are not all that unusual in fiction: the young hero at odds with society has a vision of a more attractive alternative; we know from our wider experience of novels, though, that there is probably something deceptive about this intense moment, as it is impossible to make a permanent escape to a better, freer world.

What makes this fairly familiar experience seem unfamiliar is the choice of style, which is far more lyrical than anything normally offered in a novel. One might say that the experience is being presented in the sort of vocabulary that Stephen might well have used at this stage of his life: a style appropriate to a young aesthete, emphasising such qualities as delicacy and softness, and employing lyrical repetition to add to the almost spiritual rapture of the moment. The event is reported, not by an omniscient narrator, but in the language that Stephen himself might have used.

One can also say that the style raises questions about how language can best engage with the world. The straightforward style of a realistic novel works well for presenting life as we normally think of it, just as this style is fine for reporting a romantic experience, but in both instances language shapes and processes the world, so that one can ask how the full truth of any moment can be conveyed. In *Portrait* this problem is crucial for the young man at the centre: how can he be an artist, what language can he employ, if he rejects the ways of thinking, and language, of society at large?

This may seem a rather rarefied issue, and perhaps one peculiar to this novel, since it is about a young writer, but in fact the questions it raises are not uncommon in fiction. Many modern novels try to get inside characters' minds, but in doing so they almost inevitably encounter the problem of whether language can describe what is elusive, even intangible. Many modern novelists – Virginia Woolf and William Faulkner being two of the better-known names – actively concern themselves with the problems of perception and the registering of experience in a literary text. They do so by making the text so opaque that we cannot just look through to the experience being described, but become aware of the complications that arise in the attempt to describe anything.

But even if this dimension to such works is recognised, the student is still left with the problem of how to discuss these novels: how can they best be treated in an essay? First, it is important to have some general guidelines when tacking such novels. Reading novelists such as Woolf, Faulkner and Joyce, you are likely to be baffled unless you can sum up in a few words a justification for the general nature of their work. Explanations must inevitably lie in the area of changing the angle of perception, of moving from the safe distance occupied by the narrator of a realistic novel to a less conventional perspective. This can then, as explained, lead on to the idea that the text deliberately ties itself up in knots, as a way of indicating the gap between words and reality. But, however knotted the text may become, the chances are that familiar themes and tensions will be in evidence at the core of the novel; in particular, the individual-and-society conflict.

But your account will be lacking if you just stick to content in the traditional sense (even though it can be argued that conventional themes really underpin the novel), as this will involve overlooking the oddities of presentation. The most solid and sensible approach to such novels is to work through about four passages exploring what themes are central, but giving slightly greater emphasis to the technique than might be the case when discussing a realistic novel. The novel, in your essay, will thus be represented as a new way of looking at familiar questions.

A more radical approach would concentrate almost totally on the technique, and argue that the text is not so much looking in a new way, as simply talking about the problems of looking. But whether you adopt this approach or the more conservative one, the ideas underlying your analysis are likely to be very simple and familiar. Indeed it is wise to avoid excessively original or ingenious ideas. What really makes a piece of criticism impressive is the way in which the reader uses the details of the text in a creative way to illustrate simple and central ideas about novels.

A look at one more passage from *Portrait* may reinforce this point. I have chosen the scene where Stephen visits a prostitute. Something of the significance of the scene can be grasped even before we read it: the hero, at odds with a society that restricts and restrains him, searches for an outlet for his emotional desires, but this outlet is likely to prove disappointing, as in life and novels it is far from easy to escape from the conventional world, and searching for emotional gratification with a prostitute is obviously rather grubby and suspect. Our initial assessment of the meaning of the scene is thus determined by our awareness of what usually happens in novels: few, if any, novels before *Portrait* present an encounter with a prostitute, but as an act of rebellion it has much in common with what happens in many novels.

Our sense of the meaning of the scene will alter slightly, however, as we begin to look at it in detail, and see Joyce's unique way of presenting the incident:

> Tears of joy and relief shone in his delighted eyes and his lips parted though they would not speak.
> She passed her tinkling hand through his hair, calling him a little rascal.
> Give me a kiss, she said.
> His lips would not bend to kiss her. He wanted to be held firmly in her arms, to be caressed slowly, slowly, slowly. In her arms he felt that he had suddenly become strong and fearless and sure of himself. But his lips would not bend to kiss her.
> With a sudden movement she bowed his head and joined her lips to his and he read the meaning of her movements in her frank uplifted eyes. It was too much for him. He closed his eyes, surrendering himself to her, body and mind, conscious of nothing in the world but the dark pressure of her softly parting lips. They pressed upon his brain as upon his lips as though they were the vehicle of a vague speech; and between them he felt an unknown and timid pressure, darker than the swoon of sin, softer than sound or odour.
>
> [pp. 93–4]

We can see that the passage is about Stephen's response to the advances of the prostitute, but what is interesting about the passage is the way Joyce finds a new method for describing Stephen's response. Rather than adopt an omniscient manner of narration, Joyce varies the perspective by adopting the sort of lyrical romantic style that Stephen himself might use. The passage does present a clear account of what is happening, but concentrates far more on the young man's feelings. In order to convey this impression that he is getting inside Stephen's mind, Joyce has to depart from the clear, straightforward prose that might be found in a realistic novel. The rhythm of the sentences becomes poetic or lyrical, signalling to the reader that something emotional and internal is being presented: the repetition of 'slowly slowly, slowly', for example, conveys Stephen's state of mind, rather than processing and reporting on his feelings in the manner that we might encounter in a realist text. There is a similar effect in the last sentence of the extract, where the movement of the prose again attempts to enact Stephen's feelings.

Such use of repetition and rhythmic effects can also be found in the novels of Woolf and Faulkner. We tend to expect a kind of crisp, no-nonsense prose in novels but, by confounding this expectation, by presenting a lyrical description of an experience, the internal novelist deceives the reader into believing that the text is getting close to the experiences of the mind itself. 'Poetic' is a convenient label for such a style, partly because the rhythms of poetry are different from those of conventional prose, but also because we tend to think of poetry as emotional and personal, whereas we tend to associate prose with the presentation of hard and fast facts. But the internal novelist does not necessarily have to opt for a lyrical mode of presentation; any deviation from the standard manner of prose will have a similar effect on the reader. For example, if the novelist abandons the usual conventions of punctuation, the impression on the reader is that something far more fluid is being presented than anything we might encounter in a conventionally punctuated passage of prose. Joyce at times experiments with punctuation in this kind of way (most forcibly in the last chapter of *Ulysses*), but in this passage he uses the sort of lyrical technique that we might encounter in many internal novels; he breaks away from the conventional rhythms of prose story-telling to convey the impression of getting inside the mind.

The point I am making is a simple one – that the internal novelist finds new ways of writing about familiar experiences, redirecting the emphasis, however, so that the internal experiences of the character become central. The effect is created by a modification of conventional prose, the novelist most frequently moving closer to a manner that we might more commonly associate with poetry.

But there is an added difficulty in this passage, that we might not encounter in the novels of Woolf and Faulkner. There is a consistent impression that Stephen is being mocked: notice, for example, the pretentiousness of the phrase 'they pressed upon his brain as upon his lips . . .', and the exaggeration in the description of Stephen's feeling 'he had suddenly become strong and fearless and sure of himself'. This tone is, however, easy to explain. Different novelists have different temperaments. Woolf usually offers us a sympathetic insight into the minds of her characters, but Joyce prefers to mock, showing us that Stephen takes himself rather too seriously; and, throughout *Portrait*, there is always a degree of irony, even in the most beautiful scenes. Joyce conveys Stephen's feelings, but does not hesitate also to reveal his absurdity and sense of his own importance.

There is, however, another way of responding to the exaggerated manner of this passage; it is a very perceptive and delicate piece of writing, but also rather gushing and romantic. The simple point that can be made is that Joyce is possibly also concerned here to discuss the nature of language itself. There is, very clearly, a sense of a gap between the word and the deed: Stephen cannot bring himself to kiss the girl, as if there were an unbridgeable gap between the falsifying romantic haze of the style and the reality of a sexual encounter. Again the text highlights the problem of how can language engage with reality.

This self-referential aspect of the novel, the way in which it discusses, if only implicitly, the relationship between its own use of language and the nature of experience in the real world, is one that many readers may prefer to ignore and, of course, you should concentrate on those aspects of a text that interest you most. The point of this last piece of analysis, however, has been to show how simple and consistent are the ideas that inform most criticism; they only become distinctive when the reader starts to analyse a passage in detail, and uses these simple informing assumptions to create something new.

To sum up, the best way to approach an 'internal' novel is to recognise the ways in which the work is shaped by the familiar social and personal tensions that shape all novels, but then to focus on the original ways in which the novelist alters the manner of writing, in order to look at familiar issues in a new light. The direction of your reading will probably be determined either by the idea that the novelist is striving to get inside the mind of the character, or is interested in highlighting the nature of writing itself. These simple ideas will flesh themselves out the moment you turn to discuss extracts from the novel.

III 'Martin Chuzzlewit'

The sort of internalisation described above is one way in which the artist can dissent from the conventions of realism. The other method is to become more external: drawing attention to the artifice of the story, perhaps not bothering to present believable characters, or using the sort of creaky stories that are obviously more like story-telling than life. Many novelists use such external methods – for example, Fielding, Sterne and Thackeray. But it is Dickens, and his novel *Martin Chuzzlewit*, that I focus on here.

As with Joyce's *Portrait*, it helps when studying *Martin Chuzzlewit* to forget at first what makes it so distinctive, and concentrate on how it resembles other novels. The ways in which it does should be obvious from a summary: *Martin Chuzzlewit* tells the story of Martin, a rather priggish young man, who is apprenticed to an architect, Pecksniff. He leaves Pecksniff, and goes to live for a time in America; in his absence, Pecksniff tries to woo Mary Graham, the girl Martin loves. Eventually, Old Martin, Mary's guardian and Martin's grandfather, turns on Pecksniff, and reunites Mary and young Martin.

Viewed in the most basic terms, this is clearly another novel about a young man maturing, and one could look at a number of scenes to see how Dickens handles this familiar theme. It would soon become clear, however, that Dickens is not concerned to present any very profound or penetrating analysis of the relationship between the individual and society, but seems more intent on entertaining, on producing a performance. To justify his approach we need to look at the text, trying to work out why Dickens chooses to write in this way.

The novel begins:

> As no lady or gentleman, with any claims to polite breeding, can possibly sympathise with the Chuzzlewit family without being first assured of the extreme antiquity of the race, it is a great satisfaction to know that it undoubtedly descended in a direct line from Adam and Eve; and was, in the very earliest times, closely connected with the agricultural interest. If it should ever be urged by grudging and malicious persons, that a Chuzzlewit, in any period of the family history, displayed an overweening amount of family pride, surely the weakness will be considered not only pardon-

able but laudable, when the immense superiority of the house to the rest of mankind, in respect of this its ancient origin, is taken into account.

It is remarkable that as there was, in the oldest family of which we have any record, a murderer and a vagabond, so we never fail to meet, in the records of all old families, with innumerable repetitions of the same phase of character. Indeed, it may be laid down as a general principle, that the more extended the ancestry, the greater the amount of violence and vagabondism; for in ancient days those two amusements, combining a wholesome excitement with a promising means of repairing shattered fortunes, were at once the ennobling pursuit and the healthful recreation of the Quality of this land.

[*Martin Chuzzlewit* (Penguin, 1968), p. 51]

Dickens's subject matter here is the family history of the Chuzzlewits, but, more than the alleged subject, what is most noticeable about the passage is Dickens's manner: the elaborate and pompous tone, the general inflation of language for the most commonplace things. He seems to take a comic delight in the world, in particular a comic delight in social affectation.

Trying to characterise the passage and its effect more precisely, we can say that the manner is exaggerated, a display of verbal fireworks, which seems to prevent us from accepting the world presented as in any way convincing. The sort of simplification involved can be seen in the way that pride is singled out as the ruling passion of the family. It is, then, an external comic mode: Dickens is not concerned to represent the world as it is, but to use his art to present a comic interpretation of life, in which, presumably, the characters will serve principally as amusing illustrations of his thesis.

But can this be said to have as much substance and value as a realistic picture? Well, just as internalisation (as in Joyce's *Portrait*) gets at a truth distinct from that of standard realism, so does an external method. As is clear in this passage, an external comic approach is a very good way of representing social affectation: the realistic novel tends to take people seriously, but the comic approach can pick out and exaggerate all the slightly absurd traits in human behaviour. Thus, a comic novel can present a serious vision of society, because of its ability to present a vivid picture of folly: in Dickens, this can become immensely powerful when, extended over the course of hundreds of pages, it becomes a complete panorama of chaos, of people absurdly pursuing selfish interests.

There is a more disturbing side to this in *Martin Chuzzlewit*, which our method of analysis may reveal. I have stressed several times that the best way to grasp a novel as a whole is to identify the broad opposition or oppositions that shape the text. The most common of these is the conflict between the individual and society but other oppositions can exist within a text, sometimes simultaneously with the tension between the individual and society. In *Waverley*, for example, Scott not only presented the young man's conflict with the world he was born into, but also the contrast between English and Scots society.

What all these oppositions have in common is that they set society's conventional patterns against alternatives, most commonly the rebelliousness of an individual or a less familiar society. But the novelist – and in particular the comic novelist, who starts from an assumption of the absurdity of social life – can also contrast the conventional world with motives and instincts which polite society may never acknowledge. In this opening passage from *Martin Chuzzlewit*, for example, Dickens parodies the discourse of society, but at the same time touches on disturbing anti-social behaviour. There are a number of references to murder and violence – dangerous impulses which society may not be able to control. The next few paragraphs of the novel would confirm this impression, as, beneath the comic manner, we would see repeated references to such things as 'slaughterous conspiracies and bloody frays', to war and invasion, and to civil unrest, in the person of Guy Fawkes. The tone of the opening is amusing, but there are hints of dangerous and disturbing anti-social impulses, elements in the human personality which represent a threat to the very notion of civilised society.

Not every comic novelist will suggest such submerged dangerous feelings; it is enough for the comic writer to show human folly without hinting at darker instincts in people. But such basic instincts do look as if they are going to be central in this novel. Possibly you might not spot such an opposition in the novel, but that would not be very important; a perfectly satisfactory interpretation can be built upon any opposition or oppositions that any reader notices in the text. Remember, however, that three oppositions are most likely to be in evidence: society versus the individual, a clash between two societies, and society as we generally think of it contrasted with a more anarchic concealed world. This last one is, for example, frequently encountered in Hardy's novels, which present country people at odds with traditional ways of living, and also chart the changes that alter the social fabric of Wessex; but at the same time he contrasts the artificiality of life in society with more basic rhythms, which seem to reside in the patterns of nature. Often

Hardy seems to be commenting from a great height, in a manner very similar to the detached aloofness of the comic novelist.

The comic approach, especially that of Dickens, can embrace some very disturbing ideas, but not every reader will spot this element in the novel (and other readers will, of course, regard it as something of only limited importance in the overall appeal of his work). So the most fruitful way of progressing might be to look more closely at some of the standard features of comic fiction as exemplified in this text. Some of these features – things such as comic invention, an interest in social affectation, amusing exaggeration, and fine comic writing – come together in the portrait of Pecksniff. In the scene that follows he is visited by Anthony Chuzzlewit (a brother of Old Martin) and his son Jonas:

> 'Come to say good-bye, you see,' said Anthony, in a low voice, to Mr Pecksniff, as they took their seats apart at the table, while the rest conversed among themselves. 'Where's the use of a division between you and me? We are the two halves of a pair of scissors, when apart, Pecksniff; but together we are something. Eh?'
>
> 'Unanimity, my good sir,' rejoined Mr Pecksniff, 'is always delightful.'
>
> 'I don't know about that,' said the old man, 'for there are some people I would rather differ from than agree with. But you know my opinion of you.'
>
> Mr Pecksniff, still having 'Hypocrite' in his mind, only replied by a motion of his head, which was something between an affirmative bow and a negative shake.
>
> 'Complimentary,' said Anthony. 'Complimentary, upon my word. It was an involuntary tribute to your abilities, even at the time; and it was not a time to suggest compliments either. But we agreed in the coach, you know, that we quite understood each other.'
>
> 'Oh, quite,' assented Mr Pecksniff, in a manner which implied that he himself was misunderstood most cruelly, but would not complain.
>
> [pp. 248–9]

The passage features Pecksniff and a member of the Chuzzlewit clan, Anthony. The characters are competing, but the real opposition is between the grand manner of both and the selfishness of their true selves. Pecksniff, in particular, is a bloated windbag, always acting, always putting on a performance, beset with affectation and thoroughly imbued with falseness. Dickens is not offering a subtle insight into the hypocritical temperament of his character, but working out a simple idea, and making it effective through the delight with which he imagines these pompous gestures.

This leads back to the darker side of Dickens, for what is implicit here is a frightening sense of the pretence and greed prevalent in society, and the rareness of goodness and innocence. If the realistic novel tends to accept the social world as the normal world, this sort of novel can show the falsity of all social behaviour, and point to the mean, sordid or depraved motives at the bottom of most actions. In a way, the comic novel resembles the 'internal' novel because, instead of merely looking at the visible surface, it teases out the deeper instincts that govern behaviour.

Having now looked at a couple of scenes from *Martin Chuzzlewit*, I could continue to construct my analysis by selecting further passages. My approach is very much the same as with an 'internal' novel: I start from a recognition that familiar social and personal themes are bound to be in evidence, underpinning the text. Once I have identified these conflicts I have something to get hold of, and then can continue by paying closer attention to the distinctive way in which Dickens handles these themes. My comments on any individual passage are to a large extent shaped by the very simple theory of comic fiction put forward in this chapter – that it laughs in an aloof way at human folly. But when individual passages are examined closely, this simple idea is likely to become more complicated, and reformulate itself with a different emphasis depending upon the particular novelist or novel I happen to be discussing.

With Dickens, as has been suggested, the direction in which I travelled was towards the darker side of his imagination. Another reader, of course, might have no interest in this at all, but as it is the element in his work that has caught my attention I might well choose subsequent passages for analysis that tend to endorse my theory. For example, I might choose a passage concerning Jonas Chuzzlewit and his murdering of another of the characters, Montague Tigg, which might provide a very vivid illustration of nasty impulses intruding into the social world. But such an idea is not necessarily one that need be at the centre of a discussion of the novel. I could, for example, select four scenes featuring Pecksniff and build up a perfectly satisfactory impression of the novel from them, provided, of course, that I worked with sensible, straightforward ideas, and built up a coherent case from the evidence of the scenes I examined.

In this section I have been discussing *Martin Chuzzlewit*, but at the same time I have been trying to establish some general principles about analysing comic novels. Of course, no two novels are going to be the same, so there is some difficulty in trying to establish general principles while at the same time considering an individual case. Dickens, for example, has a more disturbing side than many comic novelists; Thackeray, a near contemporary, is much more single-minded in his focus on social folly. Novelists such as Fielding and Sterne look at the art of the novel itself, although Sterne has a very morbid imagination, which in some ways can be compared with that of Dickens. It is this distinctive quality of any individual novelist or novel that criticism is, in the end, trying to identify.

The approach to getting a view of your own of the unique character of any work can be reduced to three stages. First, identify the perennial social and personal themes in evidence in the novel. Secondly, analyse a number of scenes from the novel in the light of a theory of comedy – such as the idea that the comic novel laughs at social folly. This will provide a general justification for the overall tactics of any scene in the novel, but as you consider individual passages the third step will develop, as you become aware of the distinctive qualities of any specific novel. It may seem a rather optimistic hope that such qualities will reveal themselves, but in fact they will – but only if you are prepared to look hard at, and think hard about, those passages you select for analysis.

IV

The primary idea in all the analyses presented so far in this book is that the first priority when studying a novel is to identify the underlying nature and structure of the text. If you can label a novel an education novel, a realistic novel, a comic novel or whatever, you have immediately made a considerable advance in coming to terms with it critically. The next stage is to search for the opposition or oppositions that you believe shape the text. The purpose of these initial critical moves is to make yourself aware of the family resemblances between the particular novel being studied and novels in general. This makes it much easier to proceed with the rest of your critical analysis, as you can advance from saying in what ways the novel is a very ordinary example of its genre to describing the ways in which it is an extraordinary and unique work. The emphasis here falls on the ways in which the particular novel is distinctive.

It may seem hard to identify these distinctive qualities, but in fact it isn't very difficult. All you have to do is to look at individual scenes, and spot the details that give the novel a style of its own. This does mean, however, that you have got to be quite astute at seeing what there is about any particular novel that makes it resemble a great many others; you cannot proceed to look at the details if you haven't got hold of an idea of the general picture. But in most cases this should not prove too tricky, as the features a novel has in common with other novels are usually fairly obvious.

There may, however, be novels that simply baffle you, that you can't see as a whole, and which defeat your attempt to classify them. This could well be the case with contemporary experimental novels, but it might also be true of many classic texts. For example, *Sons and Lovers* is an easy novel to classify, but by the time Lawrence wrote *Women in Love* he was producing a far more convoluted book, which the reader might feel far from confident about categorising.

The thing to remember is that, however complex the texture of the work may become, underneath there are always going to be familiar patterns, familiar subjects. As I have said, *Women in Love* is a very complicated novel, but underpinning it are familiar ideas about conformity to and deviation from traditional values and conventional ways of behaving. However complicated a text is, it should always be possible to identify certain underlying tensions; having identified them, you can then work towards a sense of the ways in which the particular novel is distinctive. And, obviously, the main critical effort must be directed towards identifying how the artist does, in the end, present a unique picture.

5

Tackling a long and difficult novel

Novels discussed:
Middlemarch, by George Eliot, published 1872
Bleak House, by Charles Dickens, published 1853

THIS chapter represents a test of the method of analysis demonstrated so far, for in it I look at two major works, both of considerable length and complexity, and, by common consent, two of the greatest English novels. One of these books, *Middlemarch*, falls within the realistic tradition; the other, *Bleak House*, is outside it. What this chapter should reveal is whether the approach adopted so far is adequate for coping even with works of this size and difficulty. The stages of analysis in the following sections are again those listed at the beginning of chapter two; I begin by working from four passages, trying to establish a coherent overall view of each novel; when I notice a feature in the text, I try to explain its presence, specifically in a way which is consistent with my developing overall view. Such simple critical strategies inform and shape the analyses that follow.

I 'Middlemarch'

The opening section of *Middlemarch* focuses on Dorothea Brooke, and shows how she comes to marry Edward Casaubon, a clergyman some thirty years her senior. As this story develops a number of other strands are introduced. There is the story of Tertius Lydgate, a young doctor newly arrived in the area, and his courtship of, and marriage to, Rosamond Vincy. Another couple who eventually marry are Mary Garth and Rosamond's brother, Fred Vincy; but in the early stages of the novel she refuses to marry him until he mends his ways. For Dorothea, the reality of marriage to Casaubon is not at all what she had expected, although they come closer together when he learns that he has not long to live. But Casaubon extracts a promise from her that, after his death, she will continue with his futile scholarly work; moreover, he leaves a codicil in his will stating that Dorothea will be disinherited if she ever marries a young relative of Casaubon's, Will Ladislaw. Will has featured prominently in the novel, but, up to this point, Dorothea has certainly never regarded him as a potential partner.

Just as Dorothea's marriage has proved a disappointment, so has Lydgate's: his wife is extravagant and foolish, flirting with Ladislaw, experiencing a miscarriage as a result of riding while pregnant, and eventually forcing Lydgate to mortgage the furniture to pay off debts incurred as a result of her overspending. One way out of Lydgate's troubles would be the assistance he might receive from a banker, Bulstrode, but Bulstrode has problems of his own, as his past dishonesty catches up with him. Lydgate then tells his story to a sympathetic Dorothea, who, deciding to help, calls the next day, but finds Rosamond and Will together; this is a decisive moment for both women: it makes Rosamond act unselfishly for once, as she tells Dorothea that Dorothea herself is the woman Will really cares for. In the meantime Dorothea has realised her own love for Will. This event helps to bring Rosamond and her husband together, and also paves the way for the marriage of Dorothea and Will.

Is there anything that can be deduced from this summary? Well, it is obviously a story that concerns itself with the ordinary dilemmas of life: with marriages, mainly unhappy marriages, with people's jobs, with their relationships with their neighbours. As always, the way to start making some sense out of a mass of material is to look for an opposition. Thinking in terms of the individual and society, we can see how various characters are at odds with society, not so much as a consequence of obvious ills in the world, more as a result of their own unrealistic expectations.

But that is only a very general impression. It is time to start looking at the evidence in greater detail. The novel begins:

> Miss Brooke had that kind of beauty which seems to be thrown into relief by poor dress. Her hand and wrist were so finely formed that she could wear sleeves not less bare of style than those in which the Blessed Virgin appeared to Italian painters; and her profile as well as her stature and bearing seemed to gain the more dignity from her plain garments, which

by the side of provincial fashion gave her the impressiveness of a fine quotation from the Bible, – or from one of our elder poets, – in a paragraph of to-day's newspaper. She was usually spoken of as being remarkably clever, but with the addition that her sister Celia had more commonsense. Nevertheless, Celia worse scarcely more trimmings; and it was only to close observers that her dress differed from her sister's, and had a shade of coquetry in its arrangements; for Miss Brooke's plain dressing was due to mixed conditions, in most of which her sister shared. The pride of being ladies had something to do with it: the Brooke connections, though not exactly aristocratic, were unquestionably 'good': if you inquired backward for a generation or two, you would not find any yard-measuring or parcel-tying forefather – anything lower than an admiral or a clergyman; and there was even an ancestor discernible as a Puritan gentleman who served under Cromwell, but afterwards conformed, and managed to come out of all the political troubles as the proprietor of a respectable family estate. Young women of such birth, living in a quiet country-house, and attending a village church hardly larger than a parlour, naturally regarded frippery as the ambition of a huckster's daughter. Then there was well-bred economy, which in those days made show in dress the first item to be deducted from, when any margin was required for expenses more distinctive of rank. Such reasons would have been enough to account for plain dress, quite apart from religious feeling; but in Miss Brooke's case, religion alone would have determined it; and Celia mildly acquiesced in all her sister's sentiments, only infusing them with that common-sense which is able to accept momentous doctrines without any eccentric agitation. Dorothea knew many passages of Pascal's *Pensées* and of Jeremy Taylor by heart; and to her the destinies of mankind, seen by the light of Christianity, made the solicitudes of feminine fashion appear an occupation for Bedlam. She could not reconcile the anxieties of a spiritual life involving eternal consequences, with a keen interest in guimp and artificial profusions of drapery. Her mind was theoretic, and yearned by its nature after some lofty conception of the world which might frankly include the parish of Tipton and her own rule of conduct there . . . With all this, she, the elder of the sisters, was not yet twenty, and they had both been educated, since they were about twelve years old and had lost their parents, on plans at once narrow and promiscuous, first in an English family and afterwards in a Swiss family at Lausanne . . .

[*Middlemarch* (Penguin, 1965), pp. 29–30]

The passage is mainly about Dorothea Brooke, elder of the Brooke sisters. One possible opposition is the difference between Dorothea and Celia, but a more promising one is the opposition between the reality of their lot and Dorothea's ideal of some sort of higher life. Presumably in the course of the work either this young woman is going to be educated, so that she will realise that she cannot escape the real problems of daily life, or else she will be backed by George Eliot in her dissatisfaction with the world she is born into. One rather suspects that the former is going to be the case, that Dorothea will change and mature.

Looking at the details, we might notice first the great length of this opening paragraph. From this we might deduce that the length suggests the fullness of Eliot's approach, how thorough she is in her analysis, how steadily she constructs a closely argued reading of the character or event. The cataloguing of the reasons why Dorothea dresses as she does suggests that Eliot is concerned to report fully on the complex combination of factors making up the whole. It is partly this that leads me to suspect that the author will be critical of Dorothea, for Dorothea is theoretic, looking for an all-embracing view, while Eliot seems to pull in the other direction, towards a complex cluster of possible views and explanations. The opening paragraph indicates a novelist dedicated to fullness and thoroughness, almost obsessive about detail.

But if this is the method, what of the woman presented? Initially we get the impression of a sensible middle-class woman, but, as the passage goes on, she begins to appear rather absurd. The inflated language Eliot employs to describe Dorothea's attitudes suggests a mocking of her high ideals. And we can also note Dorothea's egocentricity, for her grand ideals feature herself in a starring role, benevolently conducting and guiding life in Tipton. But, just as the treatment seems to become savage, Eliot turns things round, letting us know how young Dorothea is, and what a disorganised upbringing and education she has had; this goes a long way towards justifying and explaining her.

So the novel as a whole promises an account of a young woman having to come to terms with life. This familiar theme is made distinctive by the fullness with which Eliot analyses character. But more can be said about the style. Looking at the opening sentence, we can see a sort of conspiracy of understanding between narrator and reader: Eliot does not actually describe Dorothea's beauty, but takes it for granted that the reader will know what she means. There seems to be a sharing of middle-class values and knowledge, and in a phrase such as 'one of our elder poets' there is a notion of a shared inheritance. This suggests that Eliot is writing and judging from the point of view of society as a whole, even though her comments are likely to be more subtle than those of the mass of people. This confident reading of human experience is probably what most attracts readers to George Eliot, although some readers are merely irritated by an author who is so all-knowing.

As we move forward in the novel, Lydgate seems to demand attention. How does he relate to what we have seen so far? Most of chapter fifteen is devoted to a very lengthy examination of Lydgate, his past history, his reasons for becoming a doctor, the sort of man he is. I have selected an extract where Eliot seems to move towards summing him up:

> He was certainly a happy fellow at this time: to be seven-and-twenty, without any fixed vices, with a generous resolution that his action should be beneficial, and with ideas in his brain that made life interesting quite apart from the *cultus* of horse-flesh and other mystic rites of costly observance, which the eight hundred pounds left him after buying his practice would certainly have not gone far in paying for. He was at a starting-point which makes many a man's career a fine subject for betting, if there were any gentlemen given to that amusement who could appreciate the complicated probabilities of an arduous purpose, with all the possible thwartings and furtherings of circumstances, all the niceties of inward balance, by which a man swims and makes his point or else is carried head-long. The risk would remain, even with close knowledge of Lydgate's character; for character too is a process and an unfolding. The man was still in the making, as much as the Middlemarch doctor and immortal discoverer, and there were both virtues and faults capable of shrinking or expanding. The faults will not, I hope, be a reason for the withdrawal of your interest in him. Among our valued friends is there not some one or other who is a little too self-confident and disdainful; whose distinguished mind is a little spotted with commonness; who is a little pinched here and protuberant there with native prejudices; or whose better energies are liable to lapse down the wrong channel under the influence of transient solicitations? All these things might be alleged against Lydgate, but then, they are the periphrases of a polite preacher, who talks of Adam, and would not like to mention anything painful to the pew-renters. The particular faults from which these delicate generalities are distilled have distinguishable physiognomies, diction, accent, and grimaces; filling up parts in very various dramas.
>
> [pp. 178–9]

The passage is about Lydgate: there is an opposition between the potential, the promise of success, and the fact that it is not a clear path, that because of various reasons, but principally personal shortcomings, he might not achieve such success. Relating this to the first passage, we see here another character with noble ambitions, full of idealistic thoughts, but in the mixed conditions of this world these dreams will fail. Lydgate's ambitions are more practical than Dorothea's, but he has the advantage of being a man who can apply himself to a career.

Like Dorothea, he seems too egocentric: just as she envisaged herself at the centre of Tipton life, so he is a 'little too self-confident and disdainful'.

The general ideas informing Eliot's novel as a whole are now becoming clearer. She concentrates on a certain kind of egoist, and the trials of that person in the world. But it is far from being a black-and-white moral examination, for she is ready to acknowledge the nobility and sincerity of the ambition; the nobility of Lydgate's aims is made clear by contrasting him with the more wasteful young man who is only concerned with horses and gambling. Yet Eliot constantly shifts the angle of evaluation, for, just as she is disdainful of gambling, so she uses the betting idea to estimate his chances of success. Her art is extraordinarily nimble, for she is forever shifting the angle of looking, forever saying 'Yes, he has this fault, but also this virtue, but this virtue has to be set against this fault'. The object of her art seems to be to view the case from all possible angles. She urges the reader not to be dismissive, not to settle for a simple view, but to see all sides of the case. The way in which we are encouraged to look at Lydgate here is probably reproduced throughout the novel, as Eliot looks at more characters or looks at the community in which they live.

One way forward in looking at the novel would be to consider George Eliot's presentation of a number of the other characters or to look at the way in which she presents the social institutions of Middlemarch, but in this initial analysis it is, I think, more useful to concentrate on the forward movement of the plot, specifically to see what happens to Dorothea and Lydgate. To take Dorothea: almost any scene from her marriage would indicate why it fails. The extract I have chosen comes near Casaubon's death; he has asked Dorothea to continue his work, but she is aware of its futility and reluctant to commit herself. She goes for a solitary walk:

> When Dorothea was out on the gravel walks, she lingered among the nearer clumps of trees, hesitating, as she had done once before, though from a different cause. Then she had feared lest her effort at fellowship should be unwelcome; now she dreaded going to the spot where she foresaw that she must bind herself to a fellowship from which she shrank. Neither law nor the world's opinion compelled her to this – only her husband's nature and her own compassion, only the ideal and not the real yoke of marriage. She saw clearly enough the whole situation, yet she was fettered: she could not smite the stricken soul that entreated hers. If that were weakness, Dorothea was weak. But the half-hour was passing, and she must not delay longer. When she entered the Yew-Tree Walk she

could not see her husband; but the walk had bends, and she went, expecting to catch sight of his figure wrapped in a blue cloak, which, with a warm velvet cap, was his outer garment on chill days for the garden. It occurred to her that he might be resting in the summer-house, towards which the path diverged a little.

Turning the angle, she could see him seated on the bench, close to a stone table. His arms were resting on the table, and his brow was bowed down on them, the blue cloak being dragged forward and screening his face on each side.

'He exhausted himself last night,' Dorothea said to herself, thinking at first that he was asleep . . .

[pp. 522–3]

But Casaubon is dead.

The passage concentrates on the struggle in Dorothea's mind about whether or not to give him the promise he desires; in fact she has decided that she will make the promise. The details of the passage show how delicately George Eliot goes into the trials and tribulations that beset the heroine. Dorothea had a simple wish for self-fulfilment and to be of service in her marriage, but the reality of marriage is not so simple. George Eliot is concerned to show how many complications there are: for example, the husband might seem tyrannical and selfish, but he is also pathetic, which becomes evident as we see him sitting still, wrapped up, not just an old man but very much like a baby. And the complexity of the situation is also evident in Dorothea's response: there is reluctance and resentment, but, when she sees him, her immediate feeling is one of compassion and concern.

Perhaps one of Eliot's central ideas is revealed in the phrase 'the ideal and not the real yoke of marriage': she presents characters who set out with an idea but soon find themselves yoked. This applies to Lydgate as well as to Dorothea. Eliot's extraordinarily full method of description, analysis and comment renders a very vivid sense of the reality of living through such experiences.

The next step is to turn to the point at which the characters' lives seem to change direction: the point at which certain characters come to terms with how they have been using or squandering their lives. In the passage that follows, Dorothea reflects on how she feels about discovering Rosamond and Will together:

She began now to live through that yesterday morning deliberately again, forcing herself to dwell on every detail and its possible meaning. Was she alone in that scene? Was it her event only? She forced herself to think of it as bound up with another woman's life – a woman towards whom she

had set out with longing to carry some clearness and comfort into her
beclouded youth. In her first outleap of jealous indignation and disgust,
when quitting the hateful room, she had flung away all the mercy with
which she had undertaken that visit. She had enveloped both Will and
Rosamond in her burning scorn, and it seemed to her as if Rosamond
were burned out of her sight for ever. But that base prompting which
makes a woman more cruel to a rival than to a faithless lover, could have
no strength of recurrence in Dorothea when the dominant spirit of justice
within her had once overcome the tumult and had once shown her the
truer measure of things. All the active thought with which she had before
been representing to herself the trials of Lydgate's lot, and this young
marriage union which, like her own, seemed to have its hidden as well as
evident troubles – all this vivid sympathetic experience returned to her
now as a power: it asserted itself as acquired knowledge asserts itself and
will not let us see as we saw in the day of our ignorance. She said to her
own irremediable grief, that it should make her more helpful, instead of
driving her back from effort.

[pp. 845–6]

The passage is about Dorothea's response to discovering Will and
Rosamond together. The tension is between her immediate angry and
jealous response and her acceptance that it has happened and that she
should not think only of herself. We see her growing in a certain
understanding, moving away from her impetuous selfish response, and
looking at the thing from different angles: that things might have more
than one meaning, that she must think herself into Rosamond's position.

Now, having looked at four passages, it is time to ask whether I
have achieved a full enough sense of the work. The answer, of course,
must be 'No': all I have managed is to identify the main structural
thrust of the text. But I have at times, I hope, hinted at the sort of
complexity Eliot achieves in her novel. In a process of consolidation
and extension I could now look at a number of additional passages:
these would probably reinforce my impression of the general moral
assumptions informing the novel, and also make clearer the richness of
the local texture in which such ideas acquire flesh, and become real
and convincing.

I might, though, prefer to look more closely at the characters; I
have, after all, only scratched the surface of an immensely full novel.
There is much more that could be said about Dorothea, Casaubon,
Lydgate or Rosamond: and I have barely mentioned Mary Garth, a
character who seems to have fewer of the failings that characterise the
others. What I might discover would probably be consistent with the

fairly simple basic pattern I have already detected – that characters are, for the most part, presented as egocentric – but my emphasis could fall on demonstrating how perceptively Eliot presents such egoists.

I might, however, wish to concentrate on the broader community presented in the novel: I have seen how the text touches on the relationship between private lives and public lives, and how most people are more wrapped up in their own well-being than the well-being of the community as a whole. By concentrating on scenes such as meetings of the local doctors, or scenes about estate management, or scenes concerning the coming of the railway, I could probably establish a vivid view of the sort of community Eliot presents.

Formally, I might wish to look at Eliot's style. I have already seen how she seems to speak in the voice of society at large, and I might wish to explore this further; and I could also take a look at other aspects of her style, such as the frequent scientific tone in her descriptions, which seems to give her analysis the weight and value of objective scientific fact. It is almost certainly the case that such further lines of investigation will suggest themselves during the process of establishing an overall view of what the novel is about.

II 'Bleak House'

Middlemarch is a novel where we are perhaps principally interested in the seemingly real world it presents. *Bleak House* presents a frightening world, but the story as a whole is not meant to be particularly credible. If *Middlemarch* is the most complex expression (in English) of a certain tendency in fiction, *Bleak House* is arguably the finest example of a novel that makes its appeal on a basis other than realism.

It deals with an interminable Chancery suit – 'Jarndyce and Jarndyce' – and the characters involved in the suit. The principal characters are Ada Clare and Richard Carstone, wards of John Jarndyce, and Esther Summerson, a young girl Jarndyce receives into his household as a companion for Ada. Richard, who loves and eventually marries Ada, becomes obsessed with the Jarndyce suit, even to the point of distrusting his guardian, and it becomes such an obsession that he sinks into a decline. When a new will is discovered, and the suit is settled, it is found that the whole estate has been swallowed up in costs. The effect is enough to kill Richard. Running in tandem with this story is the story of Lady Dedlock, Esther's mother as a result of a youthful relationship with a Captain Hawdon. She believes that her secret is safe, but it is uncovered by a law clerk, Guppy, and Lady Dedlock then makes herself known to Esther. Subsequently she becomes a murder suspect when the solicitor, Tulkinghorn, who has also divined her secret, is murdered. Fleeing from her home, she is found dead near Hawdon's grave. Her daughter Esther, meanwhile, has accepted a proposal of marriage from John Jarndyce, but he stands down, permitting Esther to marry a more suitable partner, Allan Woodcourt.

It seems fair to assume that Dickens is condemning a society that is corrupt in various ways, and making a case for human trust and honesty. But that tells us very little about the details of the novel, so we turn to the text. The novel begins:

> London. Michaelmas term lately over, and the Lord Chancellor sitting in Lincoln's Inn Hall. Implacable November weather. As much mud in the streets, as if the waters had but newly retired from the face of the earth, and it would not be wonderful to meet a Megalosaurus, forty feet long or so, waddling like an elephantine lizard up Holborn Hill. Smoke lowering down from chimney-pots, making a soft black drizzle with flakes of soot in it as big as full-grown snowflakes – gone into mourning, one might imagine, for the death of the sun. Dogs, undistinguishable in mire. Horses scarcely better; splashed to their very blinkers. Foot passengers, jostling one another's umbrellas, in a general infection of ill temper, and losing their foot-hold at street-corners, where tens of thousands of other foot passengers have been slipping and sliding since the day broke (if this day ever broke), adding new deposits to the crust upon crust of mud, sticking at those points tenaciously to the pavement, and accumulating at compound interest.
>
> Fog everywhere. Fog up the river, where it flows among green aits and meadows; fog down the river, where it rolls defiled among the tiers of shipping, and the waterside pollutions of a great (and dirty) city. Fog on the Essex Marshes, fog on the Kentish heights. Fog creeping into the cabooses of collier-brigs; fog lying out on the yards, and hovering in the rigging of great ships; fog drooping on the gunwales of barges and small boats. Fog in the eyes and throats of ancient Greenwich pensioners, wheezing by the firesides of their wards; fog in the stem and bowl of the afternoon pipe of the wrathful skipper, down in his close cabin; fog cruelly pinching the toes and fingers of his shivering little 'prentice boy on deck. Chance people on the bridges peeping over the parapets into a nether sky of fog, with fog all round them, as if they were up in a balloon, and hanging in the misty clouds.
>
> [*Bleak House* (Penguin, 1971), p. 49]

Here we have a description of London (and such a complex one that some readers might prefer to move on to a character, to give their analysis of the novel an easier start). Looking for an opposition, we can see clearly that Dickens is presenting a rather frightening and cruel world: the weather alone, with choking fog everywhere, suggests this; the implicit alternative is a more pleasant, more hospitable world. When we examine the passage in detail, we see· what a hostile atmosphere prevails: it does not seem a city for human beings; the emphasis falls on mud, dirt and pollution, and there is also the language of disease − 'a general infection of ill temper'. While fog penetrates everywhere, soiling everything it touches, people are pushed into a subsidiary role. In the first paragraph, Dickens mentions dogs and horses before introducing the people, who are reduced to a sort of animal herd, not even allowed the dignity of being able to stand upright. In the second paragraph the cruel fog makes a physical attack on the toes and fingers of the apprentice.

Relating this to the novel as a whole, we might well expect a novel which concentrates on the inhumanity of the Victorian city. It promises to be an immensely pessimistic analysis; yet, though a terrifying vision, the passage is, at the same time, light and amusing. Here we encounter Dickens's distinctive method. There is an exuberant verbal delight in describing the city in this way; as much as what is being said, we are struck by the joy with which Dickens commandeers language to present his vision. One effect of such writing is to remind us of the presence of human qualities − in particular, the human imagination − in what might be felt to be a dehumanised world. If we consider Dickens's subject matter but ignore his manner of writing, the impression we get is of a certain sort of social novelist, anxious to expose the evils of contemporary society. When we look at his way of writing the emphasis begins to shift: the novel begins to seem less an indictment, and more a piece of fine comic writing.

This is a point to which I can return, but, piecing together my other impressions so far, I have decided that Dickens must be attacking the society of his day, and making some sort of plea for a better lot for people. To test whether this is the case, I can turn now to look at Esther, the heroine of the work. In fact, she is not only the heroine but narrates the sections in which she appears. At some point I will have to determine why Dickens employs this technique. But first I must look at a passage featuring Esther:

> I was brought up, from my earliest remembrance − like some of the princesses in the fairy stories, only I was not charming − by my godmother.

At least I only knew her as such. She was a good, good woman! She went
to church three times every Sunday, and to morning prayers on Wednes-
days and Fridays, and to lectures whenever there were lectures; and never
missed. She was handsome; and if she had ever smiled, would have been
(I used to think) like an angel – but she never smiled. She was always
grave, and strict. She was so very good herself, I thought, that the
badness of other people made her frown all her life. I felt so different
from her, even making every allowance for the differences between a
child and a woman; I felt so poor, so trifling, and so far off; that I never
could be unrestrained with her – no, could never even love her as
I wished. It made me very sorry to consider how good she was, and how
unworthy of her I was; and I used ardently to hope that I might have a
better heart; and I talked it over very often with the dear old doll; but
I never loved my godmother as I ought to have loved her, and as I felt I
must have loved her if I had been a better girl.

[p. 63]

The passage is about Esther and her godmother, in particular Esther's
inability to love her godmother. The stated contrast is between the
goodness of the godmother and the badness of Esther, but the truth is,
of course, the opposite: the godmother is cold and unfeeling, stern and
unbending, whereas Esther, who harps on the word 'love', is a good
person, motivated by warm and loving impulses. Relating this passage
to the first extract, we now begin to see something of the alternative
the novel presents to a cold, impersonal and cruel city. Dickens seems
to be suggesting the importance of personal feelings and personal
contact, to be set against an inhumane society, in which there is no
recognition of individual needs and feelings.

I have now related this second passage to my developing impression of the novel: it remains to say in what ways it is distinctive.
Most noticeable, of course, is that Dickens has handed over to Esther
as narrator. As always, our duty as critics, having spotted a feature of
the text, is to seek an explanation for it, an explanation which fits in
with a coherent overall sense of the work. Here it might be sufficient to
say that this seems a logical way for Dickens to organise his material,
but to my mind that does not really go far enough as an explanation. I
do offer an explanation here, but as always it must be remembered
that this is just a theory about the book and not a definitive interpretation; the only thing that matters in any piece of interpretation is that it
must be plausible and supported by the evidence of the text itself. In
such a spirit I offer the following reading: in this particular passage,
Esther is compared at the outset to a princess in a fairy-story, and

indeed the Esther story is rather like a fairy-story in structure in that the abandoned girl rediscovers her mother and eventually finds happiness with the man she loves. But fairy stories are untrue, and, if society is as cruel and inhumane as Dickens suggests, then there is something suspect about the novel progressing towards a happy conclusion. I would suggest, therefore, that the Esther story is offered to us as an untrue story; her whole mincing manner of narration makes her just too good to be true.

By giving part of the novel to Esther, Dickens as it were separates out two sorts of fiction. In his own sections he presents life as complex and chaotic, but in the Esther sections he presents a far more positive and purposeful story, but one that is not meant to be convincing. He is playing with the notion of imposing fictional patterns upon the chaos of the world; or, in other words, he is setting the disorder of life against the fantasy order of art. Now what led me to construct this theory was the obtrusiveness of the style in this novel – and, as suggested previously, when style obtrudes it is often the case that the novel is offering some form of discussion about the relationship between art and life. This novel seems to me to be concerned to contrast fictional neatness with life's lack of such neat patterns.

But as I have stressed time and time again, this is only one way of interpreting the evidence of the text. You may detect a quite different pattern in the work, and that is quite acceptable as long as your reading is plausible and supported by the evidence of the text itself. For example, you need not venture into the area of abstract theories about fiction and how it relates to reality. The evidence of the novel could be used just as effectively to suggest that Dickens is concerned to set corruption and social malaise against purer instincts; arguably all the characters are caught between the pull of finer instincts and the sort of self-interest that is likely to be encouraged by such an inhumane society. I could look at any number of characters or incidents to extend this idea, but the particular character I have chosen is Harold Skimpole:

> When we went downstairs, we were presented to Mr Skimpole, who was standing before the fire, telling Richard how fond he used to be, in his school-time, of football. He was a little bright creature, with a rather large head; but a delicate face, and a sweet voice, and there was a perfect charm in him. All he said was so free from effort and spontaneous and was said with such a captivating gaiety, that it was fascinating to hear him talk. Being of a more slender figure than Mr Jarndyce, and having a richer complexion, with brown hair, he looked younger. Indeed, he had

more the appearance, in all respects, of a damaged young man, than a well-preserved elderly one. There was an easy negligence in his manner, and even in his dress (his hair carelessly disposed, and his neckerchief loose and flowing, as I have seen artists paint their own portraits), which I could not separate from the idea of a romantic youth who had undergone some unique process of depreciation. It struck me as being not at all like the manner or appearance of a man who had advanced in life, by the usual road of years, cares, and experiences.

[*There follows an account of how Skimpole had once worked as a doctor in the household of a German prince, but spent most of his time lying in bed, so that*] . . . the engagement terminated, and Mr Skimpole having (as he added with delightful gaiety), 'nothing to live upon but love, fell in love, and married, and surrounded himself with rosy cheeks.' His good friend Jarndyce and some other of his good friends then helped him, in quicker or slower succession, to several openings in life; but to no purpose . . . He was very fond of reading the papers, very fond of making fancy-sketches with a pencil, very fond of nature, very fond of art. All he asked of society was, to let him live. *That* wasn't much. His wants were few. Give him the papers, conversation, music, mutton, coffee, landscape, fruit in the season, a few sheets of Bristol-board, and a little claret, and he asked no more. He was a mere child in the world, but he didn't cry for the moon. He said to the world, 'Go your several ways in peace! Wear red coats, blue coats, lawn sleeves, put pens behind your ears, wear aprons; go after glory, holiness, commerce, trade, any object you prefer; only – let Harold Skimpole live!'

[pp. 118–19]

The passage is about Harold Skimpole. At first, Skimpole seems an attractive character, with his delicate face and charming voice; in a world where there is so much cruelty, his freedom and spontaneity can be taken as a positive alternative. There is certainly a great deal of emphasis on how he values love and friendship, how he disdains money and the idea of social advancement. But it is a perverted sort of feeling, for there are social obligations in the world, and Skimpole fails to face up to his responsibilities; he is qualified as a doctor, but has made no effort to use his skills to serve humanity, being content to sponge off his friends. His vice is selfishness.

What I have done so far is to connect Skimpole with the theme of the novel as I perceived it in my discussion of the first two extracts. The novel sets a corrupt world against characters with finer instincts, and Skimpole has a part to play in the novel's panorama of self-interest. But to state the case in that way can make Skimpole seem the sort of character we might find in a George Eliot novel. What I have not yet dealt with is Dickens's distinctive way of presenting such a character, which can be summed up generally, and without any sense of its imaginative force, as an exaggerated and amusing caricature of the man. Again, as with *Martin Chuzzlewit*, the point we arrive at is that Dickens is above everything else a comic novelist, laughing in a superior way at human folly, affectation and greed.

But really to come to terms with the novel I need to go beyond this general theory of comic fiction, and to identify some of the ways in which this becomes a distinctive comic novel. With this passage about Skimpole it is easy to move on, for there is clearly considerable power in this comic portrait, power of a serious and disturbing nature. The normal parent–child relationship has broken down when Skimpole does not accept his family responsibilities, but acts more like a child; the novel is, in fact, full of bad parents. It is also powerful in the way that, beneath the comic surface, we are being offered a nasty picture of greed and a cruel lack of concern for other people. Again we see how a comic novel can simultaneously be a very dark and disturbing novel. This passage about Skimpole provides one means of access to this level in the text, but other scenes would obviously provide their own distinctive illumination of some of the qualities of the novel.

What I am doing here is very much what I did with *Martin Chuzzlewit*. The first task is to get hold of the theme or themes that shape the text, ignoring, for the moment, the distinctive manner in which it is written. When I feel that I have grasped the novel in this way I can then proceed to regard it as a typical example of a comic novel. But while looking at it in this way I am also likely to be discovering some of its more distinctive and, possibly, more disturbing qualities. What I have touched on in the case of *Bleak House* is the very serious picture it presents of a corrupt society, and also the way in which individuals within this society are likely to become corrupt themselves. In addition, I have touched on the possibility that the more positive alternative that Dickens offers in the novel is presented as no more than a fantasy alternative – that the story of Esther is a fairy-story, the sort of thing that happens in fiction, whereas in the world itself we are forever caught in a labyrinth of chaos, confusion, decay and waste.

Such conclusions as I have drawn here are, to be honest, rather in excess of what could reasonably be determined from the three passages examined, but I have been more concerned to illustrate a method than to spell out every step of an interpretation. And the method is, as should by now be clear, the same as with every other novel – working from the details of the text to build up a coherent overall view of the text. It does not matter that the conclusions I reach may be different from those of other readers, because what I am constructing is my own response to the book. But this response is not going to be of much use unless I can use it to write a reasonable essay, for essay-writing is the central method of assessment in the study of English. So it is essay-writing, and, in particular, the skills and techniques of constructing an essay, that I consider in the next two chapters of this book. The advantage of a good essay-writing technique, as we will see, is that this not only enables you to make full and proper use of your work on the text, it also structures your thinking so that you can begin to take on more advanced critical ideas. This is something I turn to after these two essay-writing chapters, in the second part of the book.

6

Writing an essay

MORE than in any other subject, success in English depends upon the ability to write a good essay. This is fine for those lucky people who are natural writers, but is very depressing for the rest of us. We are likely to delay as long as possible the actual moment of putting pen to paper, hoping that inspiration will strike. But, fortunately, there are more practical methods of guaranteeing that you will produce a reasonably competent piece of work. What you need, above all else, is a clear idea of what you are setting out to do in an essay, and some ideas about how to organise and present your material. It is often apparent to the examiner marking A-level papers that the books have been read carefully, and carefully analysed, but that candidates are very unclear about how to organise an essay. The intention of this chapter is to provide some basic guidelines.

I

The basic rules of essay-writing are very straightforward. The first rule is to **answer the question set**: when a teacher sets a certain essay-topic, or when a particular question appears in an exam, it is set because the person who will be marking your work wants to see you discussing specific aspects of the novel. The question set will point towards a significant area of interest in the book, and, however well you write, you will gain no credit at all unless you actually discuss the specified issue. This may necessitate discarding some of your best ideas, but this is how the system works; the defence of it is that your flexibility is being tested, your ability to consider the text from a new or unexpected angle.

In order to answer the question set, though, it does help to **have some idea of the sort of questions that can be asked about**

novels. Essay-topics and exam questions in English are seldom really obscure. Indeed, it has been said, and you may have noticed the fact yourself, that only a handful of questions can be set about any book. Often the question may look frightening, because of the way in which it is phrased, or because it employs an erudite quotation from a critic followed by the word 'Discuss', but the underlying question is likely to be fairly familiar and predictable. If you have studied the book carefully and sensibly you should be able to cope with almost any question set.

The sort of questions most commonly set are as follows: (i) **A question about character**, asking you to discuss the main character, or how two of the characters in the book compare and contrast, or about the author's conception of, and presentation of, character. (ii) **A question about the society of the novel**, in which you are asked to discuss the world the novelist presents, in particular the author's strength in presenting a convincing sense of the characteristic feel and prevailing values of a certain society. Or you might be asked about the author's skill in presenting the differences between two societies, or the divisions within a society. Sometimes the question may be about how the society and the characters of the novel interrelate. (iii) **A question about the author's attitudes/values/morality/view of life**, which asks what view of life the novel reveals, what the author values and what he or she condemns. (iv) **A question about style or method**: usually this will take the form of asking you to explain why the author chooses to write in the way he or she does. Sometimes, however, you will be asked more specific questions about, say, imagery in the novel: but this will only be when the feature is reasonably obvious, and already widely commented on by critics. You should never be asked 'trick' questions, i.e. questions about some feature of the novel which is not generally recognised and widely discussed. (v) **An evaluative question**: this is a very popular form of question with university lecturers; they will find some dismissive critical statement about the author, and ask you to discuss it. For example, they might suggest that Lawrence writes in an emotionally ranting way which damages the effect of his novels, or that Dickens's lack of realism is a limitation. The best way to answer this sort of question is to defend the author, explaining why his or her particular way of writing is appropriate for what he or she wishes to achieve.

Most questions set at school and university should fall into one of the above categories. At A-level, questions will, most commonly, be about characters or society, with, sometimes, questions about the author's view of life (although an idea of an author's view of life may be said to be implicit in most questions). At university, questions will generally be about the author's attitudes, or the novel's style, or will be evaluative. As you will probably have noticed, the sort of questions asked correspond almost exactly to the sort of approaches to a text recommended in the first five chapters of this book. This means that your work on studying a novel can be carried over almost wholesale into an essay. Some students find that forcing themselves to write essays is the best way of organising their thoughts about a book, and if this is the case with you, you can obviously combine your work on the text with writing up your conclusions about the novel.

But how do you set about answering the question once you have spotted what it is getting at? Again, the rules are straightforward. The first priority is **a strong, clear argument running through the answer**. Indeed, to expand that slightly, the whole secret of writing a good essay can be summed up as follows: **a strong, clear argument, closely illustrated from the relevant novel or novels**.

But I will deal first with ways of establishing a clear argument. As suggested above, the questions set on novels are always reasonably straightforward, so the general outline of the answer should also be fairly straightforward. For example, if you are asked about the main character in a novel, and the main feature of his or her personality is that he or she is idealistic and immature, it is essential that you establish this point at the outset of your essay, and then maintain it as the controlling argument of your answer. It is much better to establish a clear response than to produce an answer that does not really know where it is heading. Sometimes you may feel you are over-simplifying the issue, but it is much better to start from a simple idea, which you can make more complex as you go along, than to produce a confused answer that never really brings anything into focus.

To produce a clear response you should be able to sum up in a few words what you feel the main outline of the answer is. Some students find this incredibly hard to do. There are others, though, who are very good at grasping the essentials of what a book is about, and who can often talk confidently about it without perhaps having read it very closely. To do well in English you do need to work hard to acquire this ability to recognise the central issues. The earlier chapters of this book should have provided some guidance about how to make yourself proficient at this, for they indicated that certain themes and ideas appear and reappear in novels, and encouraged you to become adept at spotting them.

It helps to remember such basic issues as these: that novels often set individuals against society; that these individuals are often naïve and immature; that these characters often change and develop during the course of the work; that the artist is likely to be ambivalent in his or her attitude to society, finding things to praise and things to criticise; that, broadly speaking, novelists are likely to be for or against the established order, and that this necessarily affects the attitude they adopt towards their principal characters; that the style is value-laden, that it reveals the author's attitudes, and that it is appropriate to the content in ways that it is essential to grasp. Clearing the mind of too many details, and focusing on such central issues as these, should help define a clear outline of an argument.

If all else fails, and you cannot see what the essential, summarisable answer is, then turn to critics who will help you to identify the principal threads in the book. What you do need to tell yourself is that the overall thesis in your essay does not need to be ingenious or even particularly original. The argument in an essay is simply the foundation on which you build; the quality of your answer will reveal itself in the quality of your proof of your thesis. To give an example: you might be asked to discuss the relationship between Paul and his mother in *Sons and Lovers*. The answer, in essence, is straightforward: that Paul and his mother have a very close, perhaps too close, relationship, with Paul over-dependent upon his mother, and the mother reluctant to allow her son to escape from her control. Such an argument must be at the centre of an answer to this question. But two students with the same argument could produce essays of very different quality. The poor student might simply repeat this view over and over again, in a fairly vague way, making a few general references to incidents in the novel; the good student, however, would constantly be turning to the book, **showing how the relationship is actually presented in the novel**, and could in the end produce a very original essay, by selecting and emphasising details that other readers might have overlooked. The originality would reside in the details rather than in the overall thesis, but that is the sort of originality at which to aim in writing an essay.

This leads on to the next point,which is **the technique of fleshing out the basic argument**. Here it is all-important to turn to the text as often as possible, providing illustrations of how the text presents the issues you are talking about. Generally speaking, if you start with a clear controlling argument, and then turn to the text as often as possible, one of two things should happen in the course of your essay. The first possibility is that, when you have stated your general view of the problem in an introductory paragraph, a look at a number of episodes in the novel may extend your argument, introducing subtleties and nuances which you had not thought of at the outset, but which a close examination of the text reveals. The result is that when you reach the final paragraph, you can conclude with a statement that bears some resemblance to your opening paragraph, but which is altogether more subtle as a result of having looked closely at the evidence of the text. But the other thing that might happen in an essay is that a close look at the text might overturn your initial thesis. This does not matter, as your essay simply gives the impression that the text is more complex than as first appears.

To give an example: you might be asked to write about Paul Morel's father in *Sons and Lovers*. You might decide that he was an uncouth and cruel man, and decide to use this as your controlling argument, but a close examination of a number of scenes might well reveal that Lawrence was aware of the father's good qualities as well as his faults. By the time you reached your final paragraph you would have overturned your initial argument, but, by working from a clear idea, you would be totally in control, even if your idea changed direction as the essay progressed. The object is to have a simple controlling frame within which complexity can develop naturally from the evidence of the text.

This covers the basics of how to construct an essay, and I trust that there is little if anything here that any teacher would dispute. I am now going on, though, to a more precise illustration of a way of constructing an essay, and at this point it does need to be said that this is only one of many possible ways of organising and presenting material. It is a method I have found useful, and some of my students have found it useful, but it may not suit you, and your own teachers may recommend a method that you find far more congenial.

In constructing an essay, I find that it helps to work with a fairly set format, so that the mechanics of the essay largely look after themselves, making it possible to concentrate on the quality of the content. A good overall format should ensure that the essay is at least reasonably competent. One possibility is to think in terms of an essay of, say, eight substantial paragraphs. Assuming that each paragraph is just over or just under half-a-page in length, this will produce an essay of about four sides, which is a sensible and manageable length for an exam answer or class essay. These eight paragraphs can be organised as follows: an introductory paragraph, six paragraphs looking at six separate incidents or passages in the text, and a concluding paragraph.

The introductory paragraph serves to introduce the problem, and in it you give a rough outline of the case you are going to present. Do not waste words at the outset; far too many students write a flabby opening paragraph, in which they introduce irrelevant material about the period or the author's life. The opening paragraph need be no more than a dozen lines in length, and should be a statement of the areas of concern of the essay, and an indication of the line you are going to take. It is, in essence, a summary of your view of the problem posed in the question, and will only prove really effective if you can see what the question is getting at. For example, the question might be about Scott's attitudes as revealed in *Waverley*. All that need be said, at the outset, is that his values seem fairly clear – a sympathy for English restraint and a distaste for the rebelliousness and indiscipline of the Scots. As the novel develops, however, he becomes more ambivalent, never sacrificing his own taste for moderation, but increasingly ready to recognise the sterling and admirable qualities of the rebels. So, in a few words you have set up your controlling argument for the essay.

As I have said before, however, some students find it very hard to define briefly what a possible answer to the question might be: if you are very concerned that this opening paragraph should be devoted to setting out the main outline of your answer, then it should help to clarify and define what is of central importance. Writing this initial paragraph should not be too difficult, because what you are trying to do is express things in the simplest possible terms, cutting through to the essentials of what the essay is going to be about. It is the firm foundation on which your answer is going to be built.

The real substance of your essay develops as you turn to various incidents or episodes in the novel. In the second paragraph you first turn to the text, which you want to get to grips with as quickly as possible. For example, the second paragraph might well begin, 'Something of the author's attitude/The main character's personality/The social environment of the novel/The author's distinctive style . . . can be seen in the passage where . . .', and then you could proceed to outline a suitable passage. A good essay should work from the evidence of the text, rather than bring in the text to substantiate a point already made. There are two reasons for doing this: first, that it reproduces an ideal process of reading, in which you look at the text and draw various conclusions from it; and second, that you are likely to discover far more about the subtleties of the novel by looking closely at the evidence than by coming up with a conclusion beforehand and then merely glancing at the text.

But it is very easy to say 'Look at the evidence of the text': what exactly does this mean? Obviously one could not reproduce passages of the length discussed in earlier sections of this book, or the essay would become hopelessly cumbersome. The best tactic is to outline a scene, mentioning the main things that happen in it, but remembering details within the scene, perhaps odd words and phrases, that enable you to make an interesting point. Sometimes it is worth quoting a sentence or two, but only if you then fully discuss the quotation. The rule is, **if you quote, analyse what you quote**. The format of the whole paragraph is **text/analysis/conclusion**. By this I mean that you first refer to a section of text, then discuss it as shown in previous chapters, then conclude the paragraph with a sentence or two to pull together everything that you have established so far. Providing a sentence or two of conclusion to each paragraph is a good way of ensuring that your essay has a sense of direction, as it makes you review how your argument is advancing.

Obviously one scene on its own will not tell you everything about the book, so in the next paragraph you move on to another episode, building upon, and extending, the case established so far. For example, the concluding sentence of the second paragraph of your essay might suggest that, on the basis of the evidence examined so far, the author appears hostile to a certain character. Your next paragraph could then begin, 'There is, however, more to it than this . . .', and gradually, repeating the text/analysis/conclusion sequence, you can modify the direction of the argument.

In subsequent paragraphs you turn to the book again and again, working from pieces of the text, establishing a case which should steadily be growing in subtlety as the essay develops. The method is very much the same as that recommended in earlier chapters of this book, and, if that method of analysis seemed laborious, it may seem less so when you realise that you can be writing your essay virtually simultaneously with your analysis of the book. After working through about six passages, you should have a fairly substantial and very detailed argument. It is now that you write your concluding paragraph, although you should be almost embarrassed to write this conclusion, as you have illustrated and established everything so conscientiously along the way that this final paragraph will be no more than reiteration of a case already thoroughly made.

The format of an essay is, then, as follows:

(i) Introductory paragraph.

(ii)–(vii) Six paragraphs of text/analysis/conclusion, in which you develop your argument.

(viii) A concluding paragraph.

Of course, it will be necessary to be flexible in your treatment of this overall structure. You may want to write at great length about one episode, or you may not find it necessary to discuss so many passages, but it is worth having this sort of format as your initial plan. It guarantees that you have, running through your essay, a clear argument, that develops in clear logical steps, with one idea being expounded and concluded within one paragraph, before you move on to a fresh point. Having a plan like this makes essay writing much simpler; you do not have to worry about having all your ideas worked out beforehand, nor should you get lost in writing the essay. You start from a fairly simple view, and then let the evidence of the text determine the development of your argument. Quite what to include in each paragraph is a question that is more fully dealt with in the examples that follow later in this chapter.

II

In the next section I provide outline illustrations of how to answer essay or exam questions on three specific novels, but first it may be helpful to say something about the most common shortcomings in students' essays on fiction, and also something about what factors determine how well you will do at school or university.

At A-level, the most common shortcoming in exam answers is irrelevance. Examiners understand why irrelevant material is produced, but however sympathetic they may feel towards the candidate, they cannot give a good mark to an essay that fails to answer the question. Irrelevance at A-level is mainly due to panic; many people arrive in an examination room in a state of great nervousness, and are so anxious to get something down on paper that they simply start reproducing everything they know. Often, of course, one cannot avoid examination nerves, but it is essential to try to stay calm, and just as essential to devote some time to **thinking** about what you are going to write before writing it. This does not necessitate writing elaborate essay plans, but you must think about what exactly the question is getting at, and how it can best be answered. A little more thinking and a little less writing at A-level would improve a great many grades. It also helps to have an idea of the shape your essay is likely to take – as in the eight-paragraph structure suggested above. This gives you a sort of ready-made vessel into which to pour your material, and guarantees that your answer will have some shape, form and sense of direction.

Formlessness is, indeed, a shortcoming that affects both A-level and undergraduate essays, but, before turning to it, I want to discuss the most dangerous of all temptations in writing about novels – the temptation simply to tell the story. There are several reasons why students lapse into telling the story. One is that, having started to outline the work, you get carried away and forget all about the question. Another reason is the sheer bulkiness of novels: it can seem difficult to know what to select, so you include everything. But the third reason is the most problematic: you may feel that telling the story does provide a sort of answer to the question; for example, if you are asked to discuss the main character, it could be maintained that his character is made plain by a full account of all the escapades and events he becomes involved in. The trouble is, however, that many novels employ roughly similar stories, so the story cannot really be said to show in what way any particular novel is distinctive. The best way to fight against the temptation to tell the story is to follow the method outlined in this book, selecting a handful of incidents which you can assume are representative of what happens in the book as a whole.

Irrelevance and story-telling are common faults at A-level. The faults that follow are common among both A-level students and university students. The first is formlessness – the essay that rambles without any very clear sense of direction or purpose. Essays ramble either because the student is unclear what he or she is trying to say, or because he or she lacks a tight method of organising material, which can ensure that the essay is moving along purposefully. The illustrations in this book should have provided some ideas about how an essay can be logically organised; there are other approaches, but the all-important rule is to be clear and well-organised. It is better to over-simplify for the sake of clarity than to produce a confused and confusing essay, for the presentation of your ideas is just as important as the ideas themselves.

Another common fault is the exam answer that is clear and to the point, but too general in its references to the text. The fault here is a lack of sensible planning. Rather than re-read a whole novel for an exam, it is far more sensible to select a number of scenes which you think you might be able to make use of in the examination. You will get little credit for simply saying that a certain character illustrates a certain point, but a great deal of credit for discussing in detail a scene in which that character appears, showing how the text establishes the point you want to make. This problem of the too general essay connects with the 'back-to-front' essay, in which the student has all his or her conclusions ready, and then just makes incidental references to the text. It is much more productive to be constantly turning to the text, drawing your conclusions out of the evidence you examine.

A word about grades at A-level: to achieve an 'A' a candidate does, perhaps, need some special flair for the subject, but a 'B' can be achieved simply by diligent and sensible work; clear answers making frequent references to the texts can easily produce a 'B'. 'C'-grade candidates usually write clear essays, but essays which are slightly less detailed in their references to the texts, this lack of detail making the overall argument less sophisticated. 'D'- and 'E'-grade candidates write confused essays with a lack of close references. 'Failures' are students who write confused answers, making very little use of the texts. Never make the mistake of thinking that inspiration will strike on the day of the exam; you must be thoroughly prepared, knowing what extracts from a book you want to use, but in the exam itself you must be flexible, adjusting your prepared material to answer the specific questions set.

If you do well in English at school, and go on to university to study English, you may well find that your essays at the beginning are less successful than your essays at school. There are several reasons for this. One is that you will be given far less guidance at university. You might also be required to look at books in new and unfamiliar ways. But the major reason for a decline in the quality of first-year students' essays is that they forget the systematic approaches they have consciously or unconsciously acquired at school. At university, just as much as at school, you must have a clear argument running through your essays and make as many references as possible to the texts.

III

The last part of this chapter provides brief outlines of how to tackle specific essay questions. The easiest example comes first: a straightforward question about character. The novel referred to is Thomas Hardy's *The Mayor of Casterbridge*. This tells the story of Michael Henchard, a countryman who sells his wife, but then feels remorse and applies himself to a disciplined life, finally becoming a powerful corn merchant and mayor of Casterbridge. But Henchard has a fiery temperament, and most of the book concentrates on how things go wrong for him. His wife returns with her daughter after about twenty years, and Henchard remarries her. At the same time a young man, Farfrae, comes to Casterbridge and Henchard takes him under his wing. Eventually, however, they become rivals, and as Farfrae goes up in the world Henchard goes down. He loses his business to Farfrae, and then has the additional blow of discovering that his assumed daughter is really the child of the sailor to whom he sold his wife. Henchard feels he has lost everything when this assumed daughter marries Farfrae. Clearly, this is yet another novel about society and the individual: Henchard repeatedly transgresses social codes, and, although he does achieve a position in society as a result of disciplining himself, the effort proves too much, and he finishes as a social outcast.

A fairly typical A-level question might be: 'At what points in *The Mayor of Casterbridge*, and for what reasons, do you feel sympathy for Henchard?'

First, you must decide on the general outline of your answer. A clear simple argument that could serve as the basis of an essay is that Henchard, with his fiery temperament, is in many ways to be condemned, but that the novel does indicate some redeeming features. Quite what these are can be made clear in the course of the essay, but the first paragraph need say no more than that his cruelty in selling his wife, and his hasty actions in many situations, make him seem unsympathetic, although as the novel progresses we begin to see other aspects of his personality.

The second paragraph can then be devoted to establishing his shortcomings. The obvious scene to choose is the scene where he sells his wife. The episode can briefly be described, and then analysis can follow: it can be pointed out how loud and uncouth he is in the episode, particularly in comparison with his wife, who says virtually nothing. Searching for something positive, you could argue that he feels trapped by society's conventions. It could be shown how hasty and impetuous he is in his actions, and indeed this might make him seem somewhat more sympathetic, as he is not a man capable of controlling himself. The analysis could be made more telling by drawing attention

to vivid descriptive touches, such as Hardy's references to the 'occa-
sional clench of his mouth' and 'the fiery spark of his dark eye', both
signs of an explosive personality. Having described and analysed the
scene in this way, you would then need to tie the paragraph together
with a sentence or two of conclusion, which could be as simple as,
'Although there are a few touches here that might make us almost
sympathise with Henchard, the overwhelming impression so far is of
his cruelty, his self-centredness, and his lack of concern for other
people'.

It is now essential to start looking for more sympathetic traits, as
this is what the question demands, so the next scene must be chosen
with care. It might be worthwhile looking at the scene where Henchard
sobers up and realises what he has done. The next paragraph could
begin as simply as, 'There is, however, another side to his personality,
as we see when he sobers up'. This would be followed by a brief
description of the episode, followed by analysis drawing attention to the
subtleties of personality Hardy emphasises in the passage. You should
then be able to move to a concluding sentence or two in which the
initial impression of his personality would be somewhat modified.

In the next four paragraphs you can proceed through the text,
choosing four relevant scenes in which Henchard appears sympathetic.
For example, the scene where he realises that Elizabeth-Jane is not his
daughter could be discussed, as could a scene around the point where
his business is starting to collapse. Working steadily and systematically
from these and other scenes, you could present a very full picture of
Hardy's achievement. The earlier analyses in this book should provide
a more detailed idea of the sort of discussion that could be constructed.

By the time you reach your concluding paragraph there should be
very little left to say, as the thoroughness of your analysis along the way
will have covered nearly all the worthwhile points. It should prove sufficient simply to state that we can see how sympathetic Henchard
appears when we consider the work as a whole.

This question is fairly typical of the sort of questions set at A-level.
The following question, on George Eliot's *The Mill on the Floss*, might
well be set at either school or university: '"Her whole art is moral."
Discuss this comment about George Eliot, making particular reference
to *The Mill on the Floss*.'

Again, one starts with a simple outline of the general direction the
essay might take. Here, for example, one might start by saying that
George Eliot is certainly a moral artist, but that it is a very com-

passionate morality, for she views people very sympathetically and understands why they may not be able to adhere to strict moral codes.

You can then show how the generosity of Eliot's understanding is clear from very early on in the novel, selecting an incident featuring the major character which is likely to show the author's tolerant and perceptive awareness. As in the Hardy example, describe the incident briefly, and then show what is involved in it, what features of personality are revealed, and why the author chooses to emphasise what she does emphasise. Working from an extract, you will soon begin to establish a clear sense of some of the distinctive features of the writer's approach. Then, again as with the Hardy example, you can say, there is more to it than this, and turn to another example where you can add to your impression of the author's distinctive approach. About four more examples will establish a very full picture, and then you can turn to your final conclusion, in which the points you have established along the way can be reiterated and finally tied together.

Exactly the same procedure can be employed with an evaluative question or a question on style. Here is the sort of question that might well be set on Virginia Woolf's *To the Lighthouse*: "'Her art is febrile and delicate: sensitive, but essentially lightweight." Discuss this view of Virginia Woolf's *To the Lighthouse*.'

When a limitation is suggested the best approach is to reject it. You can begin by saying there is some truth in the statement, but it is far too glib a dismissal of Woolf's achievement, which is delicate but also powerful.

You can then turn to an episode early in the novel, and, having briefly described it, move on to an explanation and analysis of how the passage works, what it tries to do, and what it achieves. As in the other examples, work outwards from a number of passages, gradually establishing a full and coherent impression of how the novel works.

As described in this chapter, the writing of essays may seem a simple business, and to some extent it is, but writing anything can also be agonising. What the method recommended here should help you do is to put the effort where it really matters, in getting the content right. The method here takes care of the mechanics of essay writing; it is a mould into which you can pour your material. By being confident about that mould, knowing that it will not crack or splinter, and knowing that it will always do the basic job, you can manage to put the real effort into the really hard and demanding side of writing an essay, which is producing an intelligent discussion within each paragraph.

Only practice will make you really skilled at analysing any extract from a novel.

The method described in this chapter may seem most appropriate to working at A-level, although, in fact, it should prove quite adequate for getting a good degree at university. For, at university, it is not the frame of your essays that should alter but what you put into that frame. In the next chapter I go on to discuss some of the more complicated, and at times risky, areas you might attempt to cover within an essay. But, although the next chapter touches on more difficult ways of discussing novels, it does need to be stressed that everything that can be said about any work can be fitted into the sort of systematic framework described in this chapter. As you progress in English, it is a matter of toughening up the content of your essays, rather than altering their basic form.

7

Writing a more complicated essay

WHENEVER you write an essay about a novel, or any literary text, one of the most important things you are trying to do is to convey a vivid impression of what the book is like. That may seem such an obvious point that it hardly needs to be made, but it is not really so obvious, and certainly not so easy. For example, Dickens and Eliot are very different novelists, writing in very different ways, and an essay about either of them would only be successful if it managed to convey some clear sense of the ways in which they are distinctive. To reduce things to the simplest terms, with Dickens that might mean showing how he depends upon caricatures rather than characters, whereas with George Eliot you would probably want to show how credible and substantial her characters are. Such essays, as you can see, would be setting themselves fairly simple goals, attempting to provide clear illustrations of relatively straightforward points. But, although the targets are simple, it takes a long time, and great deal of practice, to see clearly what you are aiming for in any particular essay, and to reach the point where you can provide a vivid demonstration of the case you want to make.

There will come a time, however, when you want to extend your essays, and make them more sophisticated. Obviously, for the most part this can only be a natural development over a fairly lengthy period of time, as you begin to grasp how to write and become more assured in your response to literature. But if you are impatient to extend and deepen your work there are paths that can be pursued that provide some sort of guarantee that you will be travelling in the right direction, and it is with these ways of advancing your written work that this chapter is concerned.

The central idea to keep in mind is that **the objective of any**

more complicated essay should be to show the relevant novel's complexity. Complexity is not, of course, a characteristic of all novels, but is likely to be a quality of most novels studied at school and university. Demonstrating this complexity can, however, prove very difficult because, in the short span of an essay, there is an almost inevitable tendency to pin the novel down and limit its scope, rather than really suggest how complicated it is. Indeed, at A-level, where most candidates are looking seriously at novels for the first time, pinning the work down should be a primary aim: the objective at A-level is to show your ability to form a coherent impression of a book, and to be able to convey a vivid impression of that relatively uncomplicated understanding of the text. But this does involve a degree of falsification; in a short essay you will inevitably be producing a very simplified version of a novel which might contain as many as eight or nine hundred pages.

A novel is usually a very complex structure, as the amount of criticism that can be produced about any individual work indicates; it would seem that a novel can give rise to endless new readings and new interpretations. This is partly because the individual reader imposes something of his or her own personality on the text, but also because there is so much in any novel. If you tell a simple story in as few words as possible the meaning is likely to be fairly obvious, but if you do what novelists do, which is to tell a simple story at great length, the whole thing is likely to become very complicated. Novels may be easy to read, but are likely to prove far more difficult to sum up. Indeed, many teachers of literature would admit that, the more often they read a novel, the less clear they become about what it is saying, or how it works.

What this suggests in practical terms is that it would be a sensible target for a more complicated essay to attempt to do greater justice to the complexity of the particular novel being considered. Rather than pin everything down, or parcel everything up, a more complicated essay might try to offer a more fluid sense of the text's complexity. But the idea of writing this sort of ambitious essay may seem daunting. Both at school and university, most students are racing against time to put together even the simplest impression of what any book is doing. To suggest that you should try to get beyond this, liberating yourself from too rigid a definition of the book's impact, may seem to be asking too much. But it can be done, although this chapter can only sketch out some of the ways to proceed if you want to become a more sophisticated critic of fiction.

I

The first point that must be made is that you cannot force the pace. There is no point in trying to make yourself a sophisticated critic if you haven't yet qualified as a competent one, as more complex approaches grow out of straightforward approaches. In particular, the basic design of your essays need not change at all; if you stick to the sort of overall format recommended in chapter six (or a plan that you have worked out for yourself), you should find that you can say more or less anything you want to say within such a pattern.

As time passes, and as you read more novels and write more essays, the likelihood is that you will find that you are managing to say more complex things in your written work. The more you write, the more alert you will become to the various elements in evidence in any extract from a novel, and as you become more assured in your analysis of individual passages, so the overall sophistication of your essays will develop.

It helps, though, to bear a few points in mind. The most important thing is to be very conscious that novels do not have 'a message'. Claiming that they have 'a message', or even a summarisable 'meaning', is a very reductive approach. It assumes that the novelist wrote the work simply to get across some point of view, whereas the most characteristic advantage of the novel form for the writer is that it provides him or her with enough space to complicate matters, to introduce ambiguities and contradictions, and to avoid presenting too simple a view of the world. This has already been touched on in earlier chapters, and should be evident in the analyses of novels presented within them. If you employ the essay format of taking a few passages to build up a coherent case about the novel, by the time you get on to the third passage you should be looking for those details that complicate your whole impression of the work, emphasising those points that make the particular novel distinctive and worthy of attention.

The way forward is to attempt to accommodate more and more impressions at each stage of your essay, in order to provide a really vivid account of the density of texture of the particular novel. For example, you may be explaining how a certain character is presented, but the more closely you look the more evidence you will probably find, in any specific passage, that the presentation of the character is far from simple. You might see that the passage suggests a whole variety of, possibly contradictory, character traits, or you might notice just how many rhetorical devices the writer employs to present the character. You should be aiming to escape from the idea that the character is presented straightforwardly, and endeavouring to show either the subtlety of the presentation, or, as might be the case with a novelist such as Dickens, where the characterisation is not likely to be particularly subtle, the variety of artistic effects the writer employs in order to create his or her picture. Your object is not to reduce the novel to the simplest terms, but to perceive and present an impression of its complexity.

This of course is difficult and some students never come to terms with the problem. They may well be able to see, in a vague way, that there is a lot going on in any passage, and in discussion with other students may well be able to identify a whole range of complex effects, but they are likely to find it hard to discover such things for themselves, and find it even harder to accommodate a whole range of insights within the fairly restricted space available in an essay. Again, it helps to remind yourself that more complex ideas must develop from simple ideas about the novel. As has been said many times, novels often set a particular individual against society; this can be your controlling thesis, but a close look at a particular passage is likely to indicate a somewhat ambivalent view of the main character. If you know that this sort of ambivalence is what you should be looking for, then you will probably recognise it when it appears as a characteristic of an extract. An ambivalent presentation of the characters and the society in which they live, in which nobody and nothing is presented as either wholly good or wholly bad, is such a common feature of good novels that it is always worth looking for. You may not find this quality in a novelist such as Dickens, but it is certainly going to be there in novels that fall within the realistic tradition.

Even when you have spotted this sort of complexity of texture, it can prove difficult to describe it in an essay. This is because so much of the effort of writing an essay is directed towards providing a clear and coherent overall argument. It can prove extremely testing trying to reconcile overall clarity with an awareness of the subtlety of the local texture of the novel. But this is where it helps to keep to the sort of simple format described in the previous chapter, building up an argument by means of a sequence of text/analysis/conclusion paragraphs. Your overall argument about a particular novel may be as simple as the point that the central character experiences all sorts of problems in trying to come to terms with society, but the successive paragraphs can make it clear just how complicated that character's situation is as presented in the various incidents of the novel. It particularly helps to remember to conclude each paragraph with a couple of sentences that pull together the whole case as you have understood it up to that point in the essay. This gives you the freedom to make many different points within the analysis section of each paragraph, because you can feel confident that the concluding sentences will pull the threads together and keep your overall thesis under control.

It will, of course, take time for this sort of expertise in analysis to develop. But it does help to remember that you are trying to define the subtlety of the picture at every stage of the novel, even though the basic situation (most commonly, an individual in conflict with society) may well be one that is present in many novels.

Some novels, however, do not offer this sort of subtlety of characterisation or complexity of social analysis; with these the best way to proceed is to concentrate on technique. In a Dickens novel, for example, you might encounter a character who is an obvious hypocrite; but the novel will not, however, simply be saying that he or she is a hypocrite, nor will it simply be providing examples of his or her hypocritical behaviour, but employing a whole variety of artistic devices to create that impression. Everybody who reads Dickens can see that he produces very memorable, larger-than-life characters, but, if you can pinpoint the techniques he employs to make the characters appear as they do, then you are well set to write a sophisticated essay about Dickens as an artist.

But it is not only with a novelist such as Dickens that a great deal of attention to technique is a fruitful approach. One of the most important steps forward in writing about any novelist is to become more alert to that particular novelist's method. Particularly at university, you should find your attention moving slightly away from a consideration of the experiences described in the novel towards a fuller discussion of the technique of the work.

How do you discuss technique? Again, it helps to start from basic principles; get them right and everything else follows naturally. As earlier chapters of this book have demonstrated, in talking about technique you are essentially trying to explain why the author chooses to write in the way he or she does. You need to be aware that any piece of writing employs a host of rhetorical devices and talking about technique amounts to being able to describe and justify such elements in a text. That may sound difficult, but it isn't really; the moment you transfer your attention away from the picture presented in the novel in order to concentrate more on the methods employed to create this picture, you are likely to start noticing all sorts of things about the technical strategies of the writer. What you need to tell yourself is that the total picture is only created by putting together a mass of details; every sentence involves a mass of artistic choices. As soon as you start looking at the component pieces, as if they were pieces in a jigsaw, you will be moving towards proficiency as a technical analyst of fiction.

Many students are hesitant about approaching fiction in this way, simply because it is not a method that they are familiar with from school, and indeed this sort of interest in technique is not likely to appeal to all readers. To some it can seem an excessively cold and clinical approach, but it is only arid if it becomes technical analysis for its own sake. The best formal analysis of fiction stems from a genuine curiosity about how the novel works, and doesn't lose sight of the fact that the technique serves a purpose, which is the overall imaginative effect of the novel upon the reader.

II

Laying a great deal of emphasis on the ambivalence of the content of a novel, or redirecting your work towards paying more attention to the techniques of fiction, are the most reliable ways of moving forward as a critic. One approach stresses complexity of **content**, the other stresses complexity of **method**. Obviously the two things interact, but it makes most sense in practical terms to approach a novel either through its content or through its method. Adopting such approaches, there is really no limit to what you can say about a novel.

Such approaches also have the virtue of being solid and reliable, and solid and reliable approaches are obviously, in the long run, the best. But there are other ways of cutting a dash as a critic, and it is to a couple of these that I now turn. I use the phrase 'cutting a dash' deliberately, as these are risky rather than reliable ways of tackling a novel. Following the ideas below might not endear you to all your teachers.

One approach is to concentrate on some far from obvious feature of the novel. The overall point that you are making need not be particularly original, indeed it is better if it is a solid, conventional point, but it can be extremely effective if you illustrate this point from the evidence of some obscure or unlikely textual detail that other readers are unlikely to notice or exploit. You might, for example, notice that one character wears an odd hat, or that in the description of a building the writer includes some unusual detail; providing that you can forge some connections between such details and an overall view of the work, you can pick up and play with these details in a way that may touch the limits of ingenuity, but which can be very effective as a part of an essay. Of course, you can only adopt this approach if you are very confident about what you are doing; you must be capable of providing a solid and sensible reading of the novel, so that it becomes clear to the person reading your essay that it is only in proving this thesis that you have chosen to be possibly a touch too clever. I once had a student who methodically searched books for the oddest or the most boring passages, knowing that analysis of these passages would make her work distinctive; but to do this successfully she had to know just what she wanted to say about the novel as a whole.

An extension of this approach is to search for recurrent details; if you notice something odd, look through the book to see if it appears again in some shape or form. For example, you might notice an interesting reference to somebody's hands and if, on looking through the book, you found several references to hands, as well as some hand-shakes, you would have enough material to start constructing a reading of the novel. One of my students, writing about Hardy's *Jude the Obscure*, picked up all the references to railways in the novel, in particular showing how often the main characters missed trains; as a result, he could present a fairly familiar case about the overall significance of the novel, but prove it in an original and imaginative way.

This sort of approach exploits details within the text, working out from them to a general theory about the novel. Another legitimate approach, however, is to work from a theory of your own, seeing how the text fits in with your ideas. As you read more and more books, you may well discover that you are developing some general ideas of your own about novels and how they work. Your essays can then become a continuing exploration and development of your ideas about fiction. Or you might want to look at fiction from a certain stance; for example, at the moment an approach which looks at fiction from the point of view of how it handles issues of gender is extremely popular. A similar approach might be to look at the author's political position as revealed in the text.

But whatever approach you adopt you need to remember that

brilliant ideas do not in themselves make brilliant essays. A brilliant idea must be thoroughly substantiated from the text. And that really takes this book back to the point at which it began. You may be totally baffled by a novel, or you may be bursting with original, provocative and challenging ideas, but your case about the novel as you work it out in an essay will only really stand up if you prove everything from the evidence of the words on the page.

Proving everything from the text is also the idea that underlies the next three chapters, which are concerned with new approaches to the novel and criticism. They are chapters that you are likely to find most helpful when you have got your basic essay-writing technique sorted out, and feel a degree of confidence that you can now build a basic analysis of a novel. At the same time, it is fair to say that for many readers they may help clarify ideas and ways of thinking that they have encountered both in lectures and recent critical books, for these three chapters deal specifically with the changes that have swept through literary criticism in the past twenty years and how these might affect your thinking and writing about novels.

Part Two

8

New approaches

Novels discussed:
Jane Eyre, by Charlotte Brontë, published 1847
Wuthering Heights, by Emily Brontë, published 1847
The Mill on the Floss, by George Eliot, published 1860

IN chapter two of this book I looked, albeit briefly, at Charlotte Brontë's *Jane Eyre*. I now want to take a sceptical look at some of the things I said about it; in particular, I want to examine some of the concealed assumptions that shaped my reading of the novel. But why bother? Isn't it rather self-indulgent in a book about how to study novels to start looking back at things I have already said? There is, however, a point to the exercise. The earlier chapters of this book are written as if one can look at a work of fiction in an almost objective way, detecting a pattern in a passage and then relating it to a sense of the work as a whole. But these chapters are less straightforward than they seem; what is, perhaps, not immediately obvious is that I am nudging you in certain directions all the time. I am encouraging you, as my reader, to feel that certain things are worth mentioning and that other things are less important, encouraging you to pursue certain details, and encouraging you to accept certain assumptions about the effect and achievement of novels as a whole.

To an extent, this was inevitable: I was not only illustrating a method of analysis but also providing an impression of the tone and stance to adopt in criticism. People marking examinations are looking for a certain kind of understanding on the part of candidates, and these chapters provide some sense of a tone that will satisfy the most demanding examiner. Critical views change, however, and the fact is that the informing stance in the earlier chapters is traditional, some might even say distinctly old-fashioned. There are other perspectives that have now become central in thinking about, and in the teaching

121

of, literature. To put it more precisely, since the early 1970s there has been a flood of new theoretical and critical thinking that has shaken up novel criticism; anybody studying literature at university today, for example, will soon become aware of terms such as structuralism, post-structuralism, deconstruction, feminist criticism, Marxist criticism, psychoanalytic criticism, New Historicism and cultural materialism. The object of these last three chapters is to provide a sense of how these new ideas have adjusted, and will continue to adjust, the ways in which we might want to discuss novels.

Before starting, however, I must make it clear that these new approaches do not invalidate the old approaches. Whatever else may change, novels remain, in the broadest sense, works about individuals and society. New critical approaches might complicate our sense of these two terms, and the relationship between the two, but any critic of literature has got to be able to grasp the basic pattern, and its implications, before searching for additional complications. In other words, you have got to be able to construct a coherent sense of the nature, shape and significance of the story enacted in a literary text, and how it is brought to life, before compounding your argument. And, although examiners reward cleverness and originality in exam answers, they will also want to see plenty of evidence of basic grasp and control of texts. What appears in these last three chapters, therefore, is primarily a sense of how to take things further once you are sure of yourself, and how to take things further in a way that takes account of recent developments in novel theory. To put it another away, if the opening chapters of this book were the equivalent of driving lessons, we're now going to do a bit of motorway practice.

I 'Jane Eyre' reconsidered

An introduction to modern critical thinking could take the form of a descriptive survey of the impact of structuralism and other, related, critical approaches, but that might prove less than enthralling. It might prove more helpful if I look at some of the things I said about *Jane Eyre* in chapter two, and then suggest how critics today might adopt a different tack. *Jane Eyre*, you will remember, is a story about an orphan, Jane, and her unhappy experiences, particularly at school, before securing a job as a governess in the house of Mr Rochester. They intend to marry but the wedding ceremony is interrupted by the revelation that Rochester's first wife is still alive. Jane flees, but is eventually reunited with Rochester after the death of his wife. On the basis of looking at passages from the novel, I suggested that *Jane Eyre* offered us a sense of a heroine who is alienated from society. I praised Brontë's skill in getting inside the mind of her heroine, describing it as an 'extraordinary mind'. Jane, I suggested, is someone with no sense of balance or proportion in her personality, finishing with the comment that 'Brontë's ability to imagine and present such a character' accounts for the strength of the novel.

In some ways my comments may seem merely bland, but they now strike me as simultaneously smug and sinister. Jane is alienated from society, but most of the words I used to describe Jane are words that judge her from the perspective of society: for example, I talk about her 'overcharged view of herself as victim'; at one stage I describe her response as 'pathological'; and I refer to her inability to conceive of 'a sensible middle course'. There is an implicit suggestion in these comments that there is something wrong with Jane, and an assumption that the language of society can identify and label her faults. I might feel embarrassed about the inadequacy of this reading if it didn't have so much in common with most traditional interpretations of the novel. For example, critics often suggest that the novel deals with Jane's growth to maturity: such discussions are informed by a concept of the self as individual and unique, but there is also an assumption that the romantic impulses of the individual must be tempered by moderation. The obvious point is that such readings are written from within society; waywardness may be treated sympathetically, but there is an informing assumption that an accommodation should be made with society. And sometimes a belief on the part of the critic that it is the responsibility of novels to inculcate such a sense of moral and social responsibility.

I mentioned a 'sinister' dimension to my original reading. Think about the fact that many people are introduced to novels such as *Jane Eyre* when they are about sixteen or seventeen, in their latter years at school. It is at a stage in life when they may feel like breaking free, having little patience with the values of their parents or teachers. Is it, therefore, a complete coincidence that most of the texts studied at school deal with wayward heroes and heroines, but do so within a general pattern of interpretation that sees non-conformity as deviant, and associates conformity with maturity? At a covert level, studying literature can become synonymous with the social indoctrination of young people.

Traditional criticism is often excellent – and still very rewarding to read – but the fact is that most traditional criticism works from a perspective of the assumed common views and values of society. Looking through all the discussions of novels in the earlier chapters of this book, I am struck by the consistency with which I stress the socially ameliorative function of literature, as if novels can show people a reasonable course of action in society. This moral approach to fiction goes hand in hand with a desire, again almost universal in traditional criticism, to establish total control over a text. I have, even in this chapter, stressed the importance of establishing a coherent case about a book, but there comes a point at which the critic, in the desire for coherence, can ride roughshod over problems or awkward material in the text, pulling everything together into a pattern. One aspect of this is a concern with the author's 'intention', as if it is possible to pin down what the author is trying to say. This belief in 'intention' is part of a more general desire for a controllable and comprehensible world, a world where individuals see the advantages of acting reasonably within the system, and where authors can offer sage advice on how life should be conducted.

What happens in traditional criticism, therefore, is that the critic – knowingly or unknowingly – while appearing to put together a disinterested analysis of a text, is likely to be putting forward a fairly specific socially-constructive message. It is, of course, unfair to lump together thousands of critics in this kind of way – traditional critics of the novel such as E. M. Forster, F. R. Leavis and Wayne Booth produced far more valuable criticism than most of us are ever likely to produce – but, retrospectively, what becomes clear is that they shared what can be called a 'liberal humanist' stance: what is meant by this is a certain sense of a balance between the individual and society which should be a controlling principle both of society and literature. And just as generations of critics were committed to such a stance, the same assumptions still underpin a great deal of the teaching of literature.

Starting in the 1970s, however, an increasing number of critics began to dissent from the established informing assumptions. In order to understand why such a change came about, we could look at the growing impact of structuralist approaches to literature, but it probably makes more sense to think about how people's values have changed since the 1960s and 1970s. There was a time, not too long ago, when marriage was the norm, when divorce was unusual, and when most people would never have considered living together before marriage.

All that has changed in the course of twenty years; of course, marriage continues to suit a great many people, but marriage has changed as more and more women continue in employment. People have also started to think about the sexual politics of marriage, how it is perhaps an arrangement that has suited men more than women. And there are, of course, many who do not wish to marry, or whose sexual preference excludes them from marriage. The point I am making is that traditional criticism emerged from a society that knew where it stood in relation to social institutions and values; the disintegration of old certainties, however, means that today it is no longer possible to approach literature with the same sense of shared assumptions, the same sense of a consensus. Responding to social change, criticism has changed.

In order to see how, let's return to *Jane Eyre*: the simple issue is, what are people likely to say about this novel today if they are no longer prepared to continue talking about the way Jane would benefit if she behaved reasonably? In this passage, Jane, who is now engaged to Rochester, is called 'hard':

> I assured him I was naturally hard – very flinty, and that he would often find me so; and that, moreover, I was determined to show him divers rugged points in my character before the ensuing four weeks elapsed: he should know fully what sort of a bargain he had made, while there was yet time to rescind it.
>
> 'Would I be quiet and talk rationally?'
>
> 'I would be quiet if he liked; and as to talking rationally, I flattered myself I was doing that now.'
>
> He fretted, pished, and pshawed. 'Very good,' I thought; 'you may fume and fidget as you please: but this is the best plan to pursue with you, I am certain. I like you more than I can say; but I'll not sink into a bathos of sentiment: and with this needle of repartee I'll keep you from the edge of the gulf, too; and, moreover, maintain by its pungent aid that distance between you and myself most conducive to our real mutual advantage.'
>
> [*Jane Eyre* (Penguin, 1966), p. 301]

The first point to make is that, although I am now approaching passages from a different angle, the essential method remains the same – and will do so for the rest of this book: there really is no substitute for working closely from the text to build a case. Turning now to the evidence, in chapter two I talked about how Jane delights in manipulating Rochester, saying that this provided evidence of her perversity. In this extract (which immediately precedes the passage looked at in chapter two), we again see Jane, in her own words, working Rochester 'up to considerable irritation'. But, rather than criticising her behaviour, we might take a more positive view of the power game she is playing with Rochester. He expects her to assume the usual woman's role of being submissive, of deferring to the male, and Jane can play this part – 'I would be quiet if he liked', she states – but it is nothing more than a part she assumes, for she is uneasy with the kind of sentimental, meek role she is expected to play as fiancée. One can understand her irritation: there is a fundamental contradiction in the position of Rochester, who expects her to act rationally – in other words, to display the strength of character he will want from a wife – but also expects her to act like a sentimental, besotted girl. In such circumstances, Jane's behaviour constitutes a protest against gender roles, at the roles assumed by men and assigned to women; he is meant to be 'hard', she is meant to be 'soft', but she won't play this part. What we see instead is her taunting him, sliding in and out of roles; this is inevitable, for if she won't play the usual part there is no consistent, alternative role for her to adopt. There isn't a legitimate woman's role she can assume, so she advances into, then withdraws from, roles, either being the 'quiet' woman, or, more interestingly, acting 'hard', which serves as a kind of ironic comment on male power.

The point is, then, that, rather than dismissing Jane's behaviour as perverse (which is to judge from the male perspective of society), we can see her protesting against male authority. At this stage the novel becomes something larger, and more unnerving, than a study of how a young woman matures: it becomes a politically engaged examination of the subjects of power, authority and gender in society. Charlotte Brontë, whom some people continue to think of as just a romantic novelist, here becomes a committed critic of the social order of her day. This kind of reading, as you might have realised, is a feminist perspective on the novel (though not the only feminist perspective, for feminist criticism is diverse and has had a lot of different things to say about *Jane Eyre*). What should be apparent is that, the moment one shifts from a middle-of-the-road, traditional, male, social perspective, it becomes possible, and indeed necessary, to start seeing both Jane's behaviour and the novel as a whole in a fresh light.

But, you might object, this kind of perception about Jane cannot be entirely new. Surely there have always been feminist critics ready to see the political implications of the situations in which Jane finds herself. It is a fair point, but the thing is that, in the past, feminist sympathy for Jane's plight could only co-exist with a generally conservative view. In recent years, by contrast, the disintegration of traditional values has allowed feminist critics to do fuller justice to the implications of their stance. One way in which this becomes apparent is the manner in which current feminist analyses are complemented by, and echoed by, psychoanalytic criticism and structuralist criticism of the language of the novel.

On the question of language, an appropriate scene to look at is the interrupted wedding service. The clergyman has asked if anyone knows of any reason why they should not marry:

> 'The marriage cannot go on: I declare the existence of an impediment.'
> The clergyman looked up at the speaker and stood mute; the clerk did the same; Mr Rochester moved slightly, as if an earthquake had rolled under his feet: taking a firmer footing, and not turning his head or eyes, he said, 'Proceed.'
>
> [p. 317]

But the service cannot proceed, for Rochester's wife is still alive. What strikes me in this passage is the difference between the formal manner of the objection – 'I declare the existence of an impediment' – and another kind of language, the language of metaphor, from Jane as she describes Rochester moving 'as if an earthquake had rolled under his feet'. What can we make of this? The language of the objection is at one with the language of the marriage service: it is formal and legalistic. The authority of the law and the authority of religion are coming together, both exuding power, just as Rochester attempts to assert his power by telling them to proceed. But Charlotte Brontë stands aside from this discourse of society, showing how easily the whole house of cards collapses.

It is significant that she draws attention to the clergyman and the clerk being struck mute: the moment society ceases to function according to the set script, the usual male-written rules, there is no form of words available. Jane, however, uses a different sort of language, as she does so often in her narration throughout the novel: most commonly, as here, she draws metaphors from nature to describe human feelings and behaviour. She has to reach after a different language to say things that break free from conventional discourse, with its conventional view of the world. There are two points that need to be made here before we move on: one is that we should again be struck by the ambition of Charlotte Brontë, the way in which she is engaged in a political analysis of society that is deeply aware of how that world is constituted and shaped by language. The second point is that, although critics have always discussed the language of texts, it was structuralism that first put into general circulation ideas about the conventional discourse of society, with a specific emphasis on how the world is formed through language.

Structuralism stepped back, looking at how we normally structure the world. In a rather similar way, Jane can, at times, step back, even step outside herself. At such moments in the novel we see something striking about the whole psychological construction of the self, of the character as an individual, within nineteenth-century society. An episode that defines this well takes place on the morning of Jane's wedding. She is being dressed by her maid:

> She was just fastening my veil (the plain square of blond after all) to my hair with a brooch; I hurried from under her hands as soon as I could.
> 'Stop!' she cried in French. 'Look at yourself in the mirror: you have not taken one peep.'
> So I turned at the door: I saw a robed and veiled figure, so unlike my usual self that it seemed almost the image of a stranger. 'Jane!' called a voice, and I hastened down. I was received at the foot of the stairs by Mr Rochester.
> 'Lingerer,' he said, 'my brain is on fire with impatience, and you tarry so long!'
> He took me into the dining-room, surveyed me keenly all over, pronounced me 'fair as a lily, and not only the pride of his life, but the desire of his eyes' . . .
>
> [p. 315]

The first thing we might notice here is the patronising, domineering behaviour of Rochester, who also seems to reduce Jane to the status of a sex object. Of principal interest, however, is the way in which Jane sees a virtual stranger in the mirror. It is as if she has detached herself from her social identity and can stand back and survey the self she has constructed to play a part in the world. The point we might extract from this is that Brontë is not just examining the political and sexual dimensions of gender relations but also, at a more fundamental level, the very notion of identity, of a self.

When we begin to talk about issues such as this, we are beginning to venture into the sphere of psychoanalytic criticism. The figure of Sigmund Freud is the ultimate source of modern psychoanalytic criticism, but the person who has most influenced current theory and practice in literary criticism is the French psychoanalyst Jacques Lacan. Lacan suggests that the very young child passes from a pre-language period (he refers to it as the 'Imaginary' stage), and that, with the acquisition of language, it enters what Lacan calls the 'Symbolic Order', that is, the order of social and cultural life and language. Submitting to the symbolic order of language, the child now comes under the 'Law of the Father'. In the Symbolic Order the child becomes a subject, that is, a figure who calls itself 'I' but who is not the originator of meaning since meaning resides in the language the child has learned. The twists and turns of this theory might be a bit much to absorb this quickly, but things should become clearer if we think about how Jane detaches herself from the identity she has assumed in the world, an identity that is a product of language, a product of the social order. In a related aspect of his thinking Lacan picks up Freud's division of the mind into the controlling 'ego', the conscious or thinking self; and the 'id', the repressed impulses of the unconscious. Sanity is usually associated with the ego, but Lacan, in a neat reversal of traditional thinking, describes the ego as a carrier of neurosis, suggesting there can be no such thing as a coherent, autonomous self. In looking in the mirror, Jane distances herself from the 'I' that is constructed for the uses of society. We, as readers, begin to see the ways in which this novel might be suggesting that the idea of a coherent or unified self is merely a historical, linguistic and fictional construct.

Jane Eyre is beginning to look a lot more complicated. Rather than emphasising the difficulties the heroine has in adjusting to society, modern criticism stresses Brontë's examination of the dominant order in society, questions of gender, and the concept of the self. Such criticism takes apart solid assumptions about society, conventional roles, and, perhaps most fundamentally, the very idea of a solid self. It is, primarily, a combination of structuralist, feminist and psychoanalytic thinking that has adjusted our sense of *Jane Eyre*, but what we should also be aware of is the possibility of a New Historicist approach. New Historicism looks at texts in their historical context, but with the same scepticism about traditional patterns and values that is evident in the other approaches mentioned here. It is worth thinking, for example, about how the novel's sense of the individual relates specifically to the period around 1847 when the novel was first published. In the economic turbulence of the 1840s, with the rapid expansion of industrialisation, old patterns of social relationship were disintegrating. There was increasing emphasis upon the individual, for – as against the old, agricultural order, where the individual knew his or her place in the system – the self increasingly carried the burden for decisions and actions. Consequently, and not surprisingly, novelists around this time (perhaps most notably Dickens in *David Copperfield* in 1850) were repeatedly drawn to examining the nature of individuality, often simultaneously relishing and fearing this new importance of self. *Jane Eyre*, therefore, can be regarded as part of a much wider process of cultural and social self-examination and self-definition that was going on at the time. But Brontë's is one of the most awkward voices, for although the overall story of *Jane Eyre* stresses Jane's coming to terms with society, much of the novel not only quarrels with society but with the fundamental manner in which a woman, through language, is constituted as a subject in society.

We have come a long way in a few pages. Not everything that appears here is new – traditional critics probably touch on most of the points I mention – but, in order for criticism to really reposition itself in relation to *Jane Eyre*, there needed to be a stepping away from traditional values. Perhaps the fundamental change is the shift from a stance that sees the novel as speaking for society – offering it guidance about how society and individuals should relate – to a sense of the novel being at the centre of a political debate within society. Traditional criticism sought to tidy the text up, to deliver a meaning; current criticism, by contrast, makes far more of the unresolvable tensions in a plot, seeing them as reflective of fundamental tensions and problems within a period. In *Jane Eyre*, in particular, this becomes especially clear if, as a final step in our analysis, we consider how, although Brontë appears as an angry and dissenting voice, she is also, paradoxically, committed to middle-class values.

After the wedding has been interrupted, Rochester takes Jane to see his wife:

> In the deep shade, at the farther end of the room, a figure ran backwards and forwards. What it was, whether beast or human being, one could not, at first sight, tell: it grovelled, seemingly on all fours; it snatched and growled like some strange wild animal: but it was covered with clothing, and a quantity of dark, grizzled hair, wild as a mane, hid its head and face.
>
> [p. 321]

The obvious point to make is that, alongside the social order, there is this unfortunate mad woman who is beyond hope of reclaiming a place in society. Brontë, therefore, for all her reservations about the social world, can also see the real horror of being excluded, of being insane, of being both locked out by and locked up by society. But it is more complicated than this, for Bertha Rochester, from the West Indies, is of mixed race. This fact begins to signal a deep contradiction in Brontë's stance: for all her readiness to criticise the prevailing ideology of the day, she none the less shares some of the period's fundamental ideological assumptions. The particular form it takes here is that in the novel's representation of Bertha Rochester we see a sense that is deeply ingrained in the novel of the white race as civilised, whereas those outside the fold are uncivilised. It is a structural assumption in the novel that is repeated in the idea of St John Rivers going off to India as a missionary.

What exactly do we make of this? The interesting point is, I think, that although Brontë appears to question so much in the society of her day, she needs something to hold on to. She might appear as a critic of the structure of the established or conventional order of society, but it is as if, when it really comes to the crunch, she endorses that order by contrasting those who are genuine members of British society with the primitive and dangerous people outside that order. This includes people in the West Indies and India, but it could apply just as much to members of the working class in Britain, for what Brontë appears to cling on to above all is a sense of class identity. Time and time again in the novel we can sense Jane taking a pride in her middle-class respectability. It is a fascinating aspect of the novel: Brontë raises fundamental questions about the construction of the self, about identify, but, in a situation where she has created uncertainty, she clings on to class identity as a kind of rock in an uncertain world. Victorian middle-class self-identity, as in this case, always worked on a basis of 'us' and 'others'; the working class represented the most obvious form of an 'other', but increasingly in the Victorian period, as the Empire expanded, the colonised races could symbolise the uncivilised alternative. What we need to add, however, is that women also constituted an 'other', for, as against the rational order of men, women were thought of as irrational and unstable. But as much as Brontë might quarrel with that stereotype, she does not seem to question racial and class assumptions; indeed, there is a sense on Jane's part that it is her middle-class integrity that gets her through.

What we have got on to here is the class issue in *Jane Eyre*; a consideration of class is likely to be fairly central in all political criticism, most obviously in Marxist, New Historicist and cultural materialist criticism. A fact that we need to grasp, however, and which might not be immediately obvious, is that spotting the class bias of the author does not in any way weaken one's sense of the achievement of a text; a contradiction, we need to see, is *not* a flaw in a novel. Indeed, there are going to be contradictions in all novels, for any text, while dissecting the mores of its day, is also a product of its day and cannot be expected to rise above the period of its production. This should underline a point that has informed all of this analysis, that novels do not offer us timeless, universal truths about human nature and human conduct. On the contrary, a novel will reproduce a society's arguments with itself, all its attempts to understand itself and its confusions. *Jane Eyre* provides an outstandingly interesting example of a novel standing in a complex relationship to the society that produced it.

II 'Wuthering Heights'

I want to turn now to a novel by another of the Brontë sisters, Emily Brontë's *Wuthering Heights*. It should soon become apparent that the kind of critical refocusing that has occurred in relation to *Jane Eyre* has happened just as much here, that there has been a shift from searching for the moral and the meaning of the text to an interest in the text's complex interrogation of the political, social and cultural order of its day. Such changes in critical emphasis have been particularly welcome in the case of *Wuthering Heights* because, as it is such a highly charged dramatic novel, it has always tended to attract readings that see it as timeless, inexplicable according to the normal rules, almost a freak of genius.

The novel tells the story of Heathcliff, a foundling, who is picked up on the streets of Liverpool by Mr Earnshaw. He is brought home to Wuthering Heights to be treated like Earnshaw's own children, Catherine and Hindley. After Earnshaw's death, however, Heathcliff is bullied and degraded by Hindley. The passionate and ferocious Heathcliff falls in love with Cathy, who returns his affection even though she feels it would be humiliating to marry him. When he discovers this, Heathcliff leaves, and, by the time he returns three years later, Cathy has married a neighbouring gentleman, Edgar Linton of Thrushcross Grange. Heathcliff, at Wuthering Heights, begins to assert himself, in particular subjecting Catherine to a torrent of accusations of betrayal and cruelty. Thoroughly exhausted, she dies having given birth to a girl, another Catherine. Heathcliff also asserts his vengeance on Isabella Linton, the sister of Edgar, with whom he has contracted a loveless marriage. She flees, leaving her son, Linton Heathcliff, with his father. When Hindley Earnshaw dies, Wuthering Heights becomes the property of Heathcliff. Hindley's son, Hareton, receives no education and is allowed to become a brutish beast. Heathcliff then engineers the marriage of the younger Catherine and his son Linton, an action that enables him to secure the Linton family property. Linton, however, dies, and Catherine begins to develop an interest in Hareton, in particular undertaking his education. By this stage, late in the novel, Heathcliff is longing for death and union with Cathy. He dies, but the novel concludes with the union of Catherine and Hareton, a relationship that seems to point to a new future.

To anyone who has not read *Wuthering Heights*, this summary might suggest a novel that is as convoluted and melodramatic as a soap opera. As in the case of many soap operas, there is a 'bad' character who dominates the action: Heathcliff, as an outsider, goes through life wreaking revenge on those who have shunned or mistreated him. What fails to come across in the summary, however, is the tremendous power of *Wuthering Heights*, including such things as the enigmatic force of the portrayal of Heathcliff, the brutality of his relationships, and the intensity of his love for Catherine. It is such qualities that encourage transcendental readings of the novel; with good cause, many feel there is something elemental, and well beyond normal understanding, at work in the novel.

In order to see this, let's start by looking at a short exchange between Cathy and Heathcliff:

'Are you possessed with a devil,' he pursued, savagely, 'to talk in that manner to me, when you are dying? Do you reflect that all those words will be branded in my memory, and eating deeper eternally, after you have left me? You know you lie to say I have killed you; and, Catherine, you know that I could as soon forget you as my existence! Is it not sufficient for your infernal selfishness, that while you are at peace I shall writhe in the torments of hell?'

'I shall not be at peace,' moaned Catherine, recalled to a sense of physical weakness by the violent, unequal throbbing of her heart, which beat visibly, and audibly, under this excess of agitation.

She said nothing further till the paroxysm was over; then she continued, more kindly –

I'm not wishing you greater torment than I have, Heathcliff. I only wish us never to be parted – and should a word of mine distress you hereafter, think I feel the same distress underground, and for my own sake, forgive me! Come here and kneel down again! You never harmed me in your life. Nay, if you nurse anger, that will be worse to remember than my harsh words! Won't you come here again? Do!'

[*Wuthering Heights* (Penguin, 1965), p. 196]

Whereas moderation is the defining characteristic of the behaviour of most people most of the time, Cathy and Heathcliff veer between extremes. His torrent of accusation, for example, is coupled with an extraordinary declaration of the intensity of his feelings, and Cathy's agitation is followed by a 'kindly' response to Heathcliff. The intensity of their emotions is conveyed primarily through Brontë's consistent use of images that refer to dimensions beyond the merely social: Heathcliff's speech, in particular, is dominated by words such as 'devil', 'eternally', 'existence' and 'the torrents of hell'. By defining their feelings in this way, Brontë manages to suggest something on a grand, even cosmic, scale that has little, if any, connection with the laws of society.

This effect – this suggestion of something beyond the everyday – is also conveyed in the idea at the centre of Cathy's speech, that she will continue to suffer just as much as Heathcliff, even physically, after her death. We grasp an idea, therefore, of a passion that transcends any normal limits, that not only goes beyond society but even beyond the usual boundary between life and death. Such an impression comes across even more forcefully because of the way in which Brontë uses her principal narrators, Lockwood and Nelly Dean, to mediate and present Cathy and Heathcliff's story. Lockwood and Nelly speak in the conventional discourse of society: Lockwood in the affected, shallow tone of a gentleman who sees himself as a romantic, Nelly with a pious emphasis on respectability and good manners. There is such a gulf between Lockwood's nimsy-pimsy speaking voice or Nelly's moralising and the aggressive, passionate or lyrical language of Heathcliff that it throws into even sharper definition the ferocity of his feelings. At the heart of the novel, then, is this extraordinary, and extraordinarily expressed, mutual commitment of Cathy and Heathcliff: their love is elemental and enduring, consistently transcending the merely social.

Now, up to this point there would be little for critics to disagree about in what I have said. All readers of *Wuthering Heights* are likely to acknowledge that it presents an intense relationship in a forceful way. It is also the case that most critics are likely to pay some attention to how the mediating narrators contribute to the effect of the novel. Beyond this, however, we soon begin to see a difference between traditional criticism of *Wuthering Heights* and the kind of criticism published today. There are, broadly speaking, two traditional responses to the novel. One response concentrates on the gap between Cathy and Heathcliff and the ordinary world. Cathy, of course, succumbs to conventional pressures (and conventional needs in herself) when she enters into an economically advantageous marriage with Edgar Linton. But, for one kind of critic, this only reinforces the point that the central tension of the novel is between social convention and romantic impulses; this approach leads to the argument that the novel offers an analysis of how positive natural energies are deformed by a repressive society. Even the fact of Heathcliff's brutality does not affect the central proposition that something stunning is being suggested that is beyond the scale of ordinary existence.

This can be described as the 'romantic' interpretation of *Wuthering Heights*, for it identifies with the values associated with the two principal romantic figures. Just as common in traditional criticism, however, is the 'moral' interpretation of *Wuthering Heights*, a reading that pays as much attention to the second generation, of young Catherine and Hareton, as it does to Cathy and Heathcliff. In this reading, the point that is often made is that Catherine and Hareton achieve a balance, managing to reconcile passionate feeling with socially acceptable behaviour. It was this approach, the moral view of *Wuthering Heights*, that I was taught at school. I remember at the time that I thought there was something wrong with such an approach, but naturally, at the age of seventeen, I couldn't see what was wrong. Now I can see that it is an inadequate view because it almost totally ignores the complex process of the novel in order to stress a product – as if the novel is nothing more than an extended parable with a simple message about how people should behave.

There is far more to be said for a 'romantic' view of the novel, for that clearly does attempt to come to terms with the force of the presentation of Cathy and Heathcliff, and to make bold assertions about the significance of their relationship. Even today, nobody is going to go far wrong in an examination if they put their energies into showing how Brontë brings Cathy and Heathcliff to life, and then into trying to comment on the meaning of their relationship. What I am saying, therefore, is that, if you wish, you can feel quite happy about continuing with the 'romantic' way of reading *Wuthering Heights*. The only problem, it seems to me, is that, the longer you look, the more likely you are to start encountering a rather awkward contradiction in this approach, for it is a way of looking that suggests that the relationship in the novel passes beyond normal understanding, but at the same time this feeling is accompanied by a desire to pin the novel down, to define and contain the relationship. In other words, it is a critical stance that says the relationship is beyond social comprehension but the critic insists on interpreting it, in fact comprehending it, from the perspective of society.

By now you may have been able to anticipate the approach adopted by more recent critics of *Wuthering Heights*. This is to acknowledge the central tension, between the romantic and the everyday, but, rather than rushing to endorse one side, to dwell on the tension itself. One aspect of this approach involves paying attention to awkward passages in the novel, material that can't easily be assimilated into a simple oppositional reading. It is for this reason that I have decided to look at a rather curious passage where Lockwood is trying to find a path; I have chosen it because it seems superfluous, to have no direct bearing on the Cathy and Heathcliff-versus-the world story.

Lockwood, leaving Wuthering Heights in thick snow, is stopped by Heathcliff:

> My landlord [Heathcliff] hallooed for me to stop ere I reached the bottom of the garden, and offered to accompany me across the moor. It was well he did, for the whole hill-back was one billowy, white ocean; the swells and falls not indicating corresponding rises and depressions in the ground – many pits, at least, were filled to a level; and entire ranges of mounds, the refuse of the quarries, blotted out from the chart which my yesterday's walk left pictured in my mind.
>
> I had remarked on one side of the road, at intervals of six or seven yards, a line of upright stones, continued through the whole length of the barren: these were erected, and daubed with lime on purpose to serve as guides in the dark, and also, when a fall, like the present, confounded the deep swamps on either hand with the firmer path: but, excepting a dirty dot pointing up, here and there, all traces of their existence had vanished; and my companion found it necessary to warn me frequently to steer to the right, or left, when I imagined I was following, correctly, the windings of the road.
>
> [pp. 72–3]

How can we relate this passage to the novel as a whole? The point is, I think, that from our first introduction to Lockwood we have seen him trying to act like a kind of detective, piecing together the story about Heathcliff. But this passage emphasises how lost he is, that the moment he strays beyond the familiar world he has no guidelines. Putting this in a larger context, we may say that the novel at this stage is drawing attention to the social desire to map out and control experience: Lockwood here, for example, feebly compares what he is actually encountering with the 'chart' in his mind. Consequently, it is fair to say that the novel at this point, rather than gesturing towards some larger truth that is there if only we could perceive it, is drawing attention to the conventional procedures by which we attempt to comprehend the world. There is a precise parallel to this in the very nature of structuralist criticism, for structuralism is more concerned with the patterns and procedures of texts than with any truth that might be revealed within a text.

If we begin to apply such ideas to *Wuthering Heights* as a whole it leads to a significant redistribution of the centre of interest in the text: perhaps the novel isn't gesturing at some kind of transcendental truth, such as may be concealed beneath the snow or evoked in the relationship of Cathy and Heathcliff. Perhaps the novel is involved in an examination of a range of issues, including questions about how we organise our lives in a world where any sort of clear path is obscured. The possibility is that Brontë is interrogating her age, in particular the habitual patterns of rational thought of the period, in a broad and discursive manner, rather than just offering us her 'cosmic vision'. In some ways there might seem nothing that could be more ambitious than a novel that evokes the passion of Cathy and Heathcliff, but what I am suggesting is that if we alter our critical angle we begin to see a novel that questions the very ways in which we understand the world.

Attention to passages such as that quoted above can put a spoke in the wheel of message-laden, all-embracing interpretations of *Wuthering Heights*. Feminist approaches have a similar effect of disrupting excessively neat readings of the novel. I'm not going to quote a passage here, as I think some general pointers about how a feminist response might proceed should prove just as helpful. Taking traditional views of the novel as our starting-point again, the temptation is to yoke Cathy and Heathcliff together so thoroughly as an indivisible couple that issues of conflict of gender between the two are overlooked. But if critical attention is refocused so that we look for scenes where Cathy's role as a woman is central, then what is likely to become apparent is that the issues in the novel are a lot more complex and diverse than just romantic passion versus the normal world. Such an emphasis should confirm the impression that the traditional response to *Wuthering Heights* undersells the novel by reducing everything to a pattern. When we look at awkward scenes – in this instance, awkward details about Cathy as a woman that complicate our impression of the relationship between her and Heathcliff – the novel becomes a broader kind of examination of the social and cultural order of the time of its publication. The same effect would be achieved if we focused on awkward details about class in the novel, or the fact that Heathcliff, a foundling from the streets of Liverpool, may well be Irish (giving rise to a possible colonial dimension to the text); again it would force us to recognise that Brontë is operating on more fronts than used to be acknowledged in traditional criticism.

Where this gets us is that *Wuthering Heights*, rather than offering a timeless vision of romantic love, deserves and demands to be seen as, like *Jane Eyre*, engaging with a range of issues, reproducing Victorian society's arguments with itself and that society's attempts to understand itself. Both novels were published in 1847, a time of rapid social change; as already noted in the discussion of *Jane Eyre*, the question of the self is a central issue around this time, for people were having to define a sense of themselves as members of an increasingly complex industrial society. In *Wuthering Heights*, just as in *Jane Eyre*, questions about the self could again be said to be central, that it is around this concept of the individual subject that the novel conducts its fullest and most thought-provoking discussion.

An appropriate scene to look at is one that features the most famous speech in the book, Cathy's declaration that she *is* Heathcliff. It starts with Cathy trying to justify to Nelly her decision to marry Edgar Linton:

> 'Nelly, I see now, you think me a selfish wretch, but did it never strike you that, if Heathcliff and I married, we should be beggars? whereas, if I marry Linton, I can aid Heathcliff to rise, and place him out of my brother's power?'
>
> 'With your husband's money, Miss Catherine?' I asked. 'You'll find him not so pliable as you calculate upon: and, though I'm hardly a judge, I think that's the worst motive you've given yet for being the wife of young Linton.'
>
> 'It is not,' retorted she, 'it is the best! The others were the satisfaction of my whims; and for Edgar's sake, too, to satisfy him. This is for the sake of one who comprehends in his person my feelings to Edgar and myself. I cannot express it; but surely you and everybody here have a notion that

there is, or should be an existence of yours beyond you. What were the use of my creation if I were entirely contained here? My great miseries in this world have been Heathcliff's miseries, and I watched and felt each from the beginning; my great thought in living is himself. If all else perished, and *he* remained, I should still continue to be; and if all else remained, and he were annihilated, the universe would turn to a mighty stranger. I should not seem a part of it. My love for Linton is like the foliage in the woods. Time will change it, I'm well aware, as winter changes the trees. My love for Heathcliff resembles the eternal rocks beneath – a source of little visible delight, but necessary. Nelly, I *am* Heathcliff . . .

[p. 122]

There are several points here: we could comment on Cathy's naïvety in believing that she can separate her social self from her true self. Or, if we were attracted to the 'romantic' view of the novel, we could talk about how, in this scene, the novel offers its strongest sense yet of the nature and power of the bond between them. Or, if we chose to approach the novel along psychoanalytic lines, we could suggest that there is a sense in which the relationship between the two is 'infantile', in that they refuse to assume their places, and a sense of a separate identify constructed through language, in the Symbolic Order of society, and regress to a sense of a shared identity. To my mind, however, something rather more all-embracing is being suggested here. In *Jane Eyre*, Charlotte Brontë quarrels with, looks sceptically at, but finally endorses the Victorian period's developing sense of individual identity; in particular, she indicates her commitment to middle-class identity, as the alternative, represented by Bertha Rochester, is too appalling to contemplate. In *Wuthering Heights*, however, Emily Brontë, at a more fundamental level, seems to reject the notion of individual identity: this is conveyed here in Cathy's declaration that she is Heathcliff, a denial of separate or individual identity. It is this rejection of a conventional sense of identity that permits the romantic exaggeration of the novel.

Such an awareness might not lead us anywhere, however, unless we adopt a New Historicist approach of locating the text in a sense of cultural history. Both *Jane Eyre* and *Wuthering Heights* are the products of crisis, of unprecedented social change in the 1840s. Perhaps the central characteristic of this period is that, with the world as a whole in flux and confusion, people increasingly withdrew into themselves – the idea of oneself as an individual became a fact of increasing importance. *Jane Eyre* negotiates this transition: it presents a harsh world, a heroine who is not at ease with herself or the world, but who finally comes to an accommodation with the world even though the limits of individuality are defined by men. *Wuthering Heights* confronts the same harsh world – in fact, it presents a fuller picture than *Jane Eyre* of religious, class and family divisions – but it refuses to negotiate an answer, it refuses to accept an evolving sense of individualism as the only tenable answer to social crisis. It is this that makes *Wuthering Heights* such an unusual novel, a novel that stands apart from others in the period.

If one accepts the logic of this argument, it is easy to see why the kind of reading that merely celebrates the romantic excess of *Wuthering Heights* can be said to sell the novel short, for the romantic reading emphasises a kind of timeless passion, rather than seeing how the novel is a complex response to deep tensions and problems in the society that produced it. It is, it might be said, an awkward text that refuses to go along with the new spirit of the Victorian age. Or, at least, that is what I feel, or, to put it more honestly, the view I am led to when I take account of current critical and theoretical thinking. But recent theory is diverse, and could lead to a great many, often contradictory, readings of *Wuthering Heights*. It could be, of course, that you find this diversity of recent criticism, with its proliferation of 'isms' such as poststructuralism, feminism and New Historicism, unnerving. How is it possible to find one's way through, or adapt and make use of, so many approaches? The simple fact is, however, that you don't need to be familiar with every nuance of theory; the important thing is to grasp the kind of position from which criticism today is operating, trying to get away from the idea that the text is making a statement. Try instead to see a text as a site of struggle, where the author is deeply engaged in trying to understand the different forces, particularly the forces of cultural and political change, within his or her society.

III 'The Mill on the Floss'

I have dealt with *Jane Eyre* and *Wuthering Heights* at length because of the need to give an impression of the variety of perspectives and approaches within contemporary criticism. The awful truth, however, is that I have still only scratched the surface of current critical thinking. But rather than complicate matters further, it seems appropriate at this stage, in order to take stock, to simplify and condense matters as much as possible. I am going to look briefly at *The Mill on the Floss* by George Eliot. There are a number of good reasons for choosing George Eliot for this concluding, summary section. First, George Eliot might well strike us as an author who always seems to be making a statement. While the Victorians were always concerned with questions of the balance between the individual and society, George Eliot is the novelist who perhaps more than any other at the time spells out the duties and obligations of the individual. Her principal theme is egoism; her standard plot is an educational one, in which the principal character comes to understand that he or she has been too self-absorbed and starts to think more about his or her social commitment.

This sense that George Eliot is making a moral statement made her a favourite novelist with traditional critics. They did not, of course, just endorse the message of the novels; what they praised was the tremendous subtlety and depth of understanding with which George Eliot presented the experiences of her characters. There were critics who felt that she was sometimes too didactic, too concerned to offer sage words of advice to the reader, but there were, quite correctly, far more who praised than condemned, for George Eliot is astonishingly perceptive, extraordinarily acute in her reading of a situation. It helped that her chosen mode was realism; this not only aided the kind of solid exploration of individuals and their relationship that she offers, but also endeared her to traditional critics who felt that the realistic novel was the form best suited to embodying and expressing a liberal humanist perspective on life.

How have things changed? Do critics still take the same view of George Eliot? As you will probably guess, the answer is, by and large, no: she now tends to be seen as a more anxious and uncertain author than was the case in the past. Rather than rising above her period with a sense of how people should behave, she is now widely felt to be as confused and uncertain as anyone else in her time. Her novels were published between 1859 (*Adam Bede*) and 1876 (*Daniel Deronda*); that is to say, she made her first appearance as a novelist about ten years after the Brontës. In discussions of the Victorian period, whereas the 1840s are seen as a period of unrest, the years in which George Eliot was writing are seen as the high point of the century, when the country was enjoying tremendous prosperity, and when the kinds of class division that are apparent in the Brontës or Dickens were no longer such a problem. George Eliot can be seen as the confident novelist of these confident years. But if we look a little more closely, we might question whether this was such a confident period; perhaps there were deep uncertainties, which George Eliot's novels might give expression to.

One aspect of this is the view we take of her presentation of women. In the early days of feminist criticism, George Eliot was often represented as almost disloyal to women because she seemed to endorse the values and codes of society – codes that were, inevitably, patriarchal. But more recent criticism has praised George Eliot's feminism, the quiet anger that underlies her presentation of the situations in which most women find themselves. Even the established view of George Eliot's realism has begun to disintegrate, as critics draw attention to contradictory impulses in her work.

How can such a change come about? How can the view of a novelist be turned round in this kind of way? How can a stress on coherence be replaced by a stress on incoherence? We can start with the fact that every period rewrites texts from the past on its own terms. Critics today, prompted by a sense of their own uncertainty, go looking for uncertainty in texts from the past. But this kind of gut feeling has to be accompanied by theory, by a more organised and systematic set of ideas. Change first came about with structuralism, for with structuralism critics stopped looking through the words on the page to the world presented and transferred their attention to the words themselves. What followed from that was a fundamental shift of emphasis from the substantiality of what the text had to say to the text's difficulties, its falterings in its attempt to say anything. The moment the emphasis changed from acceptance of the text to a somewhat sceptical questioning of the text, the gates were open for every subsequent development in, and variety of, poststructuralist criticism.

Let me try to illustrate the nature and scale of this change using the example of *The Mill on the Floss*. The novel tells the story of Maggie Tulliver and her brother Tom. Maggie is an intelligent girl in a community that has no time for her, and which offers no outlet for her intelligence. She becomes friends with Philip Wakem, who appreciates her qualities and sympathises with her interests, but Tom forces her to give up Philip's friendship. Subsequently, Maggie's reputation is compromised through the irresponsible behaviour of Stephen Guest; Tom turns her out of the house, and she is ostracised by local society. Maggie and Tom are, however, finally, if briefly, reconciled when she attempts to save him from a flood that threatens the family mill; but it is the briefest of reconciliations, for they both drown. If there was one point that traditional critics always found fault with it was the ending of the novel. There was general admiration for the skill with which George Eliot evokes rural life, and the sympathetic manner in which she presents Maggie's frustrations and aspirations, but the ending was almost always criticised as rushed and arbitrary. Almost inevitably, critics today are full of praise for the ending.

But before turning to that, I want to glance at some of the other things critics used to say about *The Mill on the Floss*. One point, that seems almost bizarre now, is that George Eliot was frequently condemned for her idealisation of Maggie. One line, most commonly associated with the critic F. R. Leavis, was that Maggie is so much a reflection of George Eliot herself that the author neglects to criticise her character when she acts immaturely. What smug nonsense; it should be apparent that the stance informing such a view is one that views the world entirely on male terms. It should also be apparent that it is very easy to reverse this judgement by bringing into play a feminist perspective on the text: that *The Mill on the Floss* is a wonderful evocation and understanding of the restraints and constraints placed upon women. Indeed, one would probably take this view today without even having to think about it, but that is because attitudes and values have changed since Leavis's time. He was expressing a consensus view for his time; our immediate sympathy for Maggie, and our ability to put that in a larger context of understanding the limited opportunities historically offered to women, is a consensus view for our time.

There has been a similar shift in discussions of Maggie's relationship with Stephen Guest. It is again hard to grasp the point today, but critics used to find it hard to believe that Maggie could succumb to the attractions of such an undistinguished male as Stephen. In expressing this view, they were, without realising it, revealing a certain kind of proprietorial, patriarchal attitude towards women: it is as if the woman should conform to the critic's view of what is reasonable conduct from a respectable woman. Criticism today would take a very different line, understanding a great many of the factors that prompt Maggie's relationship with Stephen. And the vast mass of readers would tend to feel the same way; it is again a matter of how the consensus of values in society has changed – the widespread acceptance of a feminist discourse within society, the way in which it has subtly altered standard ways of thinking about gender relations, means that the instinctive response of a reader today is likely to be one of sympathetic understanding rather than moral judgement of the heroine.

But if reservations about the presentation of Maggie and the presentation of Maggie's emotional feelings seem to belong to another world, there are still readers who might feel less than happy with the ending. Their argument would be that while Eliot offers a complex picture and subtle analysis for most of the novel, at the end all of this is thrown away; that the novel ends in a kind of mad rush which doesn't have a lot to do with the novel we have been reading up to this point. Recently, however, critics, in particular feminist critics, have looked at the ending in positive terms. It can be argued, for example, that the novel has encouraged us to think within the constraints of realism, accepting the modes of analysis that characterise realism; but such a discourse is essentially the discourse of society, and, as such, the discourse of men; in particular, men in positions of power. The ending spectacularly rejects not only the convention of realism but also the values that are implicit in such a convention. In presenting the flood, George Eliot demonstrates both the inadequacy of the social choices open to Maggie and the inadequacy of the form of the realistic novel. It is, of course, the case that Maggie finds no practical solution to her problems, but in the final embrace with her brother there is a supreme moment of transcendence.

There are, obviously, not going to be all that many examples where general condemnation of a sequence in a novel will turn round so totally and so dramatically as in the case of the ending of *The Mill on the Floss*, but the kind of reversal of critical opinion in evidence here points to a pattern in modern criticism. Critics used to strive to pin the text down, to see what sort of statement it could be said to be making, to make a kind of steady sense out of the evidence. But recent criticism has looked for untidiness, for disruption, for uncertainty in a text. As against the notion of a novelist who can offer us a steady, almost timeless, judgement on life, recent criticism expects to see the novelist embodying and expressing the problems and tensions of the period of the text's production.

9

New readings

Novels discussed:

Heart of Darkness, by Joseph Conrad, published 1902
Tess of the D'Urbervilles, by Thomas Hardy, published 1891
Emma, by Jane Austen, published 1815

In the previous chapter I introduced a lot of new ideas very quickly; I now want to take stock. I'm going to continue with the new approaches I have been discussing, but I now intend to work through three novels in the methodical way I described in the opening chapters of this book. It should soon become apparent that even the most radical readings can be accommodated within, and indeed shaped and directed by, a very simple framework. In other words, although you may change the assumptions that you bring to studying novels, there is no reason to change the basic method of building a case from specific passages. What follows in this chapter are not theoretically pure readings: as most critics do, I slide from one position to another in the analysis of each novel, but it is fair to say that the analysis of *Heart of Darkness* has its basis in deconstruction, that the reading of *Tess of the D'Urbervilles* is influenced by Marxist and feminist criticism, and that the interpretation of *Emma* owes a good deal to New Historicism. Let me repeat the point, however, that everything I say is based upon the evidence of specific passages in the texts, and, more particularly, as this is something that characterises all current approaches, close attention to the language of these extracts.

I 'Heart of Darkness'

Joseph Conrad was a Polish seaman who became an English novelist. It was, in fact, his experiences, in 1890, as captain of a river steamer in the Congo that served as the basis for *Heart of Darkness*. It is a short novel, but one that has attracted a tremendous amount of critical attention. In it, the narrator, Marlow, recalls a river journey into the heart of Africa. In the course of the voyage Marlow becomes curious about a man called Kurtz, an agent with an outstanding reputation for acquiring ivory, who is also, it seems, a man with a charismatic personality. Expecting to meet an inspiring representative of western civilisation, Marlow actually encounters someone who has become thoroughly brutalised. Kurtz dies declaring 'The horror! The horror!' Marlow, drawn to pay a visit to Kurtz's fiancée, is about to repeat these words but instead tells her that Kurtz died pronouncing her name.

Is there anything we can deduce from this summary? It is difficult; at the beginning of the novel we are told that, while seamen's yarns generally have a direct simplicity, Marlow's are not typical: 'to him the meaning of an episode was not inside like a kernel but outside, enveloping the tale which brought it out only as a glow brings out a haze, in the likeness of one of these misty halos that are sometimes made visible by the spectral illumination of moonshine' (*Heart of Darkness* [Penguin, 1973], p. 30). Critics have, accordingly, attempted to do justice to the enigmatic suggestiveness of *Heart of Darkness*. Yet there is a fair amount of agreement among traditional critics that both Kurtz and Marlow learn something. One aspect of this is a sense of the rapacious brutality of imperialism: it has affected a man of such great potential as Kurtz, who in his dying words expresses a kind of desperate self-knowledge. But Marlow has also been forced to consider himself, his beliefs, his frame of values: he has been forced to call the whole purpose and meaning of his existence into doubt. What we can say, therefore, is that, while traditional critics acknowledge the enigmatic qualities of *Heart of Darkness*, they also, almost invariably, manage to extract a moral point from the novel, an insight into life that the text could be said to offer. It is an understandable critical response: confronted by something puzzling, the natural inclination is to pin the work down, to identify an authorial intention, to see what sort of statement the novel can be said to be making.

More recent criticism, however, is less concerned with any message Conrad might have for his age than with the ways in which the text is caught up in that age's deeper processes of self-examination. The river journey in *Heart of Darkness* tantalises us with the prospect that we are travelling towards some significant truth, but the real effect of the text seems to be to undermine our hope that anything will or can be revealed. Appearing at the end of the nineteenth century, *Heart of Darkness* goes beyond a critique of the mere fact of imperialism and questions the fundamental convictions upon which the whole concept of Empire – that is to say, an idea of control of the world – was established. If that idea is hard to grasp, a look at a few short extracts from the novel should begin to make it a lot clearer.

Step 1: After reading the work as a whole, take a close look at the opening page of the novel, or, if this proves unilluminating, at a passage fairly near the beginning featuring one or more of the principal characters

This is the opening of *Heart of Darkness*:

> The *Nellie*, a cruising yawl, swung to her anchor without a flutter of the sails, and was at rest. The flood had made, the wind was nearly calm, and being bound down the river, the only thing for it was to come to and wait for the turn of the tide.
>
> The sea-reach of the Thames stretched before us like the beginning of an interminable waterway. In the offing the sea and the sky were welded together without a joint, and in the luminous space the tanned sails of the barges drifting up with the tide seemed to stand still in red clusters of canvas sharply peaked, with gleams of varnished sprits. A haze rested on the low shores that ran out to sea in vanishing flatness. The air was dark above Gravesend, and farther back still seemed condensed into a mournful gloom, brooding motionless over the biggest, and the greatest, town on earth.
>
> The Director of Companies was our captain and our host. We four affectionately watched his back as he stood in the bows looking to seaward. On the whole river there was nothing that looked half so nautical. He resembled a pilot, which to a seaman is trustworthiness personified. It was difficult to realise his work was not out there in the luminous estuary, but behind him, within the brooding gloom.
>
> [p. 27]

I gain an impression of calm and security from this opening: the river is still, the wind having subsided. In the second paragraph, the details seem to compose themselves into a picture with everything fitting together. An implicit tension is between this current serenity and the unnerving journey that is to dominate the book; here, for the moment, we are in the cradle of civilisation, in 'the biggest, and the greatest, town on earth'.

What helps establish this sense of security is a series of reassuring gestures. For example, we are told the name of the ship and that the river is the Thames: names of things always gives us a sense of being able to control the world. At the same time, however, the picture is not quite as settled as it seems. The wind is only 'nearly calm': nature lurks in the background and could easily assume a fiercer, disruptive energy. I'm also struck by Marlow and his friends having to wait for the turn of the tide: again, these people are at the mercy of the larger movements of nature. What all this does is set up an issue for the novel: we are offered a sense of the precariousness of the social order that Europe has created. The journey into Africa will test this social order.

What is also apparent in this passage is the manner in which we use language to create a controlled sense of the world. There are two principal methods in evidence here: one is by naming, the other is the use of connection-making metaphors. The novel starts, 'The *Nellie*, a cruising yawl . . .': the ship is both named and categorised. Grouping things together, by categorising and cataloguing them, is one of the fundamental methods we rely upon to define and order experience. Metaphor is used here in a similar way. When Conrad writes, 'sea and sky were welded together without a joint', metaphors from industry are being used to describe the natural world; it is a method of control, a way of reaching out to control the natural world (in the same way that imperialism will be presented as reaching out to control and dominate the world). But control can prove illusory. If we look, for example, at the phrase 'The Director of Companies was our captain and host', we see that it defines and categorises him in the same way that the ship was defined, something that is taken further when his similarity to 'a pilot, which to a seaman is trustworthiness personified', is stressed. But he is, in fact, nothing of the sort, he is the director of the company, whose real place is in the 'brooding gloom' of the city.

How can we sum up what is happening on this opening page of the novel? It seems to me that the text gently undermines our secure assumptions. It offers us images of security, but then shows them to be less reliable than they might appear. As the text continues, it is likely to challenge us with an increasingly provocative undermining of the secure convictions of European society and European thinking.

Step 2: Select and analyse a second passage

In this extract, Marlow has arrived at his first shore base in Africa:

> I avoided a vast artificial hole somebody had been digging on the slope, the purpose of which I found it impossible to divine. It wasn't a quarry or

a sandpit, anyhow. It was just a hole. It might have been connected with the philanthropic desire of giving the criminals something to do. I don't know. Then I nearly fell into a very narrow ravine, almost no more than a scar in the hillside. I discovered that a lot of imported drainage-pipes for the settlement had been tumbled in there. There wasn't one that was not broken. It was a wanton smash-up. At last I got under trees. My purpose was to stroll into the shade for a moment; but no sooner within than it seemed to me I had stepped into the gloomy circle of some Inferno. The rapids were near, and an uninterrupted, uniform, headlong, rushing noise filled the mournful stillness of the grove, where not a breath stirred, not a leaf moved, with a mysterious sound – as though the tearing pace of the launched earth had suddenly become audible.

[p. 44]

What Marlow encounters in the shade of the trees are black workers who, weakened by disease and lack of food, have withdrawn to die. He is an experienced traveller, but he is now confronting things more extreme and incomprehensible than he has ever seen before. A sense of something that defies belief and understanding is conveyed in all the details of the passage. For example, there is the huge, inexplicable hole, full of drainage-pipes that are serving no purpose. The European always wants to take control of his environment, but here all such effort has proved futile. We gain an impression of a land that cannot be controlled, that cannot be maintained.

Where does this get us? The most obvious response is one that says that this passage debunks the pretensions of imperialism: Conrad, it could be said, shows the irrelevance of Europe in this context, but also manages to suggest the brutality of Europe, something that is reflected in the fate of the black workers, the inevitable victims of all western attempts at expansion and domination. At this point, however, we might begin to see a difference of emphasis between traditional and more recent criticism of *Heart of Darkness*. Traditional critics used to try to salvage something from the mess: for example, it could be said that the text achieves something positive by exposing the true face of colonialism, or – and this used to be a fairly standard response to the novel – it could be argued that Marlow becomes wiser as a result of his experiences: the phrase used time and time again by critics was 'self-discovery'.

But what, if anything, is wrong with such a response? The problem is that this kind of traditional view refuses to follow through to their logical conclusion the implications of the doubts the text is raising. By talking about self-discovery, critics make it seem as if Africa is only of note in so far as it enables Marlow to learn something about himself; in other words, Africa occupies a purely supplementary role, for what matters is the western concept of self-knowledge. Critics who refer to self-discovery could, in fact, be said to be reproducing the structure of colonialism, in that they construct a world with a white individual at the centre of it, and view everything in the novel as significant only in so far as it relates to the western individual. Just as colonialism presumes to control the world, so the idea of centring everything in the self is also a way of controlling the world.

Traditional criticism of *Heart of Darkness*, then, consistently focuses on the individual at the heart of the text rather than on the darkness itself. It was structuralism and then deconstruction that took things in another direction, that prompted a sceptical examination of the way in which we use ideas, such as the idea of the importance of the self, to organise the world. Deconstructive critics, in particular, have assumed the role of standing aside from traditional habits of thought in order to expose the unquestioned convictions that shape western thinking. Recent criticism, influenced by deconstruction, resists the temptation to search for something positive in a passage such as this; it seems to make more sense to talk about total chaos, total disorder. Things are so extreme that they undermine our western convictions; if we even talk about Marlow's 'humanity' as he confronts this terrible mess, we are attempting to cling on to something positive.

Step 3: Select and analyse a third passage

Heart of Darkness, I am suggesting, if we approach it in a certain way, can be seen as a text that deprives us of all our anchors, all points of reference. In this kind of reading, Conrad himself becomes a kind of deconstructive writer who not only explores the nature of colonialism but also the habits of thinking that engender colonialism. If we read the book in this way, as it goes on it appears more and more all-questioning, for as Marlow journeys up the river things become more and more inexplicable. In this passage, for example, just eight miles before he reaches Kurtz's station, Marlow encounters a mysterious white fog on the river:

> When the sun rose there was a white fog, very warm and clammy, and more blinding than the night. It did not shift or drive; it was just there, standing all round you like something solid. At eight or nine, perhaps, it

lifted as a shutter lifts. We had a glimpse of the towering multitude of trees, of the immense matted jungle, with the blazing little ball of the sun hanging over it – all perfectly still – and then the white shutter came down again, smoothly, as if sliding in greased grooves. I ordered the chain, which we had begun to heave in, to be paid out again. Before it stopped running with a muffled rattle, a cry, a very loud cry, as of infinite desolation, soared slowly in the opaque air. It ceased. A complaining clamour, modulated in savage discords, filled our ears.

[p. 73]

There is a frightening sound coming from the shore, but Marlow can't see from where or tell what it is. This sustains the sense of being lost, of being at the heart of a blinding fog. So how does Marlow cope? Well, one thing we might look at is the technical imagery, associated with the boat, that is set against the natural imagery of the passage. At an obvious level, as the fog descends Marlow relies upon his anchor, but what is also in evidence is a more general use of technical metaphors in an attempt to comprehend and control the bewildering experience: for example, the fog is compared to a shutter sliding up and down in greased grooves. Such an image is essentially reassuring, for it connects what is happening with something that Marlow can understand. It doesn't help all that much, though, for all that is taking place here is bewildering. One aspect of this is that everything seems to be a reversal of what we might expect in Europe: rather than being cold and damp, the fog is warm and sticky, and the day is more blinding than the night.

Such images are accompanied by Marlow's inflated style: look at phrases such as 'infinite desolation'; and 'modulated in savage discords'. There is a vast gulf between Marlow's literary elegance and the facts of what is being encountered: the passage stresses the gap between what is encountered in Africa and the language available to Marlow to describe and control what is encountered. But the inflated manner of Marlow's narration also hints at the idea that there might be some larger significance implicit in all this. Traditional critics, in fact, often complained about this vague but suggestive style in the novel. They were irritated by its imprecision. They wanted a style that actually defined things, that pinned the experiences down. Rather than the style hinting at some larger significance, traditional critics wanted that significance spelt out. In contrast, critics today are much more likely to stop at the surface of the style, pointing out that it is a style that reveals the western need to analyse and make sense of experience, but how, in being so mannered, it really draws attention to the futility of attempts to comprehend and control. The point that is made is that Conrad is not leading us to a 'truth' beyond the language of the text; on the contrary, he is self-consciously exposing the language, and, as such, the ways of thinking, of the West. Something very similar is conveyed in the whole idea of the river journey: the journey exploits our desire for meaning, our desire to move towards a significant revelation, but as actually presented the river journey confounds our desire for meaning, for revelation.

Step 4: Select and analyse a fourth passage

All of this might become clearer if we consider the function of Kurtz in *Heart of Darkness*. I have selected the moment of his death:

> Anything approaching the change that came over his features I have never seen before, and hope never to see again. Oh, I wasn't touched. I was fascinated. It was as though a veil had been rent. I saw on that ivory face the expression of sombre pride, of ruthless power, of craven terror – of an intense and hopeless despair. Did he live his life again in every detail of desire, temptation, and surrender during that supreme moment of complete knowledge? He cried in a whisper at some stage, at some vision – he cried out twice, a cry that was no more than a breath:
> 'The horror! The horror!'
> I blew the candle out and left the cabin.
>
> [p. 111]

Kurtz's dying words certainly sound impressive: it is as if he has provided some real illumination of the dark horrors of experience. This is underlined by Marlow immediately blowing out the candle, as if this source of light in the darkness of Africa has been extinguished. The episode is, at one level, deeply satisfying to the reader: the idea of the river journey has led us to expect a revelation, and here, finally, it comes. The passage can, therefore, be used very effectively to pull one's critical impressions together, to make all the relevant points about self-knowledge and self-discovery.

But what complicates matters is that the language of the extract is far from trustworthy. It is, for example, overloaded with adjectival insistence from Marlow, who speaks of 'sombre pride', 'ruthless power', 'craven terror' and 'hopeless despair'. Each of these phrases sound suspiciously like a cliché, as if the predictable adjective always precedes the noun. As such, it is either a piece of fairly inept writing or, and this seems far more likely, a self-conscious parody of a moment of revelation. The clichés draw attention to the rather hackneyed quality of the whole scene. But why does Conrad present the scene in this way? Or, perhaps more to the point, why read the scene in this, possibly perverse, way? Why not accept the scene at its face value as a significant moment?

The problem is that, as soon as one decides to concentrate on the language of the extract, it becomes impossible to be anything other than sceptical. Quite simply, the language won't support the straightforward reading, for the style deflates the moment, commenting more on our need for revelation than actually offering us a revelation. This might seem to make Conrad a trivial or less than totally serious novelist, but the point is that he offers us something rather more substantial than something to hold on to; he offers us a radical subversion of our desire for a centre of meaning.

Marlow as narrator is an oddly teasing figure in all this: in the darkness of the novel, he is our guide, but we cling on to Marlow in the same way that Marlow clings on to Kurtz. It is part of the pattern of needing an anchor, a fixed point, a way of comprehending things. But when we question Marlow the text again falls apart, refusing to satisfy our expectation that a text will reveal something tangible to us. You might still be wondering, however, what the point of such an exercise is: a deconstructive approach to fiction is one that might seem to question and deny everything, deliberately seeking, and therefore finding, a lack of coherent meaning in the text. And this would be a fair criticism if the argument stopped here, if deconstruction amounted to nothing more than formulaic scepticism, but there is more involved, as we see when we follow through the political implications of the case so far. *Heart of Darkness*, as everyone has always acknowledged, questions and criticises the rapacious nature of imperialism. But it also, as has been stated, questions western habits of thinking more generally, in particular the way in which our desire to control the world we encounter is ingrained in the language we use. This leads to the realisation that such a desire for control might well be the impulse behind imperialism, that the desire to organise, dominate and impose an order upon life expresses itself physically in the form of colonial expansion. *Heart of Darkness*, as such, is not just a critique of imperialism but a critique of the very nature of the European mind; it is not just examining the issue of colonialism, but drawing attention to the deeper structure of our culture.

This might be a good stage at which to expand a little upon the role of deconstruction in criticism of novels over the past twenty years or so. A lot of deconstructive criticism, it must be said, is difficult and sophisticated. But in a more general manner, deconstruction has encouraged many to react against the old critical impulse to pull the text together, the impulse to see what kind of moral statement the text could be said to be making. Some of the best deconstructive criticism has focused upon George Eliot, despite the fact that she is an author who seems as if she has a moral point to get across. But it is precisely this that makes her so interesting, for the moment one begins to look closely at the narrator's voice in George Eliot's works it becomes apparent that it is a far more devious and confused voice than might superficially seem to be the case. This emphasis on Eliot's language then leads on naturally to a reconsideration of the nature of her achievement as a novelist. She no longer strikes us as a moral sage. Instead, the emphasis falls upon the knottiness and confusion that are often at the heart of her work. Across the board, deconstruction has turned round traditional thinking about novels in this kind of way: rather than the novelist being seen as someone who can make sense of a society and offer it a moral message, the novelist is seen as someone deeply engaged in looking at how a society uses language to try and organise and understand itself. Rather than the novelist being seen as someone who provides answers (in the case of *Heart of Darkness*, a sense of the importance of self-discovery), the novelist is seen as someone who explores and exposes such 'answers', someone who disturbs the platitudes of conventional thinking.

Step 5: Have I achieved a sufficiently complex sense of the novel?

This might seem the right point at which to conclude this analysis of *Heart of Darkness*; the traditional reading of the novel has, after all, been more or less turned inside out. It does, however, seem necessary to proceed one step further. It is a characteristic quality of novels that they examine the informing assumptions of a society. But the novelist is, at the same time, a member of that society: it is, therefore, inevitable that he or she will betray traits of thinking, even prejudices, that are characteristic of that society. How this might affect our sense of *Heart of Darkness* should become apparent if we complement the work on the text we have done so far with some feminist and New Historicist ideas.

A suitable scene to start with is one near the end of the novel, where Marlow visits Kurtz's fiancée:

'Forgive me. I – I – have mourned so long in silence – in silence . . . You were with him – to the last? I think of his loneliness. Nobody near to understand him as I would have understood. Perhaps no one to hear . . .'
'To the very end,' I said shakily. 'I heard his very last words . . .' I stopped in a fright.
'Repeat them,' she murmured in a heartbroken tone. 'I want – I want – something – something – to – to live with.'
I was on the point of crying at her, 'Don't you hear them?' The dusk was repeating them in a persistent whisper all around us, in a whisper that seemed to swell menacingly like the first whisper of a rising wind. 'The horror! The horror!'
'His last word – to live with,' she insisted. 'Don't you understand I loved him – I loved him – I loved him!'
I pulled myself together and spoke slowly.
'The last word he pronounced was – your name.'
I heard a last sigh and then my heart stood still, stopped dead short by an exulting and terrible cry, by the cry of inconceivable triumph and of unspeakable pain. 'I knew it – I was sure!' . . . She knew. She was sure. I heard her weeping; she had hidden her face in her hands. It seemed to me that the house would collapse before I could escape, that the heavens would fall upon my head. But nothing happened. The heavens do not fall for such a trifle. Would they have fallen, I wonder, if I had rendered Kurtz the justice which was his due? Hadn't he said he wanted only justice? But I couldn't. I could not tell her. It would have been too dark – too dark altogether . . .

[pp. 120–1]

Traditionally, this scene has always been read in the same way: Marlow, having seen terrible things in Africa, can now see the need for a lie when necessary, for a civilised pretence if it comforts someone, if it shields them from life's horrors. It seems a sensible, even a non-controversial, reading of the scene. But a different impression emerges if we adopt a feminist approach. We can start from the idea that western thought is binary in structure, that is to say, people think in pairs. It is the case, however, that one element in the pair is usually seen as superior; this should be apparent if we think of the conventional setting of reason over unreason, Europe over Africa, and male over female. As a novel, *Heart of Darkness* seem to have dismantled the first of these two pairs – the European claims to reason, to being more civilised than Africa or Africans – but we might have doubts about the way in which Conrad handles male and female. This scene with Kurtz's fiancée is troubling: there is an assumption on the part of Marlow, perhaps on the part of Conrad, that the woman should be lied to, as if men can face the horror but women cannot. If we search the novel for other fleeting appearances by women they are likely to confirm this impression that the sexual politics of *Heart of Darkness* are open to question. And, at that point, the critic might want to consider the whole structure and conception of the story, the idea of the man on a romantic quest in search of, perhaps, knowledge. The quest might be treated ironically, but there is the possibility that Conrad cannot rid himself of the basic assumption built into the story of the importance of the experiences of a man, and specifically a man, on his journey through life.

A New Historicist critic might also look at how the text handles issues of gender, but, in addition, and particularly with a text such as *Heart of Darkness*, would look at how the text handles issues of race. The initial impression might be that Conrad's treatment of the topic is admirable, in that he is so ready to debunk the civilised pretensions of the Europeans. But possibly, at a deeper level, something else is going on in the novel. If we think about how Africans are presented in the novel we are likely to see them as savages, even cannibals. There is no sense on Conrad's part that Africa might have a culture of its own, or that each individual African might belong to a complex society. As such, Africa remains the subsidiary term in the pairing of Europe and Africa. Indeed, it would appear that Conrad is totally indifferent to Africa, that he only uses the continent to sustain a narrative about European identity; this is an essentially racist assumption, that Europe and Europeans matter, but Africa and Africans don't. The curious position this gets us to is that a novel that seems to take apart not only colonialism but also the habits of mind that foster colonialism, is itself characterised by those very habits of mind.

This is not, however, it must be stressed as strongly as possible, an indication that the novel is flawed or inadequate in any way. In recent years, a number of critics have focused on Conrad's racism. More traditional critics have objected, for the presence of flaws in the author's vision would to some extent undermine the established idea that the author is someone with a significant moral message for his audience, the established idea that the author is someone who is wiser than his contemporaries. But that really misses the point. If we find evidence of racist views in Conrad (or if we find evidence of a patronising attitude towards women), that tells us a lot about the kind of complex relationship the novelist has to the values and attitudes of the period of the

text's production. The novelist is a member of a society, speaking in
the language of that society. In the case of Conrad, things become
more complicated because he is speaking in an adopted language; this
perhaps helps him maintain a certain kind of distinctively Conradian
ironic detachment. But this can only extend so far: in speaking the language of society he cannot stand totally outside the values and attitudes
it has absorbed. This is true of any writer; what is also true is that the
writer who might appear to be most radical, most at odds with the
values of his or her time, might reveal in the most interesting ways all
kinds of traces of the attitudes that he or she might appear to be
rejecting. If we identify these contradictions, we are not belittling the
author's achievement, but, in spotting these problems in what the
author is saying, getting at a complex, and possibly new, sense of the
political and social cross-currents that characterise the historical period
of the text's production. All in all, we are adding to our sense of the
complexity of the text, adding to our understanding of the past, and
adding to our sense of the way in which language shapes and deter-
mines our sense of the world.

II 'Tess of the D'Urbervilles'

In the case of *Heart of Darkness*, recent critical approaches seem essential
if one wishes to do justice to the complexity of the text; traditional approaches seem to sidestep the issue, to manufacture coherence where
none exists. With Thomas Hardy's *Tess of the D'Urbervilles*, however, traditional criticism has a lot to say about the novel that is genuinely illuminating. It is a novel that deals with Tess's conflicts with the society in
which she finds herself. Tess is a beautiful young woman who is both
desired and abused by the men she encounters: she is raped, gives birth
to a child (who dies), marries before telling her husband about her past,
and is then abandoned. Desolate and feeling an outcast, she establishes
a relationship with Alec, the man who raped her, but then, on the
return of her husband Angel, murders Alec. The novel ends with her
arrest at Stonehenge and her execution.

The novel is so emphatic in its sympathy for Tess that critics have
always been alert to, and ready to acknowledge, its tremendous power
and emotional force. Beyond this, critics have also written with great
insight about how the novel sets the order of society against another
kind of order, the order of nature. Society is dominated by men and

male thought, and imposes rigid rules; Tess is outside this order, instinctive rather than intellectual, at one with nature. All of this is conveyed with great delicacy: time and time again, for example, we see Tess at dawn or twilight, where she is on the border between the day-light world of reason and the intangible, elusive world of the night. Some, less than generous, critics describe Hardy's sympathy for Tess as excessive, but the majority, although they might have reservations about some aspects of the novel, are overwhelmed by the power and beauty, even if it is a tragic beauty, of what Hardy has created.

It would be silly to dispute the usefulness of such traditional criti-cism, but it does at times have some odd, even worrying features. One of the strangest things is how often male critics of *Tess of the D'Urbervilles* appear to desire Tess; they seem too ready to comment on her beauty, too fond of ogling her, too keen on the idea of possessing her. In a peculiar way, just as the men in the novel regard Tess as a desirable object, a lot of male critics echo this sense of Tess as desirable. This might seem a trivial, even insignificant, point to make, but in fact it suggests the possibility of a fundamental flaw in the way the novel used to be read. It should be apparent that Hardy, in his sympathy for Tess, is critical of the social order that punishes a young woman, making her feel she is the guilty party when the failings are all on the part of the men who mistreat her. But, in declaring their appreciation of Tess's beauty, traditional critics are, in effect, continuing to regard women in the kind of male-centred way that the novel can be seen to condemn.

The flaw in traditional criticism of *Tess of the D'Urbervilles* would, therefore, seem to be that critics respond to a work that is radical and disturbing in a manner that is conservative, that reinforces the estab-lished social order. Such conservatism also comes across in the way that a great many critical discussions focus almost entirely on Tess, present-ing her as absolutely central in the novel. It might, of course, seem simply common sense that one should focus on Tess, but this can be taken too far: an excessive focus on Tess can reduce the novel to the status of a character study, and, as such, ignore the larger political chal-lenge, indeed the whole political dimension, of the work. Discussions that focus on tragedy are rather similar in effect: critics who present *Tess of the D'Urbervilles* as a tragic drama inevitably overlook, or play down, the other, essentially political, questions that are raised by the text.

The point I have now arrived at is fundamentally the same idea that informed the previous discussion of *Heart of Darkness*: traditional criticism is informed by a desire for coherence, by a need to extract something positive from the text. In *Heart of Darkness*, critics stress the importance of self-discovery by Marlow and Kurtz. In *Tess of the D'Urbervilles*, critics stress the bravery and pity of Tess's life. In both instances, the stress falls upon the importance of the individual: a coherent sense of self becomes the focus of all the wider issues in the novel. But the focus on the self inevitably means that any protracted discussion of these wider issues can be sidestepped; even in such disturbing novels as *Heart of Darkness* and *Tess of the D'Urbervilles*, the critic can find a positive uplift, a message that can be read, in the experiences of the principal characters. I have, of course, overstated the case: there is more variety and subtlety in traditional criticism than I have suggested here. But the general tendency I have identified is true.

It is even the case in the majority of the more traditional political readings of *Tess of the D'Urbervilles*: critics such as Arnold Kettle and Douglas Brown adopt a Marxist approach to the novel, but, as is the case with many of the older British Marxist critics, their desire to read the text in political terms is rather undercut by some surprisingly conservative assumptions that continue to inform their thinking. In particular, such critics continue to offer a liberal humanist emphasis on Tess herself. In the past twenty years or so, however, things have changed: the arrival of structuralism and subsequent developments in critical theory have prompted a general reconsideration of, and fresh developments in, political approaches to fiction. These changes have made themselves felt throughout the whole field of literary studies, but have had a particular impact on Hardy studies – possibly because, with Hardy, there was such an obvious need to find new ways of talking about the relationship between questions of language, politics and gender in his novels. The following reading of *Tess of the D'Urbervilles* cannot pretend to do justice to the variety and creativity of these new approaches, but it might provide you with some pointers about the ways in which criticism today – whether the focus be Hardy or any other novelist – can engage with questions of politics, both the politics of the critic and the politics of the text.

Step 1: After reading the work as a whole, take a close look at the opening page of the novel, or, if this proves unilluminating, at a passage fairly near the beginning featuring one or more of the principal characters

I have decided to start with a passage from chapter two, where Tess makes her first appearance in the novel:

> Tess Durbeyfield at this time of her life was a mere vessel of emotion untinctured by experience. The dialect was on her tongue to some extent, despite the village school: the characteristic intonation of that dialect for this district being the voicing approximately rendered by the syllable UR, probably as rich an utterance as any to be found in human speech. The pouted-up deep red mouth to which this syllable was native had hardly as yet settled into its definite shape, and her lower lip had a way of thrusting the middle of her top one upward, when they closed together after a word.
>   Phases of her childhood lurked in her aspect still. As she walked along to-day, for all her bouncing handsome womanliness, you could sometimes see her twelfth year in her cheeks, or her ninth sparkling from her eyes; and even her fifth would flit over the curves of her mouth now and then.
>   [*Tess of the D'Urbervilles* (Penguin, 1978), pp. 51–2]

The passage is about Tess; the fact that Hardy also makes reference to the village school does, however, enable us to say far more, for this immediately confronts us with an opposition. On the one hand is Tess, who is associated with the countryside and a traditional way of speaking, and on the other hand is the school, which imposes itself upon people, forcing them to talk in a different way. The novel, we can anticipate, is going to deal with the clash between Tess and the dominant, and dominating, order of society. What is going to be crushed by society is something intangible: if we look at the description of Tess in this extract, what we see is something fluid, that Tess is various ages at once, that she is not hard and defined. The same idea is conveyed in the detail about her mouth not yet having settled into 'its definite shape'. This is a type of description widely employed in Hardy's novels: he often sets natural shapes, natural lines – such as the contours of the countryside – against the architectural regularity of towns. His sympathies, it is clear, are entirely with what is fluid and natural.

But there is more to the passage than this, for Hardy is already managing to say a great deal about the ideological order of this society. People are brought up within an ideological framework: this is not a set of values that one chooses to accept or reject, but something that has material existence in such institutions as the church, the family and the education system. The dominant ideology in society asserts its values as reasonable, as essentially a matter of morality and common sense. In this passage, Tess is going to be taught how to speak correctly in order that she might succeed in society; this does not mean rising up the social scale, simply that Tess will take her place in society having been educated in, and with, the language, and consequently values, of those who will employ her. And that, of course, forces us to look at the village school in a certain light: it becomes part of the state's system of control, with a commitment, which it reinforces every day in the language it uses, to control waywardness and subversion. Social order is maintained because it is in the interests of those with power to keep things as they are. Tess's education, therefore, becomes a form of indoctrination in which she is forced to speak in the language of polite society, the language of her masters.

The idea of 'her masters' might encourage us at this point to look at the whole idea of the 'double standard' in sexual morality that features so prominently as a theme in the novel; the fact that the man was allowed 'a past', but that the woman in middle-class society was supposed to be pure at marriage. What we can say on this issue is that gender relations in society subserve a specific economic need. Marriage constituted along controlled lines is the cornerstone of a well-disciplined capitalist society. But society can cope with male promiscuity, whereas it sees female sexuality as a threat, as something to be feared and challenged. In teaching Tess to speak correctly at school, therefore, we can see the way in which the middle-class ruling order of the day promulgates its values as the standard, common-sense values; these are values that intertwine with every aspect of marriage and sexual morality in this society. In this cluster of ideas it is impossible to separate issues of language, politics (particularly class), and gender, as all function in relation to, and in support of, each other. What we can say about the novel so far, then, already takes us some way beyond traditional criticism, for we can see how, in looking at Tess, Hardy is not just presenting us with the human drama of this one girl's life but looking at the much broader issue of the whole ideological structure of society. He adopts an adversarial position, venting his anger at the harsh hand of society, but this does not mean that he offers a narrow, and therefore over-simplified, view; on the contrary, there is already a sense of a novelist who offers us a complex impression of how language, politics, institutions of the state, class, the individual and gender all interconnect as issues in society. Each constitutes a site of struggle, where those with power engage in conflict with those who would question, subvert or resist the dominant order of society. There is no clearer illustration of this than the idea, as presented in this passage, of standard English in competition with the local dialect, a dialect that Hardy celebrates as being 'as rich an utterance as any to be found in human speech'.

Step 2: Select and analyse a second passage

For my second passage, I have decided to look at the scene where Tess is raped by Alec D'Urberville:

> Darkness and silence ruled everywhere around. Above them rose the pri-
> maeval yews and oaks of The Chase, in which were poised gentle ruling
> birds in their last nap; and about them stole the hopping rabbits and
> hares. But, might some say, where was Tess's guardian angel? where was
> the providence of her simple faith? Perhaps, like that other god of whom
> the ironical Tishbite spoke, he was talking, or he was pursuing, or he was
> in a journey, or he was sleeping and not to be awaked.
>   Why was it that upon this beautiful feminine tissue, sensitive as
> gossamer, and practically blank as snow as yet, there should have been
> traced such a coarse pattern as it was doomed to receive; why so often
> the coarse appropriates the finer thus, the wrong man the woman, the
> wrong woman the man, many thousand years of analytical philosophy
> have failed to explain to our sense of order. One may, indeed, admit the
> possibility of a retribution lurking in the present catastrophe. Doubtless
> some of Tess D'Urberville's mailed ancestors rollicking home from a fray
> had dealt the same measure even more ruthlessly towards peasant girls of
> their time. But though to visit the sins of the fathers upon the children
> may be a morality good enough for divinities, it is scorned by average
> human nature; and it therefore does not mend the matter.
>   As Tess's own people down in those retreats are never tired of saying
> among each other in their fatalistic way: 'It was to be.' There lay the pity
> of it.
>
> [p. 119]

The passage is about Tess being raped by Alec. What is gentle and delicate is destroyed by what is aggressive and vicious. The references to the 'gentle roosting birds' and the rabbits and hares underline this idea of life being full of innocent victims. And Tess, as always, is associated with delicacy and purity, particularly in the phrases 'beautiful feminine tissue, sensitive as gossamer, and practically blank as snow . . .'. The sentence then, however, turns to the word 'coarse', which it repeats: the impression is of the hard, the coarse attacking the weak.

Amazingly, there was a time when critics used to talk about the extent to which Tess is to blame for what takes place. In fact, you might still come across people arguing this today, so let us get things straight: Tess is raped by Alec. She is entirely the innocent party, entirely the victim. But how could anyone ever have blamed Tess? This takes us back to the point that the discussion of this novel started with, that traditional criticism tended to see things from a male perspective. In raising questions about Tess's culpability, the disturbing implications of the rape scene could be ignored; it could be reduced to a human interest question about how much this particular individual might have been to blame. As such, the traditional critic was arguing that a personal issue was involved here rather than a question of political power; but, although such a response might claim to be merely a straightforward, common-sense view of the text, it is really informed by conservative political assumptions about gender relations. In finding fault with the woman, the critic is implicitly announcing a whole way of thinking about the world.

Swinging to the other extreme, critics today are far more likely to stress the ways in which Hardy sympathises with the victims of society rather than with the voice and views of society. This is something that is apparent in every aspect of *Tess of the D'Urbervilles*, but particularly in Hardy's use of language. In this extract, for example, we might wish to focus on the quite extraordinary manner of Hardy's narration: it might appear that he talks about everything except the rape itself, and, when he does talk about it, writes in a curiously inflated, almost inappropriate, manner. Look, for example, at the references to the 'ironical Tishbite' and 'many thousand years of analytical philosophy'. What is going on? The point would seem to be that in rejecting the conventional values of society, Hardy must distance himself from the voice of society. Consequently, his narrative manner is often rather self-conscious in the kind of way that is evident here. Looking more closely, we can see that he casts around for an explanation of what has taken place, talking of guardian angels, of philosophy, of how such things have happened throughout history, and, finally, what Tess's own people have always said about such events. The effect is one of moving between interpretive perspectives, as if he is at a loss for one single, confident way of explaining what has happened. And this is how it has to be, for if Hardy rejects the ideological perspective of society, he must reject the language of society, for that language, in a covert way, embodies a whole range of ideological assumptions. There is, however, no single alternative voice or perspective Hardy can adopt; he has to commit himself over and over again to this provisional, speculative, self-questioning manner of assessment.

The scale of Hardy's enterprise in *Tess of the D'Urbervilles* should by now be very clear: the novel is, of course, a tragic human drama, in which we are sympathetically involved with Tess, but Hardy is at the same time reaching out to examine the whole structure of the society of his day, including the way that society constitutes itself through language. Hardy's prevaricating, inconsistent narrative voice, that consistently challenges any claims it might make towards omniscient knowledge, is a vital element in this political examination of the structure of power in the society of his day. His project is strengthened by the choice of a central character who is both female and working-class: power is examined from the perspective of one who lacks power, and in a narrative voice that rejects the traditional all-knowing power of an author.

Step 3: Select and analyse a third passage

But . . . , the traditional critic might object, doesn't all this blind us to the beauty and strength of Hardy? Modern criticism seems to regard him as a political and linguistic philosopher rather than as an imaginative novelist. There is, however, absolutely no reason why an awareness of the larger issues in a Hardy text cannot combine with a sense of the imaginative impact of his art. Just about any passage that one chose to look at would illustrate the point; I have selected a passage where Tess and Angel Clare are together, on a farm, at dawn:

> The spectral, half-compounded, aqueous light which pervaded the open mead, impressed them with a feeling of isolation, as if they were Adam and Eve. At this dim inceptive stage of the day Tess seemed to Clare to exhibit a dignified largeness both of disposition and physique, an almost regnant power, possibly because he knew that at that preternatural time hardly any woman so well endowed in person as she was likely to be walking in the open air within the boundaries of his horizon; very few in all England. Fair women are usually asleep at midsummer dawns. She was close at hand, and the rest were nowhere.
>
> The mixed, singular, luminous gloom in which they walked along together to the spot where the cows lay, often made him think of the Resurrection hour. He little thought that the Magdalen might be at his side. Whilst all the landscape was in neutral shade his companion's face, which was the focus of his eyes, rising above the mist stratum, seemed to have a sort of phosphorescence upon it. She looked ghostly, as if she were merely a soul at large. In reality her face, without appearing to do so, had caught the cold gleam of day from the north-east; his own face, though he did not think of it, wore the same aspect to her.
>
> It was then, as has been said, that she impressed him most deeply. She was no longer the milkmaid, but a visionary essence of woman – a whole sex condensed into one typical form. He called her Artemis,

Demeter, and other fanciful names half teasingly, which she did not like
because she did not understand them.

'Call me Tess,' she would say askance; and he did.

[pp. 186–7]

I am struck by two qualities in Hardy's description of the day and of
Tess. First, there is the extreme delicacy with which he conveys the
early morning mistiness, in phrases such as 'aqueous light'. But, second,
there is also a way in which Hardy can see through the romantic glow,
and put everything in a realistic context. It is apparent in the amused
tone that informs the whole passage: he debunks Angel's dreamy idealisation of Tess, pointing out that Angel's feelings might also have a lot
to do with the fact that Tess is physically attractive and 'close at hand'.
There is also a wonderfully absurd touch in the way that Angel associates their walk to the spot 'where the cows lay' with 'the Resurrection
hour'. And Hardy is equally realistic about Tess: he can suggest a kind
of ethereal otherworldliness that there is about her appearance, but he
then intervenes to point out that this 'ghostly' appearance is just a trick
of the light at this time of day.

Angel, however, only sees the vision of Tess, and it is this that
attracts him, rather than the reality. This develops a more disturbing
dimension when we consider how he desires to possess her, how he
denies the woman an independent existence. The way in which he
does this is through language, through imposing his vision upon her.
Something similar happens when Tess tells Angel about her past: he
immediately converts it into his drama, as if it is a story in which he is
the principal victim. In this early morning passage, we might focus on
the fact that Angel first views Tess as a kind of queen, then his
thoughts turn to religion, and then, finally, he calls her Artemis and
Demeter. What we can say is that he tries to possess her through his
culture, his view of the world, his view of the social order. Hardy's
technique is delicate, however; he does not press the point, he does
not spell out what Angel is doing, but he provides a series of subtle
indications of the ways in which Angel is taking possession of Tess's
subjectivity. No wonder Tess protests: 'Call me Tess.' She is protesting
at the way in which Angel establishes a patriarchal hegemony, the way
in which men ignore the reality of women, the way in which men
deny the reality of female sexuality, converting women into fantasy
objects. Tess, of course, doesn't say this, and nor does Hardy, but my
point is that we can combine a sense of the delicacy of Hardy's

writing in the novel with an awareness of the larger political analysis that is suggested in his writing. Indeed, what makes this particular extract so effective – and the same could be said about many other passages in the novel – is the artistic delicacy with which it establishes a case about how men possess women, and how such power is inscribed in language.

Step 4: Select and analyse a fourth passage

Some of the most striking scenes in *Tess of the D'Urbervilles* are set either at dawn or dusk. Here is another:

> Or perhaps the summer fog was more general, and the meadows lay like a white sea, out of which the scattered trees rose like dangerous rocks. Birds would soar through it into the upper radiance, and hang on the wind sunning themselves, or alight on the wet rails subdividing the mead, which now shone like glass rods. Minute diamonds of moisture from the mist hung, too, upon Tess's eyelashes, and drops upon her hair, like seed pearls. When the day grew quite strong and commonplace these dried off; moreover, Tess then lost her strange and ethereal beauty; her teeth, lips, and eyes scintillated in the sunbeams, and she was again the dazzlingly fair dairymaid only, who had to hold her own against the other women of the world.
>
> [p. 188]

We see, again, Hardy's remarkable ability to convey a dreamy, almost magical, impression of his heroine, which is then set against a more realistic impression. The first is always a creation of a trick of the light and early morning mistiness (or an equally deceiving radiance at twilight), and this is always set against the cold light of day. Hardy's point seems to be the reality of Tess, and the Tess that others insist on seeing.

But there is, I think, another element in this passage: I am struck by the way in which Hardy lingers over his description of Tess, focusing in particular on her mouth. Now, in at least two ways this is very effective: he has to establish the physical presence of Tess if he wants to show how she appears differently in the cold light of day. And, in addition, the concentration on the delicacy of her physical features enables him to convey a sense of a physically vulnerable victim in a cruel world: by focusing on small details, like her lips, Hardy can suggest the unevenness of the contest, the smallness of Tess and the enormity of what she is pitted against. But lingering over Tess's physical features also suggests a particular sense of woman, a particular sense of the feminine. The fact is that, although Hardy is so ready to criticise the men in the novel, in some ways he shares their traditional view of the woman as soft and feminine. In this passage, he might appear to distance himself from the view of Tess as somehow intangible and otherworldly, but it is when he is being more realistic that he lingers over her mouth and calls her 'dazzlingly fair': it is a man's view of a woman, a view that in telling respects sees Tess as an object. The point this leads to is that, although Hardy is likely to strike us as opponent of the dominant ideology of his day, in one important respect we can see that he is complicit with the ideology of his day. Indeed, it could even be said that, like the men in the novel, Hardy desires Tess: the way in which he lingers over her mouth suggests a desire to penetrate her, to exert his power over her.

Step 5: Have I achieved a sufficiently complex sense of the novel?

We have suddenly encountered a major complication in our response to *Tess of the D'Urbervilles*. Hardy seems to challenge those – in this novel, middle-class men – who have power in society, but it is clear that, in one respect at least, he has something in common with those that he criticises. But perhaps this isn't such a problem after all. Every text is embedded in the ideological values of the period that produced it. The author might adopt a questioning role, but any novel is likely to reveal evidence of ways in which the author has so thoroughly absorbed the ideological values of his or her period that some deep-rooted assumptions will be present even when the author is adopting an overtly radical stance. What this means is that in any text we are likely to encounter apparent contradictions, even confusion. But this does not detract from a work. On the contrary, it is what makes a text interesting, for contradictions reveal the ways in which a novel is a complex product of, and reflection of, the society from which it emerges. From such contradictions we gain a sense of how a text is involved in a period's attempts at self-understanding, how a text tries to deal with changing attitudes and behaviour, and, very often, how a text struggles to comprehend and define the roles of men and women in the society of its day. Hardy's slightly suspect attitude towards Tess is a very good example of this. When feminist criticism was first becoming established, feminist critics often condemned Hardy for his proprietorial attitude towards women, but more recent feminist criticism does not rush to censure the author for his prejudices. On the contrary, it finds *Tess of the D'Urbervilles* all the more interesting because Hardy's stance is confused: his confusion tells us a great deal about the sexual and gender politics of the period, indeed the whole range of divisions and dilemmas within the period that stimulated Hardy to write, and provide the substance of, the novel.

A final passage that does not relate to gender might help extend our sense of these matters. This is a description of a piece of agricultural machinery that has been introduced into the area:

> By the engine stood a dark motionless being, a sooty and grimy embodiment of tallness, in a sort of trance, with a heap of coals by his side: it was the engine-man. The isolation of his manner and colour lent him the appearance of a creature from Tophet, who had strayed into the pellucid smokelessness of this region of yellow grain and pale soil, with which he had nothing in common, to amaze and discompose its aborigines.
>
> What he looked he felt. He was in the agricultural world, but not of it. He served fire and smoke; these denizens of the fields served vegetation, weather, frost, and sun. He travelled with his engine from farm to farm, from county to county, for as yet the steam threshing-machine was itinerant in this part of Wessex. He spoke in a strange northern accent; his thoughts being turned inwards upon himself, his eye on his iron charge, hardly perceiving the scenes around him, and caring for them not at all: holding only strictly necessary intercourse with the natives, as if some ancient doom compelled him to wander here against his will in the service of his Plutonic master.
>
> [pp. 404–5]

This is a passage that many critics have looked at over the years. It has always particularly appealed to those who want to talk about the social theme of the novel. The argument put forward most frequently is that *Tess of the D'Urbervilles* deals with a shift in the social order: the old, agricultural order that seemed in sympathy with the shape and rhythms of the land and seasons is being displaced by a new, more mechanical scheme of things. This passage, focusing as it does on the introduction of a rather brutal piece of agricultural machinery, illustrates the point; it seems as if no more need be said, for the evidence surely clinches the argument.

But the limitation of such an approach is that it tends to reduce the novel to a simple pattern of something good being replaced by something bad. My feeling is that the passage offers us a more complex sense of tensions and changes within the society of the day. The basis for suggesting this is the oddness of the passage, in particular the oddness of the writing. It is clear that the machine has nothing in common with the land, but what is surprising is the very unusual manner in which Hardy describes the man in charge of it. He is an alien, bewildering, almost inhuman character in this rural context. The point this leads to is that, rather than the text offering us a controlled impression of the experience of social change, it emerges from the centre of the struggle itself, offering us a complex sense of bewilderment, of things falling apart. Hardy, writing around 1890, manages to convey a sense of a world where insecurity is increasingly prevalent, where fixed reference points are disappearing, and where not only values but also the very conditions of everyday living are in a state of flux. Rather than the novel offering us a confident analysis of a process of change, it seems to emerge from the very centre of all the complicated cross-currents of the period.

How does this way of looking at Hardy differ from a traditional approach? I think the two words that one needs to think about are 'coherence' and 'control'. Traditional criticism tended to emphasise the coherence of the author's vision, his or her ability to pull back from and analyse the significance of the story presented. But recent criticism is far less interested in the transcendent nature of the author's vision; it is, instead, interested in seeing how the work embodies and expresses, but doesn't resolve, the various cross-currents present in the society that produced it. This moves one towards a political reading of fiction; not, however, the kind of political reading that says 'This is the author's political stance', but a political reading that tries to grasp something of the knotty web of ideological, linguistic, gender and social issues in a text.

III 'Emma'

Recent approaches to fiction all stress the open and questioning nature of a literary text; rather than a novel being seen as making a coherent statement, a novel is seen as being full of a mass of unresolvable tensions. Such a sense of fiction might, however, seem to have no relevance to the works of Jane Austen. Jane Austen, as is apparent to any reader of her novels, wishes to reassert traditional values. In the discussion of *Mansfield Park* earlier in this volume, for example, the emphasis falls upon Austen's endorsement of traditional values, albeit with a slight leavening of bourgeois individualism. In all Austen's works, the impression that comes across is of a writer with a view to propound, who presents her case professionally and with absolute control.

Emma, a story focusing on the education and development of the heroine, offers plenty of evidence of this clarity of purpose that seems to characterise Austen's fiction. Emma lives with her father, a hypo-chondriacal old man. Her governess leaves the household to marry a neighbour, Mr Weston, and Emma makes a protégée of Harriet Smith, an illegitimate girl of no social standing. George Knightley of Donwell Abbey, a friend of the family, disapproves of Emma's attempts to manipulate Harriet. One of Knightley's tenants, a farmer called Robert Martin, proposes to Harriet but Emma encourages her to turn him down. She tries instead to arrange a match between Harriet and Mr Elton, a young clergyman. Elton, though, has no interest in Harriet; instead, he has set his sights on Emma. Emma herself half believes she is in love with Mr Weston's son by his first marriage, Frank Churchill, who has lately arrived in the village. Harriet, meanwhile, has become interested in Knightley as a prospective partner. But Emma now re-alises that, without actively considering it, she has always assumed that Knightley will marry her. This, together with the revelation that Frank Churchill is engaged to Jane Fairfax, forces her to examine her conduct and resolve to behave better. Knightley proposes to Emma, and Harriet, now at liberty to think for herself, marries Robert Martin.

Emma, as we can see from this summary, matures: she changes from being vain, self-satisfied and insensitive to the feelings of others. A traditional critical response might well focus on the moral develop-ment of Emma, with a good deal of emphasis on Austen's wit and irony, in particular the understated but devastating way in which she can demolish the pretensions of those who think too well of them-selves. Austen would be seen as a morally didactic, but also very entertaining, novelist. A traditional response might also draw attention to the way in which, throughout the book, the reader stands in a posi-tion in relation to the characters that is both sympathetic and judge-mental, and this could be extended into a discussion of why we share the views of some characters – such as Knightley – while knowing that others – such as Mrs Elton – are vulgar and pretentious. All of this would go hand in hand with tracking the stages by which Emma becomes more self-aware, until the point at which, like all Austen's heroines, she can be rewarded with marriage to the man she loves, who, in this case, has represented moral authority and right judgement throughout the novel.

Given all this, Austen becomes a particularly interesting test case for recent critical approaches, for her intentions as a novelist seem entirely clear. She might, as we will see, be responding to a social crisis, a change in the economic and class structure of Britain that put enormous strain on the kind of families she presents in her novels, but her response seems to be one of retrenchment: a reassertion of traditional values. In *Emma*, everyone has their place in the social hierarchy, nobody moves up or down in society, and Emma and Knightley, who are snobs at the beginning of the novel, are snobs in exactly the same way at the end. One response, of course, might be simply to accept that this is all that can or need be said about Austen, that she is a conservative novelist with something to say who says it extremely well. It could be argued that she writes at a time when the world was still relatively stable, so does not need to raise doubts in the kind of way that Hardy, as a Victorian novelist, or Conrad, as a twentieth-century novelist, do. But, as many have pointed out, Austen wasn't writing in a timeless, stable world; her era was that of the French Revolution and rapid social change in Britain.

We might seem to have reached a critical dead end, but it is, in fact, through pursuing these historical and contextual considerations that modern criticism has found a way of approaching Austen. The thrust of traditional criticism is that Emma matures, and matures in a way that provides a kind of universal lesson in good behaviour, in reasonable conduct. I think it is fair to say that many people studying Austen today, particularly at school, are still offered this view, that she presents a timeless set of moral values. But Austen starts to become a lot more complicated, and interesting, if we pay attention to the contemporary political and social situation in which she wrote. If we adopt an approach that incorporates New Historicist thinking about literature, we begin to see how *Emma* relates in an intricate way to the cultural, political and social situation in which it is embedded. Rather than Austen appearing as a confident didactic novelist, in the kind of reversal of view that characterises much recent criticism, she appears nervous and defensive, even aware of frailties and flaws in her stance.

Writing around the end of the eighteenth century and the beginning of the nineteenth, Austen is attempting to contain the radically perturbing forces of individualism that had been unleashed by the expanding capitalism of the period. In her view, individuals must recognise the need for objective understanding of themselves and others if the fabric of society is to be preserved. It was an urgent task, for society as she knew it did seem to be under threat: there were rapid changes on the land (men such as Robert Martin, for example, could, in real life, prosper enormously at the expense of their landlords), rapid development of industry and urbanisation, and the political threat of the French Revolution and the Napoleonic Wars. When we consider all this, we can see that Austen is deeply engaged politically, albeit in a conservative role. The heroines, for example, are often potentially iconoclastic individuals, that is to say, young women who threaten established social values and arrangements; Austen's narrative, guided by her ironic commentary, overtly recuperates the heroine for the conservative social order. When we look beyond the heroine, we are likely to become aware of a whole range of similar, delicate, political negotiations being conducted within the text.

We are not, it must be stressed, going to lose our sense of Austen as a Tory novelist, but we are likely to become aware of stresses and strains, of material within *Emma* that can barely be controlled by the authoritative voice of the narrator. We might even feel that there are points where Austen almost reverses her own values. To sum up, therefore: whereas traditional criticism of *Emma* stresses order, harmony and closure, recent criticism stresses the flashpoints at which the closed system almost falls apart.

Step 1: After reading the work as a whole, take a close look at the opening page of the novel, or, if this proves unilluminating, at a passage fairly near the beginning featuring one or more of the principal characters

I've emphasised the importance of the stresses and strains in *Emma*. As I have already said a good deal about the traditional view of the novel, I'm going to skip over the initial stages of an analysis (i.e. establishing a sense of Emma and the society in which she lives), and proceed directly to the stresses and strains. I will start with an extract about Frank Churchill, for Frank, whose behaviour tends to be unsteady and frivolous, looks as if he could represent a threat to the whole secure world that Emma and Knightley occupy. In this passage, Frank initiates a word game, some form of anagrams, using a child's box of letters:

> Frank Churchill placed a word before Miss Fairfax. She gave a slight glance round the table, and applied herself to it. Frank was next to Emma, Jane opposite to them – and Mr Knightley so placed as to see them all; and it was his object to see as much as he could, with as little apparent observation. The word was discovered, and with a faint smile

pushed away. If meant to be immediately mixed with the others, and buried from sight, she should have looked on the table instead of looking just across, for it was not mixed; and Harriet, eager after every fresh word, and finding out none, directly took it up, and fell to work. She was sitting by Mr Knightley, and turned to him for help. The word was *blunder*, and as Harriet exultingly proclaimed it, there was a blush on Jane's cheek which gave it a meaning not otherwise ostensible. Mr Knightley connected it with the dream; but how it could all be, was beyond his comprehension. How the delicacy, the discretion of his favourite could have been so lain asleep! He feared there must be some decided involvement. Disingenuousness and double-dealing seemed to him at every turn. These letters were but the vehicle for gallantry and trick. It was a child's play, chosen to conceal a deeper game on Frank Churchill's part.

[*Emma* (Penguin, 1966), p. 344]

We can see that some sort of relationship is going on between Frank and Jane. Knightley does not know this, but disapproves of the manner in which Frank is behaving. Knightley, as such, represents trustworthiness whereas there is something underhand about Frank. It comes across primarily in his word game: he seems to operate with a secret language as opposed to the public language, and this suggests a much broader idea of a furtive way of conducting one's life as opposed to an open and honest way. The issue is deeply rooted in language, for society constitutes itself through a public syntax of manners and morals. As against such a public scheme of things, Frank is a games player, a frivolous man. He is playing with a puzzle, and is a puzzle himself to Knightley and the other characters in the book. People, it is clear, should be open and knowable, and in not being so Frank isn't just a frivolous man but a substantial threat to good order at Hartfield; it is as if a private, secret world threatens the established, public order.

There is, of course, the slight complication that Frank is fun, whereas Knightley isn't, and the complication that Emma finds herself drawn to such a man. But the most important point to grasp is that Frank isn't just individually wayward, that the details about his conduct dramatise a comprehensive sense of the ways in which the established, public moral code of the times is under threat. Every detail about Frank's behaviour is pertinent in this respect, for every detail conveys a precise point about a way in which he represents a threat to the country's ideological order. If we put the details together, what we see is the way in which he embodies the personal and the private, how he represents self-interest as against the general interest.

Step 2: Select and analyse a second passage

We have, so far, identified the enemy, identified the nature of the threat. What we need to do now, however, is look at Austen's response to this new force, this new attitude in society. I have already mentioned that at one stage in her life Emma half-imagines she is in love with Frank. In this passage we see Emma talking about Frank after she has discovered that he and Jane are to be married:

> 'Well,' said Emma, 'I suppose we shall gradually grow reconciled to the idea, and I wish them very happy. But I shall always think it a very abominable sort of proceeding. What has it been but a system of hypoc-risy and deceit, – espionage, and treachery? – To come among us with professions of openness and simplicity; and such a league in secret to judge us all! – Here have we been, the whole winter and spring, com-pletely duped, fancying ourselves all on an equal footing of truth and honour, with two people in the midst of us who may have been carrying round, comparing and sitting in judgment on sentiments and words that were never meant for both to hear. – They must take the consequence, if they have heard each other spoken of in a way not perfectly agreeable!'
>
> [p. 390]

There are two ways in which one might read this passage. The first interpretation would endorse the idea of Austen's moral control of her material and the novel; the second reading would be far less confident about the degree of her control. To illustrate the more straightforward reading first, we might pick up Emma's insistence upon correct behav-iour, on absolute moral standards: look at phrases such as 'a very abominable sort of proceeding' and 'hypocrisy and deceit, – espionage and treachery'. Such behaviour is set against 'openness and simplicity' and 'truth and honour'. In the old order, the interests of the self were always the same as the interests of society, but things are now sliding towards a position where the interests of self and of society are opposed. Emma, along with Austen, is fully aware of the nature of the threat.

What complicates this simple moral reading, however, is if we acknowledge Emma's agitation, her anger. It isn't a balanced or fair condemnation of Frank. On the contrary, it is excessive, verging on spitefulness. Emma obviously resents the fact that she has been duped, that her judgement has proved fallible, but one might add that she is trying to deny her emotional feeling for Frank here, that she has been stirred by emotional feelings that the world she inhabits is not prepared to countenance or admit. In going on the attack, as she does here, she is censoring out her feelings, trying to deny that those feelings existed. The agitated manner of her speech suggests that something wayward has entered her life, but she is now fighting to get things back under control, to banish instability. The novel needs to move towards its end, but closure can only be finally achieved if Emma denies what has in fact taken place.

All of this lacks real significance, however, unless we place the agitated feelings of Emma in a broader context. What it seems fair to say is that, although the novel opts for retrenchment, for a reassertion of traditional values, at the same time as it is denying a new individuality there are, oddly enough, stirrings of that kind of individual, private feeling on the part of the heroine. The threat is externalised in the person of Frank Churchill, but a radical shift in attitudes – towards the private self, towards interiority – is taking place generally in society at this time, and, in the very act of attacking such a threat, Austen cannot avoid showing how the seeds of this new attitude are present within the mind of the heroine of the novel. One could even argue that the novel acquires its main thrust of energy from acknowledging what it overtly wishes to deny.

Step 3: Select and analyse a third passage

The logical move at this stage would be to look at further evidence from the text of ways in which the old order is challenged. One might choose to look again at Frank, more specifically at an extract dealing with his relationship with Jane Fairfax. Jane is a fascinating figure, for, whereas Emma is outspoken and on public display, Jane is enigmatic, involved in a secret love affair, and uninterested in the public rituals of friendship and the social round. In particular, she is lukewarm about being a friend to Emma. What we might conclude is that, again, a large idea is finding expression, an idea not only of a retreat from the public into the private but also a new sense of a division between the self and society. Austen might defend the old order, but she seems to understand a fundamental current of change in the social order.

Jane and Frank both represent external threats to life at Hartfield; so, too, do a group of gypsies who appear in the novel, inducing a state of near panic in the district. But the threats to good order are not only eternal: the obvious thing to do would be to focus on a number of incidents in which Emma displays an odd instability in her character, but, rather more teasingly, there is also the question of the tone of the narrator, in particular the kind of control that the narrator exercises; the text strives to appear logical and coherent, but there are many ways in which it is not. Part of this is the strong playful, non-serious element in Austen: as much as she might applaud openness, much of the plot actually centres on the riddle of Jane and Frank's relationship. Consequently, although the novel might overtly be aiming to assist in the moral regeneration of Austen's social peers, there is a level at which she is drawn towards what she most seems to oppose. *Emma* might, therefore, seem to be a morally didactic text with a timeless message about good conduct, but when we set it in its period we see that Austen is simultaneously appalled by and drawn to the changing values of the time of its production.

Step 4: Select and analyse a fourth passage

I have, so far, concentrated on threats to the old order. It is apparent that there is a good deal of ambivalence and ambiguity in Austen's stance. This becomes even clearer if we look a little more closely at the old order, specifically at one of the central figures in the old order, Emma's father. He is, although the characters of the novel would, of course, be too polite to say so, an old fool, nervously obsessed with his health. Quite simply, the old order doesn't seem in a very healthy shape. The kind of order Austen defends would be male-centred, with the father passing the baton on to his son in a confident way, but the society she depicts lacks such energy and purposefulness. Indeed, the general impression of family life we receive from the novel is alarming. Where are the healthy family groups, the families that must be the backbone of the kind of society that Austen desires? The novel is full of broken and divided families, and spinsters; in fact, it all seems pretty close to a shambles. And when we look at a family, for example we might decide to look at Emma at home, the atmosphere seems suffocating. Much of the book, we could even say, seems motivated by a flight from family.

What is emerging is a much more troubled novel than might initially appear to be the case. But we wouldn't really have a way of making sense of this unless we worked from an awareness of the kind of social crisis and process of social change that was taking place between 1780 and 1820. The history of the period provides us with a context that helps us understand Austen's restatement of a conservative position, but the history of the period also helps us see why Austen's vision might be more precarious, more self-doubting, than might initially appear to be the case. But history does not just serve as a background to the text, for our understanding of the tensions within the novel adds to our understanding of the stresses and changes that were taking place in the period between 1780 and 1820; in other words, historical events provide an access to the experience of the text, but the experience of the text then enables us to arrive at a fuller understanding of the historical process of the period of the text's production.

Step 5: Have I achieved a sufficiently complex sense of the novel?

We might appear to be arriving at a valid new view of *Emma*, a view that is in line with and the product of recent critical thinking. I am, however, far from sure about how to regard the novel as a whole; one reason for saying this is that, the more we look at *Emma* the more likely it is to strike us as a very peculiar, very divided novel. Consider, for example, the character of Knightley, who appears to receive Austen's total endorsement and approval. Austen can be scathing about men's limitations, but Knightley, although he might strike the reader as a snob and a bore, does not seem to have failings; he is a stable or fixed point.

The problem is, however, that while the text seems to move steadily and reassuringly towards closure with Knightley – for at the end all the uncertainties of the novel resolve themselves as Knightley declares himself to Emma, takes his place at the centre of the pattern of the text, and, consequently, enables all the other pieces in the coherent jigsaw of relationships to slot into place – another contradictory discourse seems to be going on at the same time. This should be apparent in the following passage, where Knightley and Emma declare their love for each other:

> Her way was clear, though not quite smooth. – She spoke then, on being so entreated. – What did she say? – Just what she ought, of course. A lady always does. – She said enough to show there need not be despair – and to invite him to say more himself. He *had* despaired at one period; he had received such an injunction to caution and silence, as for the time crushed every hope; – she had begun by refusing to hear him. – The change had perhaps been somewhat sudden; – her proposal of taking another turn, her renewing the conversation which she had just put an

end to, might be a little extraordinary! – She felt its inconsistency; but Mr
Knightley was so obliging as to put up with it, and seek no farther explanation.

[p. 418]

In focusing on the declaration of their mutual love, this scene takes its
place as one of the constructive threads in the novel; the text, as such,
is moving towards the establishing of a full and satisfying sense of a
traditional order. Things are turning out as they should turn out. But
the actual texture of the speeches from Emma and Knightley hardly
bears out this simple view of the intention of the passage.

It is apparent that there is an agitated quality to Emma's thoughts,
but perhaps the most striking feature here is Austen's use of a nervous,
chopped, interior monologue. We are offered the thoughts flowing
through the characters' minds. It is a stylistic effect at a far remove
from the ironic wit and detachment with which Austen usually narrates. What I find interesting about this is that, in a novel where there
is a great deal of emphasis on openness and a public syntax, there is a
sudden dramatic shift here towards interiority. Public considerations are
now irrelevant; the only touchstone is private feeling, private experience. The curious thing is that this new sense of interiority – a new
self-awareness that was taking shape at around this stage in history – is
articulated within a very traditional closure pattern in fiction: that is to
say, the novel is moving towards its conclusion on the basis of re-estab-
lishing traditional values, but, in the very process of reasserting a conventional social *and* fictional pattern, the text acknowledges a new
aspect of personal emotional feeling. Emma's reward is intimacy; language, particularly public language, falters throughout the whole proposal scene. In fact, straight statement is replaced by a sense of physical
contact between the two, even hints of sexuality in their mutual attraction.

This might not, however, seem all that significant until we put it
into a historical context. There is, between 1780 and 1820, a shift from
the public to the private. One aspect of this is the growing importance
of 'romantic love'. In many countries, even today, the notion of
romantic love does not exist; marriage is a social arrangement based
upon the economic status of the two partners. Love is something that
might develop later. As against this, there is the concept of romantic
love where one person reveals his or her inner soul to the partner. The
terms in which Emma and Knightley declare their feelings constitute

such a form of exposure and intimacy. There is a stress on authenticity of feelings: Knightley validates Emma's feelings, and thus her authenticity, and she validates his feelings. It is, of course, perfectly true that from every kind of traditional consideration Emma and Knightley should, and will, marry, but the important point is that their decision to marry is not based upon traditional considerations. It is an arranged marriage only in the sense that Austen as narrator has arranged it, but Austen invests the proposal scene with a totally new kind of significance. Specifically, the terms on which their love is declared separates the personal from the social, with Emma's 'self' being fulfilled in spite of, and in isolation from, any more public consideration.

To conclude, Austen might look traditional, and all the overt signs of her novel indicate that she is traditional, but a new ideological position is taking shape in *Emma*. No wonder Austen is so keen to cling on to Knightley as a symbol of the old order, for her new stress on romantic love and the individual is a central part of a new bourgeois spirit that will ultimately and inevitably undermine the world she wishes to preserve. *Emma*, as such, stands as a fascinating revelation of, and illustration of, the nature of the changes in the society from which it emerges. Rather than Austen rising above her age, her novel dramatically immerses itself in that process of social, cultural and political change. It is, perhaps more than anything else, this kind of interest in a text's involved and complex relationship with the period of its production that is the principal focus of novel criticism today.

10

New novels

Novels discussed:
Waterland, by Graham Swift, published 1983
The Color Purple, by Alice Walker, published 1983

ONE of the most enjoyable challenges of a literature course is writing about contemporary fiction: novels which have appeared in recent years and which, for the most part, have not yet attracted a vast body of critical writing. Some modern novels, it must be admitted, are likely to prove difficult to come to terms with, especially if they are radically experimental both in form and content, but the majority of recent novels, particularly those set for examinations, are likely to prove very accessible. You should be able to see how they raise questions that are relevant to your own life and the world we live in today. With classic novels, one often needs some pointers that one is tackling the text in an appropriate way, but the relevance of contemporary novels means that all readers are going to be that bit more confident about what matters in the text.

But there are one or two possible problems. Sometimes students forget to stick to the text; if they have read a novel about, say, the way in which the apartheid system used to operate in South Africa they might drift off into offering their opinions on the subject at the expense of discussing the text. Or, if the novel is about, say, a young person's experiences as an adolescent, there can be a temptation to focus on the one aspect of the issue that really catches your attention or which is relevant to your own experiences, and to neglect the broader impression of the text. In both examples, the student has underestimated the complexity of the work; because the novel has proved accessible, the student has used it as a springboard for talking about life, rather than focusing upon the actual words on the page.

Sometimes, however, the student is very much aware of the complexity of the text: a novel might have held your attention, and in a muddled way you might be able to see what themes it is dealing with, but you find it hard to say what it all amounts to. It is two novels that could be said to fall into this category that I deal with in this chapter (as always, I am, of course, only using the specific examples as illustrations of the kind of way in which you might set about discussing a great range of novels. Try to see the logic of the method, rather than focusing on my, possibly questionable, interpretations of these two novels.) The two novels I have picked out for attention are Graham Swift's *Waterland* and Alice Walker's *The Color Purple*. Most readers, I think it is fair to say, enjoy reading both novels, but, by the end of both of them, often feel rather overwhelmed. In the case of *Waterland*, they will have encountered a novel that touches on war, murder, death, marriage, history, childhood and families. In the case of *The Color Purple*, a novel dealing with the experiences of Celie, a black girl growing up in the Deep South of America between the wars, they will have been confronted with racism, rape, incest, child abuse, domestic violence and a range of associated issues. Both novels are powerful, both contain an explosive brew of topics, but almost overwhelmingly so. How is it possible to start organising an impression of such complex texts?

The answer, of course, is to set about organising a response in exactly the same way as with any other novel, that is to say, in the systematic manner that I have been illustrating throughout this book. It is again a case of working from short passages and building an impression. The only difference is that, because a modern novel might well have made a profound impression on you, you might find that you want to move around the book in a very free and flexible way, perhaps deciding to focus on those episodes that have stayed most clearly in your memory of the novel. But remember that you must stick to passages, you must stick to the evidence, or your ideas are likely to be wild and woolly. Unless one works from specific passages, there is always a danger of going off course, of misjudging and misrepresenting, and perhaps never really managing to define at all your experience of the text in question.

I 'Waterland'

Waterland is a novel in which a history teacher recalls his family history. On the cover of the paperback edition, there is a quotation from a critic who calls it 'a tale of empire-building, land reclamation, brewers and sluice minders, bewhiskered Victorian patriarchs, insane and visionary relicts, an amazing panoply of professional burghers and local eccentrics that together constitute a history of England over the last 300 years . . .'. It's not a very illuminating quotation, but it does give us a taste of the amazing variety of things, people, issues and themes there are in *Waterland*. How do we find a central pattern in a novel that contains so much? The only approach must be to select a passage, preferably from fairly early in the novel, and to look at it with a principal objective of establishing your sense of the work's 'subject'. This is, of course, the crucial move, as all your other ideas will be built upon this firm foundation; it means, therefore, at the outset, we must take things slowly and steadily.

Step 1: After reading the work as a whole, take a close look at the opening page of the novel, or, if this proves unilluminating, at a passage fairly near the beginning featuring one or more of the principal characters

I want to start more or less at the opening, about half-a-dozen lines into the novel:

> We lived in a fairy-tale place. In a lock-keeper's cottage, by a river, in the middle of the Fens. Far away from the wide world. And my father, who was a superstitious man, liked to do things in such a way as would make them seem magical and occult. So he would always set his eel traps at night. Not because eel traps cannot be set by day, but because the mystery of darkness appealed to him. And one night, in midsummer, in 1937, we went with him, Dick and I, to set traps near Stott's Bridge. It was hot and windless. When the traps had been set we lay back on the riverbank. Dick was fourteen and I was ten. The pumps were tump-tumping, as they do, incessantly, so that you scarcely notice them, all over the Fens, and frogs were croaking in the ditches. Up above, the sky swarmed with stars which seemed to multiply as we looked at them. And as we lay, Dad said: 'Do you know what the stars are? They are the silver dust of God's blessing.'
>
> [*Waterland* (Picador, 1984), p. 1]

We can start with the setting: the family live in a lock-keeper's cottage in the middle of the Fens. A fen is a district of low wet or flooded land; the Fen district is such an area in eastern England. This obviously ties up with the title of the novel, but what sort of significance can we read into this setting? It seems to have something to do with the idea that in a fen district there is a sense of land reclaimed from the sea, but only just. It is a precarious business, as we see later in the novel when floods come and consume the land. All the time in such an area, people are striving to keep things dry and solid, fighting against being overwhelmed. The occupation of lock-keeper is important in this context: it is the boy's father, the lock-keeper, who is responsible for trying to maintain some sort of control over potential chaos.

But what sort of chaos? Other details in the passage begin to define this for us. There is the mysterious world of the night. There is also a limitless universe, suggested in the image of the sky swarming with stars. It is an impression of a dark and baffling world. Perhaps even at this stage we can guess that the novel is going to explore some of the darker aspects of experience. What I think we can also explain, even this early in the novel, is the initial feeling we had that the novel contains a great deal, but more than we could precisely pin down. The secret of how it creates this impression is the symbolic setting, which suggests a great deal but doesn't spell things out or define them in any way. As this passage makes clear, the novel sets itself an ambitious brief, but does it obliquely through these teasing allusions to the mysteries of darkness.

What we should also be alert to in the opening of the novel, however, are the various ordering strategies that people rely upon to counter the sense of an incomprehensible world. The most obvious strategy in this extract is that people tell stories, for stories impose a shape upon experience. The passage begins with a reference to a fairy-tale place, and at the end the boys' father begins to tell them stories about the stars. At this point you could introduce the fact that the narrator of the novel is a history teacher who is telling the story of his own life and the story of his family: history, biography and autobiography are all forms of story-telling about the past. Late in the novel the narrator tells us why he took up teaching: it was what he saw at the end of the Second World War that convinced him that the job was important, that as against waste and destruction there had to be some positive attempt to order and explain, to create a narrative. We see the personality of the history teacher in statements such as 'one night, in midsummer, in 1937, we went with him, Dick and I, to set traps near Stott's Bridge'. It is a cumbersome sentence, but is so because of the number of precise facts it includes: we see the narrator wanting to pin things down and explain them.

Let's take stock. It might be that you are not studying *Waterland*, but are reading this chapter to gain some ideas about how to tackle recent novels in general. It should prove most useful, therefore, if I reiterate the general strategy that has informed how I have started to get hold of this novel. I have tried to get hold of a broad issue; if you can identify a broad issue, a subject for the work as a whole – and it is almost invariably the case that this can be detected in the first page of a novel – then you will have achieved a purchase on the text, and have a sense of a pattern that can help you organise and focus all your subsequent impressions.

Step 2: Select and analyse a second passage

So far we have a sense of the inexplicable nature of life and a sense of how we try to create order – an area of dry and secure land – primarily, the novel would seem to be suggesting, through the construction of stories. But the references to the boys' father suggest an additional idea of a family order, of some form of continuity from generation to generation. And there is also the idea of belonging somewhere, of having a place that one can call home. In order to move forward with the novel, we need to find another scene that will enable us to build upon these impressions. We might choose scenes almost at random, perhaps at even stages throughout the novel, or we might, as I intend to do here, choose scenes that made a particular impression on us when we read the novel. It is the latter that I intend to do here (specifically because it is always very satisfying to be able to relate scenes that one liked, or details that particularly caught one's eye, to one's developing sense of the work as a whole). This is a passing moment in the novel, where a woman screams in a supermarket. It is a detail that might seem to have little to do with the broad pattern of the novel; it certainly is not a part of the central narrative, the main story that is being told, but it must have a bearing on the work as a whole:

> They've got their cat food, dog food, washing powder, paper tissues, cling film and aluminium foil. But there's something someone hasn't got. Because amid the jostling trolleys, baskets and commotion a woman suddenly begins to wail. She screams and screams and won't stop . . .
>
> [pp. 135–6]

In trying to make sense of this we need to remind ourselves that the novel is dealing with a dark world, and how we try to create order within this world. The thing about a supermarket is that it is a hygienically wrapped, brightly lit, safe world in which everything has been scrubbed clean, in which people do not even have to touch messy goods that have come from the earth. And just in case we do get dirty there is washing powder to clean away the dirt, and paper tissues to clean up any mess. Normally, however, we wrap things up in film or foil. Even animal life has been reduced to domestic cats and dogs, which we feed with tinned pet food.

But suddenly, as the woman begins to scream, the horror behind it all surfaces: there is a sense of an emptiness, a void, behind the semblance of civilisation. It is this dark and terrifying side of life – and how we cope with such darkness – that Swift seems to be concerned with throughout the novel. Taking stock of how our analysis is progressing, a look at a second passage has allowed me to endorse, yet also extend, my initial impressions. What I can now add, however, is some sense of how these themes belong to the last quarter of the twentieth century. The supermarket scene prompts us to think about how we live in a world where we are overwhelmed with material goods. It is an ideal consumer's world (the novel more generally, in dealing with the rise of a family brewing firm, is among other things, dealing with the creation of a consumer society). But it is a world where people are perhaps closer to breaking-point than has ever been the case in the past. I feel that this scene in the supermarket, and, indeed, Swift's novel as a whole, manages to convey in an extraordinarily effective way this peculiarly modern awareness of the juxtaposition of the safe and the terrifying.

All novels are built on a conflict, but it is a feature of recent novels that the conflict is more extreme. In a great many current novels, we are likely to be struck by the combination of an affluent, consumer society and a brutality or emptiness that is more extreme than anything encountered in the past. This is, it could be argued, a post-Second World War awareness, an awareness that can never leave us after the excesses of Nazi Germany, a realisation that as civilisation has seemingly developed it has also proved itself capable of nastiness on an unprecedented scale. Even this woman's breakdown seems a peculiarly modern condition: there has always been madness, but psychological illness is not only common but somehow seems a product of the world we live in today. Swift's novel offers us a very vivid impression of such anxieties of modern life, but we are likely to find a comparable sense of a materialistic society and its disturbing underside in a great many current novels.

Step 3: Select and analyse a third passage

In the anxious world of modern fiction, we might well ask what do people hang on to. The answer, of course, is that they hang on to the things that people have always clung on to: most importantly, they cling on to the idea of the family, as this provides a sense of having roots, of belonging and being wanted, and having an identity. It seems appropriate, therefore, at this stage in our consideration of *Waterland*, to look at one of the many passages in the novel about the author and his family: in these extracts he deals with the Atkinson line and the Crick line:

> It was Atkinson who in 1815 built the lock and sluice two miles from the junction of the Leem and Ouse, christening it the Atkinson Lock. And it was another Atkinson, Thomas's grandson, who, in 1874, after violent flooding had destroyed lock, sluice and lock-keeper's cottage, rebuilt the lock and named it the New Atkinson . . .
>
> [p. 14]

This is the Atkinson side of the narrator's family, the thrusting, ambitious side, but the narrator is also a Crick, and the Cricks never showed any such ambition, were always content to work as 'humble servants'. The narrator speculates on why this might have been:

> Perhaps because of that old, watery phlegm which cooled and made sluggish their spirits . . . Because they did not forget, in their muddy labours, their swampy origins; that, however much you resist them, the waters will return; that the land sinks; silt collects; that something in nature wants to go back.
>   Realism; fatalism; phlegm. To live in the Fens is to receive strong doses of reality.
>
> [pp. 14–15]

There is a difference between the family who try to control things and the family who have always accepted things as they are. If we look at the Atkinsons, there is the obvious factor of their building and rebuilding the lock, their energy for controlling their environment. And we can see traces of this in the narrator's own voice, the narrator who records dates, facts and names, as if naming things will control the world. It is, in fact, often said that one of the defining features of the realistic novel is the desire to name things, for in naming things an illusion is created that one has acquired control of the world. We see it

again here in the way the Atkinsons twice apply their own name to the
lock, as if they can stamp their identity – and control – on nature.

But nature fights back: it is anonymous, vengeful, indifferent to
the ambitions of the Atkinsons. And the Cricks seem always to have
accepted this grimmer truth about life; the illusions of the Atkinsons are
set against the realism of the Cricks. The narrator underlines this by
making it clear that the Cricks are nearer the truth. It is, as we shall
see, a world where not only the illusions of the Atkinsons amount to
nothing, but where other comforting fictions – in particular the fiction
of security within the family – are exposed as equally illusory.

Step 4: Select and analyse a fourth passage

The breaking of illusions assumes its most alarming form in the novel
when dark and disturbing forces intrude into everyday life, when the
quiet routines, the complacent assumptions of ordinary existence, are
torn apart. One way in which Swift introduces this kind of extreme
disruption into *Waterland* is through incest. Incest has often featured in
novels, though, it must be said, much more frequently in eighteenth-
century and twentieth-century novels than in the Victorian period; that,
of course, is hardly surprising. It is not so much that the subject would
have been morally taboo for the Victorians, more the fact that their
social convictions were sufficiently confident to make such an extreme
threat to good order as incest an irrelevance. (In Dickens, however,
specifically in *Hard Times*, there are overtones of incestuous feeling
between brother and sister.) One of the most powerful novels employing the subject of incest is F. Scott Fitzgerald's *Tender is the Night*, a
novel which, to my mind, has a great deal in common with *Waterland*.
In Fitzgerald's work, the heroine, Nicole Warren, has been a mental
patient; the underlying cause of her mental problems, it emerges, is
sexual abuse by her father. In *Waterland* there is a similar situation: the
narrator's mother has been sexually abused by her father. The narrator's brother, Dick, is the product of this incestuous relationship.

The novel, it is clear, has moved into a problematic and disturbing area, but how do we, as readers, cope with this? How do we
manage to relate the theme of incest to our developing impression of
the novel? The best approach is to return to the basic pattern we have
detected in the text, the basic division between the creating and ordering impulse of society and something alarming that is at odds with
humanity's attempts at civilised control. If we reflect on this tension, we

should be able to see that incest is a very powerful concept for illustrating it, for incest represents a fundamental violation of every principle of an ordered existence. In particular, if it takes the form of a sexual relationship between the father and his daughter, everything we might think of in terms of a solid patriarchal order in society, of trust within families, of family continuity, and of a child acquiring independence and an identity with the help of her parents, falls apart. In *Waterland*'s use of incest, therefore, the darkest urges of the night-time world emerge and destroy everything we value, cling on to, and need in our everyday world.

Step 5: Have I achieved a sufficiently complex sense of the novel?

There are other, equally unnerving incidents in the novel where the darker, more disturbing impulses in humanity intrude into everyday existence. For example, in the year 1819, a member of the Atkinson family, Thomas, suspects that his wife is having a relationship with another man. The moment arrives when he grew:

> surly, angry, and, whilst giving vent to the most unwarranted accusations and abuse, rose up from his chair and struck his wife hard across the face.
> [p. 66]

She hits her head as she falls to the ground, and 'never again recovered her wits'. What are we to make of this? How do we relate this to our developing sense of the novel?

It is possibly feminist criticism more than anything else that has provided us with a framework for reading such a scene (and such scenes, involving male violence against women, are going to be found in a great many modern novels). The point would seem to be that the Atkinson family are strong, are makers of their own destiny, but a facet of such power is that it is always not only masculine but excessively masculine. The man creates a dynastic line; he is concerned with what he can pass on to his son. The woman is seen very much as a possession, a kind of adjunct to the man. Thomas Atkinson is proud of his young wife, but fears, without any grounds for doing so, that she might be sexually independent. The theme of male violence against women is, as has been said, a common one in recent fiction – we will see it again in *The Color Purple* – but, in addition, it often combines with a fear of female sexuality. This can be explained in various ways: the man's hegemony is challenged if he feels his wife has sexual feelings, particularly for anyone other than himself. But also, at a deeper level, men are said to fear female sexuality because it is an unknown territory, an aspect of life that they can neither comprehend nor control. This is in part connected to the fact that the man's sexual organ is external, whereas the woman's is internal, and, as such, unseen and ungovernable. In a phallocentric culture, women's sexual feelings consequently come to be seen as a threat to male power.

It is this kind of modern thinking that Swift has taken up and used to considerable effect in his novel. In the violent behaviour of Thomas Atkinson, violent behaviour that is closely associated with his fears about female sexuality, we see again the precarious thinness of any concept of a civilised order within society. In the seemingly safe, even dull, domestic regime of marriage, terrible violence can erupt unexpectedly, almost from nowhere. There is a poem by Robert Lowell called 'For the Union Dead', in which he writes about a monument commemorating a group of dead soldiers, in fact a black regiment who fought in the American Civil War. The poem, after drawing attention to the monument, then goes on to mention how the soldiers when they died were thrown in a ditch; one of the lines of the poem is 'The ditch is nearer'. It seems an apposite comment on the bleakness of so much of the vision of *Waterland*.

It is not just incest and domestic violence that create this grim impression; the novel also deals with drunkenness, murder and war. But first, let's say a little more about gender issues in the novel. Some of the saddest material in *Waterland* deals with the narrator's wife, Mary. As a teenager she becomes pregnant: the baby is aborted, and then she is more or less kept prisoner in her father's house. But there is a sense in which her punishment lasts a lifetime, for she is barren, a problem that understandably causes her immense distress. In presenting the material in this way, Swift is taking up a traditional plot structure in novels: if a woman transgresses, she is punished, and the most common form of punishment is incarceration, she is kept prisoner. What we can say about Swift's distinctive treatment of such material, however, is that he writes at a time when feminist thinking has made a considerable impact; with some earlier novelists, particularly Victorian novelists, we might well feel that they are showing us more about women's lives than they quite realise. In Swift's case, however, his novel seems informed by an acute contemporary awareness of the politics of gender and the nature of the issues involved; it is something that is reflected in the non-judgemental, totally sympathetic, tone that informs the entire account of Mary's life.

We might pursue the gender issue a lot further, but I want to touch on a couple of other points in the novel. One scene that particularly struck me when I read *Waterland* for the first time was an episode where a special ale is brewed in 1911 to celebrate the coronation of the new king. It is an astonishingly powerful brew, provoking extraordinary scenes of drunkenness. What are we to make of this? It helps if we return again to our most basic proposition about a structural tension in the novel between social order and threats to that order. Social order is reflected in the fact that the beer is called 'Coronation Ale': it is meant to commemorate and celebrate patriarchal continuity, the continuation of the dynastic line of the royal family. But the drunkenness it causes indicates how close we are at all times to irrationality and violence. This is the nice contradiction in the idea of the family brewing firm that runs throughout the novel: as a firm of brewers they are building up a business, establishing work, and contributing to social continuity and development. But the family fortune is based on exploiting, and trying to control, a commodity that provokes anti-social behaviour. It creates a telling paradox: that the social order depends upon the existence of disorder.

This intimate relationship of the desire for order and the endless presence of disorder is comprehensively explored in the novel in the ways that it deals with murder (specifically, the murder of Freddie Parr), death and war. The narrator grows up in wartime, his father returned as a shattered man after his experiences in the First World War, and the pupils in the school where the narrator works are worried by the prospect of nuclear war. In war, the irrationality that is present throughout the novel appears in its most destructive and extreme form. But the narrator is always concerned to counter, to find something to set against, that sense of destruction and waste. He recalls his experiences in Germany in 1946, at the end of the war. He stresses that he did not encounter concentration camps or any of the really horrifying scenes that we, as readers, might expect him to concentrate upon. Instead, the focus is upon what we might almost call the 'ordinary' destruction of war, the bombed and destroyed cities. It was what he saw at that time that led him to become a schoolteacher:

> Let's just say I made the discovery that this thing called civilisation, this thing we've been working at for three thousand years, so that now and

then we get bored with it and even poke fun at it, like children in school, because sometimes it takes the form of a pompous schoolmaster – is precious. An artifice – so easily knocked down – but precious.

[p. 207]

As against the novel's grim sense of waste and destruction, there is this sense that order is worth striving for; his contribution as a teacher of history might be minimal, but he is making some effort to challenge the forces of destruction and irrationality. He can see the artifice of society, but it is precious.

And, in a sense, that completes our critical consideration of this novel, but I want to pull the threads together here, as this might provide some ideas about recurrent patterns and themes in recent fiction. First, there is Swift's sense of the precarious thinness of the civilised order of society. This is a perception that is at the heart of a great many modern novels: in contemporary fiction we are likely to encounter random acts of brutality and scenes of sexual violence. Such scenes are often disturbing to read, but they are the only way in which the author can convey the feel of the world today. They also have to be seen, however, in relation to a rather traditional 'humanist' position that we encounter in a great many modern novels: the narrator of the novel – and the history teacher in *Waterland* is a very good example of this – displays his own commitment to order. It is something that is reflected, oddly enough, in the very act of writing a novel, for writing implies a belief in the power of the written word as a force against chaos. This is cleverly handled in *Waterland*: the narrator is about to be made redundant, for they have abandoned history at his school. He realises he is, and presents himself as, a rather old-fashioned voice, and can see the ways in which his views might simply be irrelevant, but there is, none the less, something positive about his middle-aged, middle-class, male voice. This combination of a sense of the horrors of the modern world and a voice from a slightly different world confronting it is something that we encounter in a great many British novels today; Swift exploits the combination very effectively, but in some novels we might feel that there are problems in the discontinuity between the author's awareness of how things are and the polite, educated voice in which he (the problem applies more to male novelists than women novelists) continues to narrate.

It is possible to imagine another kind of novel, however, in which there is not the same kind of steady narrative voice. The term postmodernist fiction is used to describe novels where there is a far greater impression of the frenetic disorder of the world, and where there is no consistent, coherent voice to guide us through the maze. But there is obviously far more to the modern novel than just the kind of works Swift is producing and postmodernism. Different novels are going to raise different issues and confront us with fresh critical challenges; each work is going to have to be confronted as a distinctive and individual achievement. But, having said that, one isn't going to go far wrong with any modern novel if one works with some of the assumptions that have informed this discussion of *Waterland*: assumptions such as the fact that everybody understands, and to some extent clings on to, the old order of families, parents and children, and marriage, and that in order to create a narrative the author has to show us this conventional order being destroyed or falling apart. A feminist novel, for example, might mock the patriarchal assumptions that are at the heart of any traditional vision of society, but the novel creates its effect by exploiting, even as it distances itself from, the conventional view. You might find the modern novel you have to study extremely baffling, but everything should start to fall into place the moment you can see how it works with an idea of social order even as it creates an impression of anarchy, repression or disorder within society, and even as it creates instability and incoherence, or a sense of doubt and uncertainty, through the method and tone of its narration.

II 'The Color Purple'

The Color Purple, by the black American writer Alice Walker, is an epistolary novel, that is to say, a novel that consists of letters from, or to, one or more of the principal characters. It focuses on the life of Celie, a young black woman who has been raped by the man she believes to be her father. She bears his children, and is then made to marry an older man for whom she has no feeling except contempt. The novel consists of Celie's despairing letters to God and to her sister Nettie, who has gone to Africa as a missionary. The novel also includes Nettie's letters to Celie. As with *Waterland*, one is likely to have a strong reaction to *The Color Purple* for it is a novel that makes a forceful impression on both black and white readers. For white readers, the response might be in part a guilty one, a realisation of how immune they have been from a knowledge of the reality of racism, but the response is also likely to be a degree of confusion, for, in addition to racism, what we encounter in the text is a disturbing picture of the violent sexual behaviour of the men in Celie's life. The other thing every reader is immediately going to be aware of is the unusual manner of the narration of the novel: it is not the fact that Celie is writing letters to God that is odd, but the unconventional English of her letters, a style very different from what we normally expect to encounter in a novel. What we might add to that is that the story in the novel as a whole twists and turns in a number of directions that seem to move well beyond the usual limits of realistic fiction.

As with *Waterland*, therefore, there is clearly a lot to discuss in *The Color Purple*. Because there is so much, we have got to set about making sense of the novel in a systematic way. But, before we start, there is an additional complication that we perhaps need to take account of here. I am very conscious of the fact that, as a male, white, British university teacher, I am not the best-qualified person to offer a view of this particular novel; I am very much in a position of viewing the experiences it presents from the outside, from a safe distance. My view of the text is naturally going to be influenced by the educational and cultural context that has produced me. But there is nothing I can do about that. I should try to be alert to the fact that other readers might see this book in a very different way, because they approach it with different assumptions, but I have got to have confidence that the kind of systematic method of analysis that I have been using throughout this book should enable me to say something about *The Color Purple* that does have some substance and relevance.

Step 1: After reading the work as a whole, take a close look at the opening page of the novel, or, if this proves unilluminating, at a passage fairly near the beginning featuring one or more of the principal characters

This is Celie's third letter. We have already gathered that she is fourteen, that her mother is dead, that she has been raped by her father, had a child, and had that child taken away. She has now given birth again:

Dear God,
   He act like he can't stand me no more. Say I'm evil an always up to no good. He took my other little baby, a boy this time. But I don't think he kilt it. I think he sold it to a man an his wife over Monticello. I got

breasts full of milk running down myself. He say Why don't you look decent? Put on something. But what I'm sposed to put on? I don't have nothing.

I keep hoping he fine somebody to marry. I see him looking at my little sister. She scared. But I say I'll take care of you. With God help.

[*The Color Purple* (The Women's Press, 1983), p.5]

This is horrifying; such things must happen, but most of us are fortunate enough never to have experienced anything so terrible. But what can we say beyond that? And why is Celie writing letters to God to tell him about the life she is having to endure? That, in fact, probably provides us with a good route into the novel. Celie is physically vulnerable, but she is also lost and bewildered both emotionally and mentally. In her first letter to God she begs him to let her 'know what is happening to me'. She has to turn to God because there is nobody else she can turn to; she is a child, but cannot turn to her mother, who is dead, and obviously cannot turn to her father. But there is something double-edged about turning to God, for it underlines the way in which Celie lives in a patriarchal culture. It is the male who is the source of authority, and the woman lives in the shadow and fear of men. Celie is caught in an awful muddle: her trust in her father has been brutally destroyed, but all she can do is turn to another kind of father in the hope of some guidance. Her little sister is more fortunate: the little girl is scared, but Celie has promised to protect her. Celie herself, however, has no other female she can turn to for support.

Let's stand back and think about this first step in building a response to *The Color Purple*. It is a novel that makes much of its appeal at an emotional level. We are, I think, keeping faith with the emotional impact of the novel, but we are also beginning to grasp the bigger issue that is involved, the political issue behind the individual case. It is Celie who is suffering, but Celie is at the same time representative: through her extreme case, we gain access to a much broader issue of how men mistreat women, and how women suffer, particularly if they are both poor and black, and thus at the bottom of the social structure of the society depicted. A political reading of the significance of Celie's life is, consequently, implicit in every detail Walker includes in the novel. But it is a political reading that connects seamlessly with a psychological reading: we have begun to see something about the nature of identity, how Celie cannot have any kind of sense of identity in the situation in which she finds herself, for she cannot think of herself as a child. Her father is destroying her sense of identity, her sense of herself.

There are, however, surprising as it might seem, some positive elements involved. Celie is a victim, but the letters give her a voice, they allow her some way of authenticating a sense of herself as someone with an identity, as someone with something to say. One aspect of this is the unconventional style. Walker attempts to reproduce the voice of the child, but there is more to this than just an attempt at realism. Celie speaks in a voice that is different from the voice that we normally encounter in novels because she writes from a perspective that is not the polite perspective of the majority of the novel's readers. This again makes Celie far more than a victim; indeed, Alice Walker has achieved something remarkable in giving a voice to a silenced and abused woman.

Is there anything else we need to add? We have already made a lot of progress from this one letter, but there are two more points – one straightforward, the other immensely complex – that we might add here. The simple point is that Celie is not only born into a man's world but a world where money rules, where even a baby can be seen as a commodity that can be bought and sold. The second, complex point is about incest. I have already mentioned in the discussion of *Waterland* that incest is the ultimate, and most unacceptable, form of social transgression, but does it have any additional significance here? The additional factors are class and race. Thomas Atkinson, in *Waterland*, was rich and powerful. Celie's father is poor and black. He is, consequently, at the bottom of the social pyramid, and will always have been treated as barely human; not surprisingly, he has been desensitised. He is, therefore, although we might find it hard to accept, a victim in the same way that Celie is a victim. As a victim, he looks for someone weaker than himself that he can victimise in turn. The poor, black American female is, consequently, on the receiving end of the harshest treatment inflicted upon anyone in American society; she is a victim of both racism and sexism. A point that is often made these days is that racism and sexism resemble each other, for both discriminate against those who are perceived as weak, yet simultaneously perceived as a threat.

Step 2: Select and analyse a second passage

It is the case with any novel that we have to bring our wider experience of life to bear on it in some kind of way, otherwise we would have no way of understanding the significance of the situations and characters presented. But with recent fiction we are likely to be far more alert to the fact that we need an awareness of broader political debates in the world today in order to make sense of the text. In the case of *The Color Purple*, we are confronted with the text's larger political and social resonances from the word go; to some extent the text makes us understand these political realities, but it helps if we already have an awareness of issues such as gender politics and racism, for this enables us to see a lot quicker what the book is getting at, and to spot the nuances and complexities of the picture it presents. The only danger in such an approach is that sometimes it can lead to the reader ignoring the actual details of the text; there is the possibility that the text might be used merely as the excuse for social comment. With *The Color Purple*, it does illustrate a lot of contemporary ideas about class, race and gender and so, consequently, the student might be tempted to write about class, race and gender rather than the experience of the novel. The fact is, of course, that one has to strike a balance, keeping close to the text and yet at the same time raising the larger questions. This is where the method of working from passages helps, for it keeps on pulling you back to the text, keeps on returning you to how these broad political and social issues are examined in this specific novel.

With this advice in mind, let us turn to the text again: in this extract, the person speaking is Sofia, the wife of Harpo who is the son of Mr ——, the man Celie has been forced to marry:

> She say, All my life I had to fight. I had to fight my daddy. I had to fight my brothers. I had to fight my cousins and my uncles. A girl child ain't safe in a family of men. But I never thought I'd have to fight in my own house. She let out her breath. I loves Harpo, she say. God knows I do. But I'll kill him dead before I let him beat me. Now if you want a dead son-in-law you just keep on advising him like you doing. She put her hand on her hip. I used to hunt game with a bow and arrow, she say.
>
> [p. 38]

From Sofia we hear again about the oppression that women have had to endure: her father, brothers, cousins and uncles are all ranged against her, and the threat, it is clear, is physical. But Sofia fights back. Look at how she places her hand on her hip and talks about hunting: she is physically assertive, and full of confidence that she can outmatch men at their own games.

What is the more general point we might extract from this scene?

The crucial words are 'power' and 'resistance'. Literary texts turn again and again to the subject of power, how people wield power in society, how they strive to dominate others. The structure of this power is aggressively masculine: we are born into a patriarchal culture, and those with power fight to preserve it. But a text that deals as explicitly with power as *The Color Purple* does is also likely to deal with the subject of resistance, of how those on the receiving end of bullying are prepared to fight back.

Sofia fights back, but can Celie do the same? Sofia provides an inspiring example, but can Celie follow her lead? Her life is, as the letters let us see, fragmented and unhappy. She isn't getting anywhere, has been separated from her children, and separated from her sister Nettie. Nettie, by contrast, has made the break for freedom, escaping from this society. But, although Celie might appear to have nothing, the letters are of great importance. One aspect of the exercise of power is silencing all those who are seen as opponents or different. Celie, however, although she is beaten down, refuses to be silenced. In her letters she articulates her position; the letters are her form of resistance, her way of fighting back.

Step 3: Select and analyse a third passage

The letters, however, are only part of the story; Celie needs support, needs to find other women who are resisting, needs to find ways of contesting the power of men. Help comes in the person of Shug, who uses her sexuality, who uses men, who is, in all senses, a strong woman:

> And when I come here, say Shug. I treated you so mean. Like you was a servant. And all because Albert married you. And I didn't even want him for a husband, she say. I never really wanted Albert for a husband. But just to choose me, you know, cause nature had already done it. Nature said. You two folks, hook up, cause you a good example of how it sposed to go. I didn't want nothing to be able to go against that. But what was good tween us must have been nothing but bodies, she say. Cause I don't know the Albert that don't dance, can't hardly laugh, never talk bout nothing, beat you and hid your sister Nettie's letters. Who he?
>
> [p. 105]

There are a number of elements here: there is the cruel way in which Shug used to treat Celie, the relationship between Shug and Celie's husband Albert, and the division in Albert's personality, how he was a different man with Shug from the man we see at home. The key to interpreting all this would again seem to be power. Shug treated Celie like a servant, but is equally in charge in her relationships with men. The curious thing is that Albert, who is a tyrant at home, was very different when he was with Shug, when he had to make an effort to compete rather than simply being able to dominate.

The presentation of Shug, therefore, complicates our impression of power relationships in the novel: she is a sexual woman, who talks about her physical relationship with Albert, but she is not available for abuse or mistreatment by men. She speaks confidently, and is very much in control of her own destiny. We are learning more and more about the nature of both power and resistance. Putting this in a larger context, one of the reasons why Alice Walker has received so much praise is because there is such a strong positive dimension to her novels. She is sometimes contrasted with black male writers of an earlier generation who seemed only to write about oppression. The sense of oppression in *The Color Purple* is brutal and overwhelming, but Alice Walker makes her characters fight back, articulating a voice, a position and a sense of independence from the very heart of oppression. Shug's is a proud voice; all of *The Color Purple* strives towards finding such a voice.

Step 4: Select and analyse a fourth passage

Celie's sister Nettie has become a missionary in Africa. Some readers, of course, might say that this seems a little too good to be true, in fact positively utopian. But a lot of feminist fiction has to have an idealist strain, for it is attempting to break the usual bounds of society, which means, in terms of novel form, stretching things beyond the limits of realism: it is playing with a new dispensation, a sense of how things might be, rather than merely commenting on things as they are. A look at one of Nettie's letters should underline this. In this extract, she tells Celie about the Olinka tribe in Africa:

> As long as they could, the Olinka ignored the road and the white builders who came. But eventually they had to notice them because one of the first things the builders did was tell the people they must be moved elsewhere. The builders wanted the village site as headquarters for the rubber plantation. It is the only spot for miles that has a steady supply of fresh water.
>
> [p. 192]

It is easy to fit Nettie into a scheme of things: here is a black, American woman who is making something of her life, who has broken out of the vicious circle of domestic violence and oppression. She is happily married, liberated and fulfilled.

If we are going to do justice to a novel, however, we must be able to relate the details of any passage we look at to a sense of the work as a whole. What, then, can we make of these details about the Olinka tribe? The way to arrive at an answer is to work through things in a simple step by step way. The Olinka are being driven away from their village. They are, therefore, victims in the same way that so many other people in the book are victims. The people victimising them are the representatives of the rubber company, which means that the Olinka are victims of western capitalism, but rather more generally they are victims of colonialism. The white settlers assert their power, they mistreat those they encounter, they deny them a life, and any protest they might make is likely to be silenced and ignored. What this should indicate to us is the comprehensive range of Walker's political analysis in the novel, the way in which she can see the parallels between the pattern of power relations within a family and the power issues involved in colonialism. What is particulary telling in these passages about the Olinka tribe is that they are recognised as constituting a complex society, with a culture and values. That might seem obvious, but is very different from Conrad's presentation of African people in *Heart of Darkness*, as discussed in the previous chapter. For Conrad, the Africans are merely savages. But Conrad views things from the perspective of Europe. Walker, by contrast, sympathises and identifies with the oppressed.

Step 5: Have I achieved a sufficiently complex sense of the novel?

I have stressed the positive elements in *The Color Purple*, and the novel ends on a very upbeat note: Celie is reunited with her lost children, and Nettie has returned from Africa with her husband Samuel, her children Olivia and Adam, and Adam's wife Tashi:

> They make a fine couple. Speak a little funny, but us gitting use to it.
> What your people love best to eat over there in Africa? us ast.
> She sort of blush and say barbecue.
> Everybody laugh and stuff her with one more piece.
> I feel a little peculiar round the children. For one thing, they grown.
> And I see they think me and Nettie and Shug and Albert and Samuel

and Harpo and Sofia and Jack and Odessa real old and don't know much what going on. But I don't think us feel old at all. And us so happy. Matter of fact, I think this is the youngest us ever felt.
Amen.

[p. 244]

Contention has been eliminated. The extended families are reunited, and a feeling of happiness prevails. Adam and Tashi speak a bit funny, but it doesn't matter: in other words, a general spirit of tolerance dominates. Nobody is looked down on or discriminated against because they are different. It is, of course, a utopian ending, but entirely appropriate in a novel that has ventured to be positive, emphasising, among other things, the restorative and healing effects of 'sisterhood', of solidarity and mutual support among women. It is a utopian ending, therefore, but one informed by a sophisticated political awareness of contemporary feminism.

Alice Walker does, however, have her critics. It has been suggested, for example, that *The Color Purple*, particularly in the earlier stages, presents a negative image of black people by focusing so much on rape, incest and violence. This is a difficult issue for the black writer; if a white author presented a similar picture of the behaviour of a group of white people, it would not be read as an illustration of a widespread problem. But when a black writer presents such material it does, whether we like it or not, to some extent confirm the prejudices of the most bigoted white reader. This is one criticism that has been voiced, and really there is no way of resolving the issue. Another criticism, however, is rather more clear cut: this is the view that, when it comes to the crunch, Alice Walker is really a rather conservative writer. It might seem a surprising judgement, for everything about *The Color Purple* looks radical, confrontational and questioning, but it has been suggested that the answer that is finally arrived at in the novel sidesteps the political problems that the work has raised. In particular, it could be said that the cosy family scene with which the novel ends endorses an apolitical model of change as a familial dialectic. To put that in simpler terms, there is something rather twee about the way in which this powerful political novel ends with a family barbecue; the whole thing seems to be reduced to the level of a kind of television situation comedy.

If one wanted to pursue this line, it could be taken a lot further. Towards the end of the novel, around the stage that Celie has sorted out her life and started to feel happy, she begins making trousers. She enjoys making them, but feels she should find a job. Shug gives her some advice:

> Let's us put a few advertisements in the paper, she say. And let's us raise your prices a hefty notch. And let's us just go ahead and give you this diningroom for your factory and git you some more women in here to cut and sew, while you sit back and design. You make your living, Celie, she say. Girl, you on your way.
>
> [p. 181]

Our response might be positive, for Celie has found a role in life: she is going to become a successful businesswoman. But some might argue that there is inconsistency in a novel that, having offered a forceful critique of the power structure of American society, suddenly turns round to celebrate the heroine's new vocation in business. It seems like an evocation of the American Dream in the most traditional terms, that the person with nothing can make a fortune in America. Both feminist and black critics have criticised this as a sell-out.

It is this slightly dismissive attitude towards Walker that predominates in criticism at the moment, but my feeling is that this attitude will change as critics find fresh issues to discuss, and fresh levels of complexity, in her work. It is this fact, that there will always be a new way of looking at an author, new perspectives to explore, new angles on a text, that keeps criticism alive and interesting. And what adds to the pleasure is that this is a debate in which we can all participate, for every time you open a novel, and start to discuss it, either in class or in an essay, you are adding to, and reformulating, the existing view of that text. As you focus in on passages from a novel, and as you assemble your impressions into a larger case, you will, however much you might doubt it, be making your own original contribution to the critical debate.

Further reading

What edition of a novel should I buy?

This problem is unlikely to bother you at school, as you will probably
be supplied with a copy of the novel; and at college or university the
lecturers will often specify particular editions. But there will be times
when you want to buy a classic novel and find that it is available in
as many as half-a-dozen paperback editions. In most respects there is
little to choose between them. All are likely to provide a reliable text,
so there is a very good argument for purchasing the cheapest. If,
however, you want to do some sustained work on the text, it might be
worth choosing an edition with a substantial Introduction and equally
substantial Notes: if there is a detail in the novel that you do not
understand, it is always helpful to be able to turn to the back of the
book and find an immediate explanation, and the critical Introduction
is likely to stimulate, and help give a shape to, your own thinking. It
may, therefore, sometimes be worth paying more for the edition
which strikes you as having the most comprehensive Notes and the
fullest Introduction. The editions referred to in this book are, where
there is a choice, the *Penguin Classics* versions, simply because they are
probably the most commonly available and the most widely used.

What critical books should I read?

The most directly useful books are those which offer close discussion
of the particular novel you are interested in; sometimes this is com-
bined with an edition of the text. There are, to my mind, two outstanding series of this kind. One series is *Routledge English Texts*
(General Editor: John Drakakis), which provide an Introduction, and
then, in addition, after the text of the novel, offer a Critical Com-

mentary. Three volumes in the series which strike me as including a particularly interesting Critical Commentary essay are *Wuthering Heights*, edited by Heather Glen, *The Mill on the Floss*, edited by Sally Shuttleworth, and *Heart of Darkness*, edited by John Batchelor. The other series combining text and critical discussion which I would recommend is *Case Studies in Contemporary Criticism* (General Editor: Ross C. Murfin; published in America by St Martin's Press and distributed outside North America by Macmillan). The volumes in this series offer an Introduction, the complete text, and then a substantial selection of recent critical essays which are chosen to represent the range and variety of current critical approaches. There are, to date, only a limited number of books in this series, but the editions of *Wuthering Heights, Frankenstein, Heart of Darkness* and *A Portrait of the Artist as a Young Man* are likely to prove immensely useful and illuminating to any student of literature.

Another very useful kind of critical book is that which provides a selection of essays about a single text or author. Two series of this kind are *Modern Critical Interpretations*, focusing on individual texts, and *Modern Critical Views*, dealing with a number of works by one author (General Editor of both series: Harold Bloom; published in the USA by Chelsea House). Each of the volumes in these series contains about ten essays, illustrating a broad range of critical approaches. They are very good, but offer little in the way of explanation of, or guidance through, the critical essays. For this kind of annotated and directed reading of criticism, one has to turn to the *New Casebook* series, published by Macmillan, and edited, as a series, by the editors of the *How to Study Literature* series, myself and Martin Coyle. The volumes in this series provide about ten essays, usually on a single text, together with an Introduction that explains the kind of critical thinking that is going on in the essays. All the essays illustrate current critical approaches; as such, the books in the series provide a very direct way of coming to grips with the priorities and methods of current theoretically-inspired criticism. The books complement, rather than replace, the original *Casebook* volumes (General Editor: A.E. Dyson; published by Macmillan), which offer a broad selection of critical views from the date of a text's first appearance up to the early 1970s. The *New Casebook* volumes, by contrast, focus on recent criticism. A rather similar series, but focusing on authors or topics rather than individual texts, is *Longman Critical Readers* (General Editors: Raman Selden and Stan Smith). The volumes on George Eliot, edited by K. M. Newton, on

D. H. Lawrence, edited by Peter Widdowson, and Charles Dickens, edited by Steven Connor, are particularly recommended.

When you are confronted by a number of books about one author on a library shelf, the best book to start with is the most up-to-date one; there is every likelihood that the author will discuss earlier criticism, and provide some sense of the range of current ways of looking at the novelist under consideration. Read just enough criticism at school to discover what literary criticism is and to stimulate your own ideas. At college or university, start to read more, but as a complement to your own thinking rather than as a substitute for thinking. Don't plagiarise critical books, either directly or by too great a reliance on other people's ideas and examples. It is, however, perfectly legitimate to use a critic's ideas if you apply them to an example in the text that you have chosen yourself. When you do that, you will be saying something new.

What general books about the novel should I read?

Some of the most interesting critical books are those in which a critic looks at a number of novels by several writers. This format allows the critic to develop an original, and sometimes provocative, view of fiction. The most successful books of this kind amount to the focusing of a new approach in critical thinking. Perhaps the first book about novels to make a real impact in this kind of way was F. R. Leavis's *The Great Tradition* (1948): in a very assertive manner, Leavis declared that the great English novelists are Austen, Eliot, James, Conrad and Lawrence. What Leavis appreciated in fiction was a certain moral seriousness, which he found in these writers. Leavis's views shaped the taste of several generations of students, and the influence of his views informs a great many critical books published in the 1950s and 1960s. It might even be said that the influence of Leavis only really began to wane with the first stirrings of structuralist criticism in the Sixties. To see how British thinking about the novel developed from around this time, an excellent critic to look at is David Lodge. In a series of books – the ones I would recommend are *Language of Fiction* (1966), *The Modes of Modern Writing* (1977), and *After Bakhtin* (1990) – Lodge comes to terms with the new theoretical thinking that was emerging, primarily from France, from the Sixties onwards, and shows how it can be applied to, and provide us with new ways of thinking and

talking about, fiction. One of the great merits of Lodge is the clarity
with which he writes; each of his books offers a very accessible sense
of a critical method that the student is likely to feel that he or she can
emulate in some kind of way.

Another critic who is likely to inspire the student, although he
might simply dazzle with the inventive brilliance of his readings
of fiction, is J. Hillis Miller. Miller was one of the first American aca-
demics to take up deconstructive criticism; at times, deconstructive
analyses can become rather dry and difficult, but in Miller we always
see deconstruction in action as he grapples in a very direct way with
most of the major novels from Britain and America. Any book by
Miller is going to provide an excellent demonstration of just how good
and interesting novel criticism can be, but I would particularly recommend *Fiction and Repetition* (1982). There are now a great many feminist
readings of fiction (indeed, several major publishers have produced
series of feminist re-readings of fiction), but the book that anyone with
a genuine interest in feminist criticism should perhaps start with is
Sandra Gilbert and Susan Gubar's *The Madwoman in the Attic: The
Woman Writer and the Nineteenth-Century Imagination* (1979). Gilbert and
Gubar's book has been much criticised, but it would be hard to conceive of a book presenting a more absorbing and all-embracing introduction to a particular area of study.

A list like this, of interesting and helpful critical books could, of
course, run on and on. I could, for example, direct the reader to
valuable books on psychoanalytic criticism, etc., but rather than
provide a comprehensive guide, it might be better if I conclude here
by drawing attention to the two recent critics whose work I have
found most interesting, and whose books, I know from my experiences
as a teacher of literature, have interested, and indeed inspired, a great
many of my students. One of these critics is D. A. Miller who, in
Narrative and its Discontents: Problems of Closure in the Traditional Novel
(1981) and *The Novel and the Police* (1987), starts with issues of narratol-
ogy (a concern with how narratives work), but then, however, opens
up questions of ideology, politics and the social role of the novel. The
other critic whose work I have found really stimulating is Mary
Poovey, particularly her two books *The Proper Lady and the Woman
Writer: Ideology as Style in the Works of Mary Wollstonecraft, Mary Shelley and
Jane Austen* (1984) and *Uneven Developments: The Ideological Work of Gender
in Mid-Victorian England* (1989). Both these works combine feminism
with a New Historicist interest in seeing how the text functions in a

particular society, with an emphasis, as there is in so much current criticism, on how such matters are constituted and debated primarily in the language of the literary text.